SILVER WINGS

Walter J. Boyne

SILVER WINGS

A HISTORY OF THE UNITED STATES AIR FORCE

Foreword by General James H. Doolittle
USAF (RETIRED)

Introductory Note by Lee Ewing
EDITOR OF *Air Force Times*

A ROUNDTABLE PRESS BOOK

 SIMON & SCHUSTER

New York   London   Toronto   Sydney   Singapore   Tokyo

To all the men and women of the United States Air Force and the organizations that preceded it, and most especially to their spouses and their children.

SIMON & SCHUSTER
Simon & Schuster Building
Rockefeller Center
1230 Avenue of the Americas
New York, NY 10020

FRONTISPIECE:
The North American P-51 Mustang was the long-range escort fighter that decided the air war in Europe.

A Roundtable Press Book

Directors: Marsha Melnick, Susan E. Meyer
Project editors: William L. Broecker, Ross Horowitz
Design: Nai Y. Chang

Printed and bound in Hong Kong

10 9 8 7 6 5 4 3 2 1

Library of Congress Cataloging-in-Publication Data

Boyne, Walter J., 1929-
    Silver wings : a history of the U.S. Air Force / Walter Boyne.
        p.   cm.
    Includes bibliographical references and index.
    ISBN 0-671-78537-0
    I. United States. Air Force—History. I. Title.
UG633.B696 1993
358.4'00973—dc20
                                                                                    92-42939
                                                                                    CIP

Contents

Foreword

BY GENERAL JAMES H. DOOLITTLE, USAF (RETIRED)

In the past, some historians have treated the history of the United States Air Force and its predecessor organizations as a catalog of equipment and campaigns, briefly highlighting the great leaders and famous pilots. *Silver Wings* is refreshingly different, for it treats the history of the Air Force in a very human way, viewing it as it really was and really is, an assembly of intelligent, wonderfully motivated people, who are also, by definition, proud and productive members of their communities.

From the very beginning of the Aeronautics Division of the Signal Corps in 1907, through the Air Service, the Air Corps, the U.S. Army Air Forces, and including the still-evolving U.S. Air Force, the long history of success and achievement has been based on hard-working men and women of every rank, and their families, who have often sacrificed much to serve the nation's interests.

Silver Wings covers the amazing technical progress of the last eight decades, and presents insight into the great campaigns, from Saint-Mihiel to the Persian Gulf. But more importantly, it also shows just how that progress was made possible by the devotion of thousands of unsung heroes, who did their jobs brilliantly without concern for recognition or reward. Anyone who served, or the family members of anyone who served, will find in this book reminders of that service, sometimes nostalgic, sometimes amusing, sometimes poignant, but always fascinating.

General James J. ("Jimmy") Doolittle flying his own B-25 to visit the 12th Bomber Group in Sicily on October 20, 1943.

Introductory Note

BY LEE EWING

The story of the United States Air Force is a proud one, and Walter J. Boyne is ideally suited to tell it. A veteran pilot, gifted author, and distinguished historian, he writes of airplanes and flying with feeling and authority gained during a lifetime in the cockpit. Boyne knows the Air Force is far more than aircraft, missiles, and satellites—it is people. With his novelist's flair for storytelling, he brings to life air power's rogues and heroes, recounting feuds, fiascoes, and daring triumphs. In this intriguing account of the birth, growth, and newfound maturity of the Air Force, Boyne pays tribute to all who design, build, and support aircraft, but his focus is never far from those who wear the silver wings.

To put the Air Force in context, Boyne traces its heritage to the pioneers of flight. Airplanes, like balloons and dirigibles, were first used for observation and reconnaissance, but their lethal potential soon became evident. In World War I, the skies over Europe for the first time became an arena for swirling combatants. What was not clear was precisely how this new way of fighting could be used most effectively. The prevailing wisdom was that airplanes should support ground forces, chiefly by providing aerial reconnaissance and artillery fire direction. But a handful of visionaries thought otherwise. In Italy, Guilio Douhet urged aerial bombardment to bring about swift victory. In the United States, Billy Mitchell saw air power as a potent new kind of cavalry that could win wars in the third dimension.

From the first dogfights over Pearl Harbor to the atomic bombing of Nagasaki, air power played a vital role in the allied victory in World War II. Yet the value of air power remained in dispute even as its advocates succeeded in winning independence for the new U.S. Air Force. Politically manacled in Korea, U.S. air power was not decisive. In Vietnam, too, political restrictions and lack of a clear national strategy prevented its effective use for most of the war. In the invasions of Grenada and Panama, air operations were important, and the strength of the Air Force during the Cold War was a critical factor in the forty-five-year struggle that led to the demise of Communism.

Despite the Air Force's impressive record, it was not until the United States deployed forces to the Persian Gulf that visions of a decisive air war sketched by Leonardo da Vinci and colored by mavericks like Mitchell became real. In telling the story of the air campaign that led to the stunning Allied victory in the Gulf, Boyne spotlights an aspect of the war that has received too little attention: it was the first war in which space-based satellites provided commanders priceless advantages. Like a modern-day Mitchell, he suggests persuasively that while early airmen's dreams of victory through air power finally were achieved in the Gulf War, future warriors also must become adept at the use of space power if they are to command the high ground.

Preface

This is not a history in the usual sense of a careful listing of dates and well-known events. It is instead a retrospective appreciation of two critical elements in the development of the Air Force: the key leaders and the men and women whom they shaped into the most powerful military force in history. It is also a new perspective on the meaning of air power, analyzing what it was supposed to mean in the past, what it means now, and the surprising way it has evolved for the future.

In doing this, there is less emphasis on familiar events that have been well covered in the past, and more on the interesting sidelights that have humanized the process. For example, rather than recount again the details of Billy Mitchell's sinking of the battleships, this book deals with the politics behind the affair. In a similar way, the familiar stories of the most well known aces are not repeated; instead the emphasis is on lesser-known but often even more important people whose stories have not been told. As the text tracks the people, so the photo captions track the amazing development of technology, which saw a growth from the Wright Military Flyer to the Northrop B-2 in less than nine decades, well within the lifespan of many people.

Space limitations preclude detailing every individual, every unit, or every battle of the Air Force; they also prohibit telling of the valorous efforts of the Army, Navy, and Marines. The intent is to honor all the people, military and civilian, who served with the Air Force or any of its predecessor organizations.

Since 1907, the flying services that eventually became the United States Air Force have been blessed and cursed by a leadership that included, in almost equal measure, radical visionaries and hidebound conservatives, the radicals seeking the holy grail of true air power in flashy demonstrations, the conservatives trying to build up the supply, training, and logistics necessary for sustained military operations. Both parties wanted the same thing, an independent air force capable of carrying out war-winning operations in the enemy heartland; each was unaware that such capability would be unobtainable for years. From Billy Mitchell's first orchestrated air battle at Saint-Mihiel through his battleship blasting, to the mushroom clouds over Hiroshima and Nagasaki, the radicals' thrust was for the quick, surgical air strike that would solve political problems on a cosmic scale. In counterpoint, at lower levels, the conservatives

OPPOSITE:
Wilbur Wright, calm and methodical as always, inspects the Wright Military Flyer —the world's first heavier-than-air military aircraft.

kept a skeleton force in being, working hard to develop a modern striking force. Both groups were doomed to failure until the inexorable march of technology thrust the means of true air power upon them.

Ironically, when the air power they had sought for so long materialized for the first time in 1945 with the wedding of the B-29 and the atomic bomb, it was so overwhelming that it could not in conscience be used again. It would require another forty-five years to re-create a different form of true air power, this time with nonnuclear weaponry mated to stealth technology, precision-guided weapons, and a degree of rigorous training never before envisaged. And this true air power would amazingly enough have its foundation in space power.

The American air forces were blessed by the people attracted to serve—eager, well-motivated, selected for their physical and mental attributes. No matter what the difficulties—inadequate budgets, low pay, public indifference, and for a time, public hostility—the service was able to generate both the leaders and the followers necessary to meet the needs of the next emergency. Perhaps the best example of this resilience can be found during World War II, when, after twenty years of penny-pinching budgets and token production levels, the U.S. Army Air Forces were able to achieve a total air supremacy in every theater of war within a three-year period.

Since the 1920s, the concept of air power has been defined as the attainment of aerial supremacy over the battlefield, combined with the destruction by aerial attack of the enemy's ability and will to wage war. In the beginning, enthusiasts believed that both tasks would be relatively easy, and the horror of death from the air would be so great that the exercise of even a primitive air weapon would be successful. Yet for many long decades, air power was not nearly so destructive as its proponents hoped it would be, either on the battlefield or behind the lines. This should not have been a surprise. Centuries of warfare had proved that cities could survive under frightful siege conditions, just as the static warfare of 1914–1918 proved that iron discipline could keep troops in the trenches no matter how horrible the conditions. Even in the middle of World War II, when bomber forces began to acquire genuine strength and a relative degree of accuracy, and when complete air supremacy had been obtained, the enemy troops in the field fought on, and enemy civilian populations maintained a high morale and productivity even after absorbing frightful punishment. Air power never broke the will of a civilian populace, even though the atomic bomb came close to it, permitting the Japanese nation to accept a way out of a lost war to which they were bound by political tyranny.

A decade after the Second World War, the rush of technological development changed the nature of the Air Force's internal conflict. With the advent of nuclear weapons, intercontinental bombers, and the prospect of intercontinental ballistic missiles, air power became an absolute reality, and the efforts of the conservative and radical theorists were merged in the need to harness and shape the efforts of the visionaries rather than oppose them. The best passive result of that effort was the termination of the Cold War without ever having to resort to the use of nuclear weapons: the race to maintain parity broke the Soviet Union's already moribund economy. The best active result was the decisive aerial triumph of the Persian Gulf War, where the insistence on the importance of training and logistics permitted air power to be exercised in a combined operation highlighted by Stealth fighters and smart bombs. The efficiency of these weapons, while perhaps not so great as originally thought in the flush of televised victory, was still so superior to any weapons of the past as to create a new measure of air power.

This new expression of air power as defined in the Gulf War acknowledges that breaking the will of a people is, if not impossible, then counterproductive. The experience in Iraq shows that air power can now be defined as attaining aerial superiority and eliminating the enemy's ability to wage war by destroying key elements in his command and control structures. The United States Air Force is currently reorganizing to adapt to this new concept so that it can meet the challenges of the future, just as it met the challenges of the past. And it will meet those challenges as always, through the men and women who serve it.

CHAPTER ONE

In the Beginning 1907–1916

As he was in so many things, Benjamin Franklin was a visionary in air power, speculating that a 10,000-man balloon-borne invasion force could drop behind the lines of "enemy princes" and render their territories indefensible. Franklin was correct in spirit, for balloons were the first expression of American military aviation, and their employment would presage the turbulent interchange of ideas that would characterize the development of what is today the United States Air Force. In the long and fertile passage from Franklin's idea to today's balanced force of Stealth bombers, smart bombs, and agile fighters, the service almost continuously faced three enduring problems.

The first was financial. The country that gave birth to the airplane was never willing to finance an air service until war was at hand. Then money flowed in a torrential stream, often too great for any organization, much less an impoverished military service, to handle sensibly. The second problem was technological. It took far longer to develop the airframes, engines, and equipment necessary for attaining air power than even most experts imagined. The third problem was doctrinal: how best to define air power, and how best to use it.

Fortunately for the United States, the answers to all three problems were supplied by the men and women of the Air Force and its predecessor organizations. No matter how limited the finances were, they stalked the future through research and development. The R&D money was spent on everything from oxygen masks to cannons, but the major thrust was for bigger engines and the airframes to handle them. The people absorbed the shortfall by accepting poor salaries, bad housing, and limited medical care. When questions of doctrine arose, there were long periods of internecine warfare among strong-minded advocates to force a decision.

These responses were buttressed by the support of industry, an essential element in the recipe for air power, one that has garnered both public acclaim as "war-winning" and public scorn in the phrase a speech writer provided to President Dwight D. Eisenhower, "the military-industrial complex." The truth of the matter is that air power, like most sciences, is too complex and expensive to develop in government isolation; there is no way that the specifications for even a simple weapons system can be created without the participation of industry. Despite the enduring impression fostered by the post-1960s media,

OPPOSITE:
The perplexed reaction of General John J. "Black Jack" Pershing's troops with the arrival of 1st Aero Squadron's Curtiss biplanes, depicted by Jim Dietz in his painting Black Jack's New Scouts.

the aviation military-industrial complex has been mission-oriented and surprisingly unrewarding to most manufacturers. One has only to go down the history's list of bankrupt companies, from Burgess, Orenco, Elias, Berliner/Joyce, and others of the early days to today's wounded and staggering industry, to realize the truth of the aphorism that if you wish to take a million dollars from aviation's coffers, you must first bring $10 million to it. That may sound satirical amid the myriad stories of $100 wrenches and $1,000 coffee pots, but ninety years of records on rates of return, stock prices, and bankruptcies speak for themselves.

One cannot ignore the fact that in what has become a huge industry there have been individuals and companies who have taken criminal advantage of the system. But the percentage is small, and the aviation industry would fare well in an objective comparison with other industries, banking, or even government.

To return to Benjamin Franklin, it is fitting that a fellow Pennsylvanian, John Wise, would partially fulfill the founding father's air power prophecy. Born in 1807, Wise made his first balloon flight, from Philadelphia, on April 30, 1835. It was the start of a distinguished career as an aeronaut that would continue until he met an airman's fate at the age of seventy-one, when he and his balloon *Pathfinder* disappeared over Lake Michigan.

A veteran airman by the time of the Mexican war of 1846–1848, Wise proposed to the War Department the building of a huge, 100-foot-diameter balloon, which he planned to fly over an enemy fortress to drop bombs and torpedoes. The Army promptly turned down his proposal, initiating a seventy-year ostrich policy toward aviation. When the Civil War erupted at Fort Sumter on April 12, 1861, Wise and five other balloonists volunteered for combat duty with the Union forces. (Two other aeronauts sought to fly for the Confederacy.) The Federal balloonists, by nature both persistent and cantankerous, distinguished themselves at first only by claims for primacy and an inability to deliver.

After some initial abortive attempts with other balloonists, Lieutenant Henry L. Abbot of the Topographical Engineers called upon Wise to provide an $850 hydrogen balloon of 20,000 cubic feet capacity. The Army had it transported to Centerville, Virginia, where it was inflated. In a classic forecast of future clashes between ground and air officers, the Signal Officer of the Army, Major Albert J. Myer, ordered that the balloon be brought immediately to Bull Run. The inflated balloon was attached like a Macy's float to a horse-drawn wagon that promptly pulled it through a line of trees. Pierced by the branches, the balloon collapsed, enfolding the wagon train in an India-silk embrace and depriving the Union forces at the Battle of Bull Run of the aerial eyes that might have won the Civil War on the spot.

Wise, a civilian, encountered further frustrations with the bureaucracy, chiefly the unwillingness of the Union Army to buy portable gas-generating equipment so that inflated balloons did not have to be hauled like great, easily punctured whales from point to point. His resignation was not the end of

Union aerial activity, however, for two other veteran balloonists entered the scene to begin the classic battle between line and staff that continues today.

The first was John La Mountain, who made repeated observations of Confederate lines and, on August 3, 1861, had created America's first aircraft carrier by mounting his balloon on the deck of the steam tug *Fanny*. Later in the year, the *George Washington Parke Custis*, an engineless 112-foot-long vessel, was also outfitted for balloon work.

ABE LINCOLN AND AIR POWER

La Mountain's achievements were overshadowed by a rivalry that was building with a younger balloonist, Thaddeus S. C. Lowe, who had an instinct for promotional activity and sought appointment to command a Union Army balloon corps. Flying, appropriately enough, from what is now the site of the National Air and Space Museum, Lowe observed Confederate activity in Virginia. With great flair, Lowe combined two new sciences in a public relations masterstroke by reporting by telegraph from the balloon directly to the President of the United States, Abraham Lincoln. The brilliant move convinced the man at the top of the practicality of the balloon as an observation platform, and secured for Lowe ascendancy in what would become the newest branch of the military service, the Army Balloon Corps.

La Mountain was furious at being finessed by Lowe, and responded with a ferocious display of airmanship. With an insight into weather unusual for the times, La Mountain began daring free-flight reconnaissance sorties, crossing the Confederate lines at a low altitude for his survey, then releasing ballast to climb to altitude for winds that would return him to Union lines. Foreshadowing the future, La Mountain resigned in February 1862, when he realized his brilliant flying was eclipsed by Lowe's superior staff work.

An aerial tug-of-war between the personalities of two brave, forceful men would become characteristic of the service. La Mountain was a flyer, a can-do type who disdained danger. Thaddeus Lowe had a capacity that many later air commanders would share—the ability to see his equipment not as an object but as a system. He developed a corps of seven balloons, each supported by portable gas generators, wagons, telegraphic equipment, and the necessary personnel to man them. Unfortunately, he had some faults that other air commanders would also share, particularly an inability to abide regulations and a tendency to give operational matters precedence over paperwork.

Over the next two years, Lowe's Balloon Corps achieved success after success, most notably at Fredericksburg and on the Chickahominy River. More significantly, the Corps' successes set in action a chain of events that would have monumental effect upon two world wars in the next century. A German military observer on leave from the King of Wurttemberg's army, Count Ferdinand von Zeppelin, was inspired by Lowe's successes. After a successful military and diplomatic career, he would invent the airship that gained notoriety in bombing raids on London in World War I. In reaction, the English established an air defense organization that presaged the 1940 system that won the Battle of Britain. There were graver consequences, for the Zeppelins had sown the seeds of terror bombing from which the Germans reaped a horrible harvest in World War II.

Despite the excellent work of Lowe's people, the local ground commanders too often lacked the ability to use the aerial intelligence they received. Like all the balloonists, Lowe was a civilian. He was paid $10 a day, about the same as a colonel, but he held no military rank. Obsessed with the details of his operations, he failed to keep a careful record of all his business transactions, a fatal error in Washington politics then as now. When he ran into political difficulties, his faulty paperwork was held against him and he was forced to offer his resignation. It was accepted, and within weeks all aerial activity ceased in the Union Army.

A TENTATIVE COMEBACK

The next balloon did not enter the U.S. Army's inventory until July 1, 1891, when Brigadier General Adolphus W. Greely, Chief Signal Officer of the Signal Corps, established a balloon section. Funds were scarce, and when the United States went to war with Spain in 1898, it still possessed only one balloon. It was used briefly at the battle of San Juan Hill during the Cuban campaign of 1898, exciting the attention of that great Rough Rider, Teddy Roosevelt, who subsequently became a patron of air power.

The peacetime Army was a small, very social organization, trying to compensate with perks what it could not provide in promotion or pay. Not as snobbish as the British army, where officers' records were marked PM for "private means" or PO for "pay only," the American Army allowed an officer with an independent income greater leverage. Even though a Balloon Detachment had been established at Fort Myer, Virginia, in May 1902, it was not until 1906, when the socially prestigious International Gordon Bennett Balloon Race was won by Lieutenants Frank P. Lahm and Henry B. Hersey, that flying began to have career cachet. On August 1, 1907, the Signal Corps issued an order establishing the Aeronautic Division, the direct ancestor of today's United States Air Force. The new division was to "have charge of all matters pertaining to military ballooning, air machines and all kindred subjects." Captain Charles de Forest Chandler was commander, and he had two enlisted men, for a total strength of three. Only six months later, one of the enlisted men deserted, reducing the new service's enlisted force by 50 percent in a single day, the nadir of American air power.

Despite the fact that the Wright brothers had been begging the War Department to purchase an airplane for three years, the first air machine pro-

cured by the new division was a lighter-than-air craft, Signal Corps Dirigible Number I. It was an intractable sausage of a machine, built to a specification that would have made Count Zeppelin laugh. His impressive (if unreliable) silver dirigibles flying over Lake Constance were monsters, almost 500 feet long, powered by two 105-horsepower engines, and capable of speeds of 30 mph. In contrast, the new U.S. machine was to have a speed of 20 mph, carry two people (combined weight not to exceed 350 pounds), and be able to stay aloft for at least two hours. Veteran daredevil Thomas Scott Baldwin submitted a low bid of $6,750 and delivered his airship to Fort Myer on July 20, 1908. After it squeaked by its acceptance tests (its airspeed was just under 20 mph), Baldwin was instructed to train three young lieutenants to fly it. They were men of vastly different personalities: nervous, intense Thomas E. Selfridge; tall, smiling, aristocratic Frank P. Lahm; and feisty Benjamin Foulois. Ironically, all would become famous in heavier-than-air flight.

The dirigible was stationed at Fort Omaha, Nebraska—later the home of the Strategic Air Command—where it fell into disrepair and was ultimately condemned. The three pilots had little enthusiasm for it; their eyes were on a future that began inauspiciously.

THE FIRST STEPS TOWARD MILITARY AVIATION

The Wright brothers had tried on three occasions to get the War Department to purchase their aircraft; they were refused each time, the last in a wonderfully obtuse memo from the Board of Ordnance and Fortification, stating that "the Board does not care to formulate any requirements for the performance of a flying machine or take any further action until a machine is produced by which actual operation is shown to produce horizontal flight and to carry an operator."

Fortunately, Teddy Roosevelt pressed for the purchase of an aircraft while the Wrights continued to pressure the Army. Finally, in December 1907 the Aeronautic Division prepared Specification No. 486, which called for a competition to create an aircraft that would carry two people, with enough fuel for a flight of 125 miles, and be capable of a top speed of 40 mph. Further, the aircraft had to be easily assembled and moved on a standard Army wagon, requiring no more than one hour for unloading and assembly.

The specification was considered unreasonably demanding, for despite the Wrights' claims, no one thought that such incredible performance was achievable. Yet the critics missed a seemingly innocuous element of the specification that was the most rigorous of all—the machine had to be "sufficiently simple in its construction and operation to permit an intelligent man to become proficient in its use within a reasonable length of time."

There had been more than forty bidders for Specification 486. Although several were obviously frivolous, more than half were closely examined by the

Army. The field was narrowed finally to three, but only the Wrights were able to bring a machine to Fort Myer in the late summer of 1908.

In fact, the two brothers were separated. Wilbur was in France demonstrating the Wright airplane to skeptical Europeans, so Orville was charged with the military demonstration in Virginia. With their usual meticulous care, each brother took his time in preparing his aircraft. And, when ready, each dazzled his audience, Wilbur turning Europe on its aeronautical ear while Orville set one record after another at Fort Myer. His first was an altitude record of 310 feet, and then, in rapid succession, five endurance records ranging from 38 to 75 minutes. For a period of fifteen days, from September 3 to 17, Orville showed the U.S. Army that the age of flying was at hand.

The inherent danger in flying—even with Orville Wright, one of the two most accomplished pilots in the world—was soon demonstrated. The Wrights had approached the art of flying with diligence and care, making thousands of glider flights before undertaking powered flight. Unfortunately, the new crop of Army flyers were going to be given a few flights and then be turned loose, with tragic results. The underpowered Wright aircraft were difficult to fly and, with their center-mounted engine and pusher propellers, dangerous in a crash. The resulting losses would almost paralyze Army aviation for a decade.

The success of the Wright brothers was built upon careful trial-and-error experimentation. In a step-by-step process, the two men, working almost as a single person, outstripped all other aviation pioneers in a brilliant four-year period. Here a re-creation of their 1902 Wright is shown in flight.

Orville Wright flying over Fort Myer, Virginia, on September 9, 1908. In the five years since Kitty Hawk, the Wright brothers had made improvements in their biplane design without altering it significantly, and its technology was still far in advance of anything yet developed in Europe.

The two-person capability of the airplane had been demonstrated when the first U.S. military observer and the man in charge of the test program, Lieutenant Lahm, went for a flight. Then, on September 17, Tom Selfridge was the passenger.

Orville Wright had mixed feelings about Selfridge; he liked him as an individual—everyone did. But Orville, always suspicious of potential competition, was concerned because Selfridge was a member of Alexander Graham Bell's Aerial Experiment Association. Bell was the Wrights' arch rival. Well aware of the hazards of flight, Selfridge manifested the same signs of nervousness that he had during the balloon trials—an edginess that some interpreted as fear.

THE FIRST MAN TO DIE

An elemental aviation problem was unfolding, the hazard of uncontrolled experimentation. Even careful Orville Wright did not consider the possible consequences when he installed new propellers on his aircraft, each eight inches longer than any used before. Outwardly, everything seemed as routine as flying could be in 1908 when, precisely at 5:14, in the calm of a Virginia afternoon, they were launched down a monorail track by means of a catapult the Wrights had devised.

A few days earlier, Orville had made seventy-one successive circuits of the parade ground; this time, at an altitude of about 150 feet, he had barely com-

Lieutenant Frank Selfridge and Orville Wright shortly before takeoff on the tragic flight of September 17, 1908. Selfridge's hands are relaxed now; in a few moments he will have a stout grip on the struts, for neither man wore a safety belt. The Wrights were still wedded to a skid-landing gear, and used a wooden track for takeoff.

pleted the fourth circle when one of the new propellers cracked, setting in process a series of structural failures that hurled the Wright Military Flyer to the ground.

The startled crowd raced to the scene. What had moments before been an airplane was now a shattered heap, the white linen wings shrouding the two broken but still conscious flyers. Orville was later to relate that Selfridge had muttered "Oh-oh" when the plane had started its dive; in the wreckage, the lieutenant said his last words: "Take this damn thing off my back."

Orville had broken his left thigh and several ribs, along with other minor injuries. Selfridge's skull had been fractured; he died following surgery, the first of many to lose their lives in aircraft accidents.

The crash did not diminish the Army's newfound enthusiasm for aviation, and there was no shortage of volunteers to fly. The Wrights returned to Fort Myer in June 1909, to complete the trials for the $25,000 contract. They had carefully improved their airplane, modifying it so that a propeller could no longer foul on the bracing wires. With their typical ability to go to the heart of a problem, they created and installed the world's first flight instrument, an eight-inch weighted string that served both as a yaw indicator and as a stall-warning device. When the string was stretched back toward the pilot, the plane was flying straight and level; if it veered to the side, it indicated the plane was yawing to the side. If the weight was too low, it indicated that the nose was too high, and a stall was imminent. (This simple idea was good enough to be

The *Wright* Flyer *had plunged more than fifty feet straight down before it began to respond to Orville's efforts at the controls; at twenty-five feet above the ground he felt the airplane beginning to recover, but he had run out of altitude. The skids hit first and, in his word "the machine turned up on edge." Both men were pinned in the wreckage.*

Lieutenant Selfridge, his skull fractured, about to be removed to the hospital. His death was the first of many that would occur in Wright aircraft.

Wilbur Wright had dazzled France with his flying. He is about to dazzle his sister Katharine in a flight on February 15, 1909, at Pau, France. Amid the aviation technology of side-by-side seating, Wright-type controls, and pusher propellers is a fashion statement—Katharine's skirts are "hobbled" with a string. She was the greatest fan of the two brothers and their constant travel companion.

revived on the six-jet Boeing B-47, which first flew thirty-eight years later on December 17, 1947. The B-47 was a complex aircraft with a massive array of instrumentation. Its 116-foot wingspan was only four feet shorter than the distance of the Wrights' first flight, yet externally mounted on its forward fuselage, directly in front of the pilot, was a length of string installed as a yaw indicator.)

Frank Lahm, Dirigible Balloon Pilot No. 2, flew with Orville for an hour and twelve minutes, satisfying the duration of flight requirement in the specification. The most crucial test, aerodynamically and financially, was the speed test. Benny Foulois, chosen in part for his light weight, set up the course and flew over it with Orville. He had surveyed a five-mile track between Fort Myer and Shooter's Hill in Alexandria, Virginia. More than 7,000 people were assembled at the parade ground to witness the test.

Foulois equipped himself with two stopwatches, binoculars, a compass, and an aneroid barometer, then sat down next to Orville. They hurtled down the track, climbed to 125 feet, and departed for Alexandria, bucking a headwind that held their speed down to 37.75 mph, less than the desired qualifying time. But things changed when they circled back toward Fort Myer, gaining height as their speed picked up to a sizzling 47.431 mph. Orville climbed to 410 feet to set a new altitude record, and then spiraled down to an enthusiastic crowd that included the new President, William Howard Taft.

The two men had set three world records: speed, an average of 42.5 mph with two persons aboard; distance, a cross-country flight of ten miles; and altitude. For the speed record, the Wrights gained a $5,000 bonus. The Army gained the commitment to aviation of one of the most outspoken and underrated leaders of his time, Benny Foulois.

A TOUGH LITTLE HOMBRE

Quick with a grin and faster still with a shot of bourbon, Benjamin Foulois was the prototypical mustang, the man from the ranks who would never quite be accepted by West Pointers, especially those he eclipsed in rank. The son of a plumber, he had earned his commission leading riflemen in the jungles of the Philippines. A natural leader, small, wiry and pugnacious, he fought again in Cuba in 1907, "pacifying guerrillas," and was then assigned to a course at the Infantry and Cavalry School at Fort Leavenworth, Kansas. Never a distinguished student, Foulois nevertheless gained attention with his thesis on "The Tactical and Strategic Value of Dirigible Balloons and Aerodynamical Flying Machines." Without any practical experience, and almost a decade ahead of William (Billy) Mitchell, Foulois forecast massive fleets operating in advance of the ground forces, and engaging enemy aviation at the outbreak of the war. No one else had ever written on the subject, and his expertise had won him assignment to train on the new Signal Corps Dirigible Number One.

In a scenario straight out of Hollywood, Foulois's most bitter rival would be Billy Mitchell, the son of a senator and the man most remembered today as the great American visionary of air power. Given a commission at eighteen, and a self-proclaimed aviation expert before he had ever flown, Mitchell was everything that Foulois was not: well-spoken, flamboyant, a politician when he had to be. The two men instinctively disliked each other, and after 1916 held different positions on almost every issue. Yet their wrangles over the years yielded enormous dividends to air power. Mitchell was constantly stretching the boundaries of imagination, and often the truth. Foulois was perhaps even more outspoken than Mitchell in the early years, but for most of his career his modest manner and sincerity deflected the criticism on which Mitchell appeared to thrive. Foulois had another quality, the determination to do the best he had with what he was given—or could beg, borrow, or requisition. Neither man ever compromised; sadly, as we shall see, both were chewed up and spit out by the service to which they had given their lives.

COLLEGE PARK, CRADLE OF AVIATION

Young Foulois loved flying, but hated the dirigible, which he felt was too slow and unwieldy ever to have a future. He set a pattern that would haunt his distinguished career by voicing his disapproval, even though this was counter to the opinion of the Chief Signal Officer.

The result was predictable. He was disciplined by not being assigned to the first group sent to learn to fly at the newly established Army flying school at College Park, Maryland. Still in existence, and the oldest active airport in the world, College Park was for a brief time the incubator for future leaders of U.S. air power. There, on October 26, 1909, Second Lieutenant Frederick E. Humphries received three hours, three minutes, thirty-six seconds of dual-pilot flight time before becoming the first U.S. military aviator to solo. Frank Lahm, with three hours and seven minutes of instruction, followed him.

Life was simple, almost serene, at College Park, if one excepted the natural hazard of flying. Actual air work could be done only in virtual calm, usually early in the morning and late in the evening. Jimmy Doolittle later told the story that a pilot would stick a finger in his mouth, then hold it in the air; if one side cooled faster than the other, there was too much wind to fly. In the long intervals between flights, the pilots and mechanics exchanged ideas, fostering the close rapport between officers and enlisted men that would always characterize the U.S. flying services. Both groups had to love flying to endure a profession so hazardous that private insurers would not issue policies to them. The hazard was demonstrated on September 28, 1912, when Lieutenant Lewis C. Rockwell was to fly in one of the school's tricky Wright B pushers. Rockwell was completing requirements for his Military Aviator rating, and on this flight needed to carry a passenger to a height of 500 feet. Corporal Frank S. Scott volunteered to go along. The Wright B had a fatal flaw inherent in the relationship of its center of gravity to its thrust line; when the aircraft was gliding at low speeds, a sudden application of power would cause the nose to pitch down. Just as Rockwell was about to land, he applied full power; the aircraft pitched forward into the ground. Scott was killed instantly, the first enlisted man to lose his life flying. Rockwell died a few hours later.

Foulois arrived back from his exile as a delegate to the International Congress of Aeronautics in Paris, and wangled orders to College Park. He had received only a few minutes' instruction from Wilbur Wright before the single Army machine was damaged beyond immediate repair. The air forces of the U.S. Army were reduced to one untrained pilot, a handful of mechanics, and one aircraft in disrepair. General Allen ordered Foulois to take Aeroplane No. 1 to Fort Sam Houston, Texas, where he was first to repair it and then teach himself to fly, as there were no funds available for further tutelage from the Wrights.

CORRESPONDENCE-COURSE FLYING

In San Antonio, Foulois, grim-faced, cap turned to the rear, took the overhauled Military Flyer for its first flight in what became a combination of first

Some elements of the Wright design have appeared again in the most modern aircraft. This Grumman X-29 research aircraft has canard surfaces just as the Wright Flyer did.

ARMY'S FIRST AIRPLANE · WRIGHT TYPE-B.
T SAM HOUSTON · TEXAS · 1910

Benny Foulois, second from the right, and the world's first military airplane. Foulois taught himself to fly by corresponding with the Wrights. It was an amazing feat, as the Wright airplane was not easy to fly, and he had to learn the hard way, rebuilding the aircraft after crashes on many of his early flights.

solo, first landing, and first crash. In the ensuing weeks, the tough little soldier learned to fly by correspondence, carefully noting what he thought made him crash, writing the Wrights for an answer, and then, perhaps ten days later, trying again. After being thrown from the airplane in one hard landing, Foulois had the saddle makers at Fort Sam make a strap to hold him in—the world's first safety belt, and the direct ancestor of every airplane and automobile safety belt in existence.

Obsessed by his new career, and delighted to be literally a one-man Air Force, Foulois poured his own money into spare parts to keep the progressively battered No. 1 flying, tinkering with it and modifying it as he gained experience. Eventually, he fitted it with a tricycle landing gear—the Army's first—and freed himself from the intractable skid undercarriage of the original Wright design.

Later, in a Wright Model B loaned to the Army by publisher Robert B. Collier, Foulois accomplished three significant aviation milestones: the first military reconnaissance of our borders, the first photographic reconnaissance that resulted in aerial mapmaking, and the first use of the radio to communicate intelligence to ground stations.

Despite Foulois's successes, a strong current of antagonism persisted in Congress and within the Army itself, in part because of the high accident rate. In 1911, one fatal accident occurred for every sixty-five hours of Army flying—and there were continual cries to shut the experiment down. The casualties resulted from a number of factors. On all of the early airplanes the margin between top speed and stall speed was small, perhaps the difference only between 40 and 30 mph. The primitive biplanes were unstable and easy to overcontrol, inducing either structural failure or a "high-speed" stall. Pilot training was inadequate, and it was difficult to get enough flying time to maintain even a limited proficiency. The pusher aircraft were particularly deadly, for a crash left the pilots crushed under the engine. Six Wright Model C aircraft, not much different in appearance from the original 1903 Flyer, were procured; within the year all had crashed, killing five pilots. In 1914, pusher aircraft were condemned, virtually wiping out the inventory, but removing one certain hazard.

Limited as the funds were, the Aeronautics Division reopened the flying school at College Park in June 1911, the beginning of a migratory training program that would move successively to Augusta, Georgia; San Diego, California; and finally San Antonio, Texas. At College Park, three lieutenants who would be famous in the future—Henry H. Arnold, Thomas DeW. Milling, and Roy C. Kirtland—immediately began setting records and testing bombsights, machine guns, cameras, and radios.

PENNY WISE, POUND FOOLISH

The enthusiasm of the pilots remained unmatched by congressional generosity. By 1914, only $400,000 had been appropriated by Congress for military aviation; in contrast, Germany and France had each expended $22 million and Russia had spent $12 million. France had more than 350 certified pilots; the United States had only 26. The great lead that Wilbur and Orville Wright had conferred had been squandered, and the country was totally unaware of it. The advances in Europe were not merely numerical; the United States lacked the enormous aviation infrastructure required for the development not only of obvious needs such as engines, instruments, and weaponry, but also for the provision of basic raw materials—linen, castor oil, spruce, and improved metals.

The United States lagged furthest behind in the area hardest to make up, that of engine development. Although Europe was literally bristling with new and more powerful engines, 90-horsepower Curtiss V-8 engines remained the industry standard in the United States.

Reports on the growth of European strength convinced the doubters that airplanes were here to stay. On July 18, 1914, President Woodrow Wilson signed a law establishing the Aviation Section of the Signal Corps, with an authorized strength of 60 officers and 260 enlisted men. The first aeronautical ratings were established: Junior Military Aviator and Military Aviator.

In recognition of the accident rate, flying assignments were limited to unmarried officers of the line; when regularly assigned to flying duty, they could draw 35 percent extra pay. Benny Foulois, the hard-bitten man of the line, had uncharacteristically done behind-the-scenes congressional politicking to authorize flying pay, even though he did not benefit personally because he was not "regularly assigned" to flying duty. But he knew that the demonstrated

Future general of the Air Force, Henry H. "Hap" Arnold in two photos with his friend and colleague Thomas DeW. Milling. Lieutenants at College Park in the top picture, they had both learned to fly in the left seat of the Wright biplane; Milling has secured the coveted spot here. In the lower photo, twenty years later, both men are majors and fly a Boeing P-12B pursuit plane. Arnold's ineffable smile blazes in both photos.

Even with their prescient view of the future, Orville and Wilbur Wright could not have imagined the intelligence-gathering capacity of the Boeing/Grumman E-8 J-STARS aircraft, the prototype of which distinguished itself in combat during the Persian Gulf War. The electronics revolution enabled the J-STARS E-8 to monitor air and ground action in a way never done before.

The Wright factory in Dayton, the first in the world for serial production of aircraft, very much set the pattern for factories around the world. It was not yet mass production, but it was the beginning of a standardized approach to the problem.

hazard made the inducement not only necessary but fair, for it was an actuarial calculation of the cost of providing insurance to compensate for the income lost by a fatal accident. Justifying the extra pay was a task that would plague the service from that time forward, no matter how many times it was proven that military flying was inherently dangerous.

The new branch of the service had about 20 airplanes, none of them up to the still primitive European standard. France and Germany each had about 180 aircraft; England had about 100. The difference with the United States grew almost geometrically over the next three years as the pressure of war forced aircraft development in Europe.

The Burgess Model 1 Weight-Carrying Scout Seaplane, the seventeenth aircraft purchased by the Signal Corps, became the first stealth aircraft when it was fitted with a muffler to permit it to fly reconnaissance missions without being heard. Here, on San Jose Beach at Corregidor in the Philippine Islands, Lieutenant Herbert A. Dargue is in the cockpit. Powered by a 60-horsepower Sturtevant engine, the Burgess retained much of its Wright heritage. It was used for both photographic and radio experiments, and received the first radio transmission to an aircraft on December 7, 1914.

Lieutenant Frank P. Lahm, an aristocrat on horseback or in the cockpit, with the first Army aircraft, a Wright Model C, at Fort McKinley in the Philippines, 1912. Six examples of the Wright C were purchased by the Army; all crashed, five of them killing their pilots.

The danger of flying aircraft powered by pusher engines was so acute that Thomas D. Milling and fledgling aeronautical engineer Grover Loening built their own tractor-engine design. Here Milling is landing at North Field, San Diego.

The air was still too new for interservice rivalry, and the Army experimented with flying boats at North Island, San Diego, in 1914. This is a Curtiss Model F, with a 75-horsepower Curtiss engine. Of clean, advanced design, the Model F was used by both the Army and the Navy and was in production through 1918. Lieutenant Walter Taliaferro is standing at left.

FOULOIS VERSUS PANCHO VILLA

Foulois's pioneering work continued with the use of aircraft in two separate Mexican border campaigns. The first, in 1914, literally never got off the ground; the aircraft sent to Vera Cruz arrived only after the action was over. The second was against Pancho Villa in 1916, a campaign in which ill-equipped American regulars were sent into hostile country against a native

guerrilla force. The Mexican forces would disappear into the countryside, frustrating the American troops floundering after them.

Foulois brought the 1st Aero Squadron to Columbus, New Mexico, and made the first U.S. military reconnaissance over foreign territory on March 16, 1916, flying thirty miles into Mexico. By May, he had 8 airplanes, 13 trucks, 16 officers, and 122 enlisted men under his command, and the unfounded expectations of the War Department at his back.

The planes were Curtiss JN-3s, fitted with wheezing 90-horsepower Curtiss engines that functioned poorly in the harsh New Mexican environment. Their very low rate of climb made the small fields available to them extraordinarily hazardous, and the intervening 12,000-foot mountain peaks could not even be approached, much less climbed over. The weather posed other problems, causing the propellers to delaminate and engines to overheat.

Foulois's men were ordered into Casas Grandes, Mexico, 125 miles south of the border, where flying conditions were even worse. After a harrowing night flight, six Jennies ultimately reached the base. There, the squadron began reconnoitering from the air and, where necessary, landing in enemy territory and operating on foot. It was during one of these operations that Foulois became the first American airman to become a prisoner of war, captured by the Mexican *rurales* and imprisoned until released to the American consul.

By April 1916, Foulois had only two planes left, and the new aircraft furnished him—Curtiss JN-4s and R-2s—were so poorly built that the unit was never able to perform useful field service again.

General Pershing expressed his appreciation, however, and the 1st Aero Squadron's pioneering efforts must have made an impression on Congress,

The 1st Aero Squadron, commanded by Captain Benjamin Foulois, on the trail of Pancho Villa in the spring of 1916. The Curtiss JN-3 aircraft with their 90-horsepower Curtis OX-5 engines were inadequate for the task; maintaining them in the heat and dust of the Mexican climate was virtually impossible. Although perhaps a great advance over the Wright biplanes, they were not at all comparable to the aircraft then fighting in Europe.

which authorized $13,281,666 for further aeronautical development. While money could not make up time, it was at least a step in the right direction.

The lag in engine development could not immediately be overcome, but good use of the funds was made creating new training schools and forming seven new squadrons. Even so, when war was declared on April 6, 1917, the Aviation Section had about fifty-five airplanes, with less than half in commission, and none combat-worthy. Although the service had 131 officers and 1,087 enlisted men, there were no plans for building an air force. No one had been sent to Europe to observe the fighting. An entire world war had raged for three years, and the Aviation Section had been oblivious to it. It was a mistake that would not be repeated one war later.

Sadly, after the Wright's great leap forward, the brothers became absorbed more in patent-protection problems than in advancing their basic design, and they were soon eclipsed by European designers. The lovely Antoinette monoplane, produced by Leon Levavasseur, is shown here.

CHAPTER TWO
The Birth of Air Power 1917–1918

Historians usually look at the American air effort in World War I through two very different lenses. With one, they find the glory of the air combat at the front, where Captain Eddie Rickenbacker and balloon-buster Frank Luke created legends. With the second, they discover the waste and error of the production programs, which by November 11, 1918, had delivered only 196 American-made copies of de Havilland DH-4s to combat units. Unfortunately, both lenses are obscured. Most of the inferences made from gazing through them have been very wrong, and instead of destroying myths, they have intensified them.

The American combat record *was* distinguished by heroes, as we shall see, but it was also marred by the inevitable hardships a fledgling air arm would encounter meeting a well-equipped veteran enemy. In fighter-versus-fighter combat, the exuberant U.S. airmen had confirmed victories for 781 aircraft and 73 balloons. American losses were 289 planes and 48 balloons brought down in battle. Later attempts to confirm all of the victories indicate that the claim for 781 victories was undoubtedly inflated, as is the case for all air forces in all wars. Nonetheless, it was by any count a splendid showing for young cubs thrown in against old lions. Later, we will examine how the American bombing and observation squadrons, roughly handled because of the aircraft they were flying and their inexperience, still pressed on to carry out their missions.

In assessing the American production effort, blame is usually placed on rapacious businessmen who tailored procurement to their own advantage, pocketing millions and sabotaging the national effort. There is no doubt that there was waste, or that some individuals lined their pockets. The year 1917 was not far removed from the days of the great robber barons, and the freebooting spirit of the business community was not inhibited by much in the way of regulation. More important than the greed factor, however, was the lust for power that boiled in the services, in government, and in industry, both at home and abroad, a general mad scrambling for primacy that impeded the war effort.

THE AIRCRAFT PRODUCTION FIASCO

The real people responsible for what was termed "the aircraft production fiasco" were the men in the military and Congress who were responsible for the

Corporal Edwin Charles Parsons, once a captain in Pancho Villa's Aviation Corps, was the twenty-first volunteer for the Lafayette Escadrille. An eight-victory ace, Parsons is shown here in his Nieuport 11, equipped with Le Prieur rockets for attacking balloons. The rotary-engine Nieuport was nimble but somewhat fragile.

OPPOSITE:
The Arizona Balloon Buster, *by Merv Corning, depicts Lieutenant Frank Luke's victory over a German observation balloon. Luke was a wild, undisciplined fighter who might have been court-martialed if he had survived, but was instead awarded the Medal of Honor for heroism.*

armed forces. They failed utterly to plan for involvement in the war not only after August 1914 but, incredibly, even after April 6, 1917, when the United States declared war. All the desperate attempts to catch up could not eliminate that failure. As the National Advisory Committee for Aeronautics (NACA) had solemnly warned, the one thing money could not buy was time.

Despite time constraints, the total lack of an industrial base for aviation, inexperience, and the false hopes and subsequent disillusionment from the flood of patriotic enthusiasm that welled up once war was declared, a complex aviation industry was in fact created within the incredibly short period of a year. Had the war lasted until mid-1919, most of the jingoistic predictions of clouds of American-designed and American-built aircraft would have been fulfilled. Certainly, the creation of the Liberty engine, even with its limitations, was a triumph of will over red tape, as was the production of the much-maligned "flaming coffin," the de Havilland DH-4. Another achievement, lesser-known, was the British use of the U.S.-designed Curtiss H-12 and H-16 flying boats for North Sea submarine patrol.

The United States was not alone in its production problems. After years of wartime experience, the British aircraft industry was still capable of colossal mistakes. The B.H.P.-powered de Havilland D.H.9 was a far worse failure on all counts than the "Liberty plane," as the American DH-4 was inevitably called. Even more notorious was the highly touted A.B.C. Dragonfly engine, intended to be the standard British fighter power plant for 1919, and around which the new fighter types were designed. The Dragonfly simply vibrated itself into pieces and out of production. The French had similar disasters, largely glossed over. The 220-horsepower Hispano-Suiza engines used to power Spads and a number of other aircraft had an appalling maintenance record; at one point, almost two-thirds of all Spads were grounded with engine problems. The

The only American-built combat plane to see active service at the front was the de Havilland DH-4 "Liberty Plane," powered by a 400-horsepower Liberty engine. Of the 4,346 built, 283 were transferred to the Navy and the Marines. This photo of a DH-4 at Colomby-les-Belles, France, clearly shows the distance that separated the pilot in the forward cockpit and the observer in the rear; the fuel tank was between them.

This strikingly handsome Packard-LePere LUSAO-11 triplane is an example of how far indigenous American designs had come by the end of World War I. Designed and built at McCook Field's Engineering Division, the LePere was a long-range observation plane powered by two Liberty engines, capable of a top speed of 112 mph. Two prototypes were built, and the first was delivered in February 1919.

Germans were hardly immune. Their problems ran from recurring shoddy workmanship in Fokker aircraft to a chronic inability to develop more powerful engines for their fighters.

THE PLANNING FAILURE

Still, the American planning failure was comprehensive. Even though Congress had authorized a Council of National Defense on August 29, 1916, until March 1917 there was not even a draft paper suggesting how large an air service should be organized, how many men would be necessary, or how many and what type of planes would be needed. There was absolutely no planning for the development of an industrial base, with its aircraft factories, trained workers, component suppliers, parts makers, and vendors of raw materials. As weak as the U.S. Army ground forces were, at least they were able to form cadres to train the millions of men required to bolster the Western Front. And, although equipment was scarce, an industrial infrastructure was able to provide the raw materials, machine tools, and factory space to turn out rifles, cannons, uniforms, and other items of equipment.

It was totally different with the Aeronautics Division, which existed only as a barely tolerated experiment. There was no concept of the variety and number of skills required by a modern air service, from mechanics to pilots to surgeons to seamstresses, or any vague idea of the enormous base that would be required to train personnel. In terms of hardware, only 20 percent of the 224 airplanes the Army had purchased since 1908 remained in service. The industry that had starved so long consisted of a dozen small aircraft builders and the giant Curtiss Aeroplane and Engine Company. Taken together, in 1916 this infant industry had been able to deliver only 83 airplanes out of 366 ordered, and many of these were crashed almost upon receipt.

In a hauntingly familiar style, Congress sought a quick solution for public consumption: if there was no air arm, create one overnight by throwing money at the problem. The Air Service, which up to 1916 had total appropriations of less than $500,000, tasked Captain Foulois to draft a program for an expansion to meet the needs of a 3-million-man Army. Foulois worked with Captain Edgar Gorrell, one of his colleagues from the Mexican expedition, to prepare the estimates and guide them through the legislative maze, their zeal augmented and focused by the May arrival of the famous Ribot telegram discussed below. The result was the single largest appropriation in congressional history, $640 million, and the command to go forth and darken the skies with airplanes.

THE MYTHS ARE BORN

In retrospect, the congressional naïveté was understandable. The United States of 1917 was still a provincial country, just peeking beyond its own frontiers with the recent acquisition of the Philippines. Bumptious with wealth, proud of their automobile industry, still flushed with the industrial successes of the Civil War, and puffed by their recent victory over Spain, the people of the United States believed that a little thing like building airplanes could not be much more difficult than building Model-T Fords.

National leaders, intoxicated with the rush to war, exacerbated the optimism and fueled the myths. The newly formed Aircraft Production Board, intended to select and standardize aircraft types for production, issued a statement that allayed fears and elicited boasts. The Aero Club of America, which of all organizations should have known better, called for air raids that would strike Germany in its vitals and lead to permanent victory.

Even the monumentally unprepared Secretary of War, Newton D. Baker, argued that although a few million troops would not tip the scales on the Western Front, a few thousand aviators could. He glibly told a cheering nation that it would take time to train and equip armies, but thousands of aviators could be trained and thousands of airplanes manufactured without interfering with the rest of our military buildup. The militantly patriotic press responded with enthusiasm, portraying a cartoon Kaiser terrorized by American warplanes swarming overhead. Inevitably, the patriotic furor had a reverse effect; the Germans launched their own *Amerikaprogramm* to expand their aviation industry to cope with the anticipated American buildup.

The total failure to prepare was all the more inexcusable because even though the traditional corps of military observers had not been sent to the front, many enthusiastic, well-connected young men had already gone to France to fly with the British and French air forces, including the soon-to-be-immortal Lafayette Escadrille.

As popular as the Lafayette Escadrille was, as feted as its heroes were, until the spring of 1917 no one within the War Department or the Air Service made an intelligent inference from its activities as to what would be required when the United States entered the war. It is inexplicable that despite having American airmen engaged in combat, flying first-line equipment, the American Air Service and the aviation industry learned nothing from them and continued to operate in a void, neither building strength nor creating modern designs.

The problem might have been mitigated if all the Allies had been as helpful and forthcoming as England (with the single exception of Rolls-Royce, which adamantly refused cooperation unless paid adequate royalties). In contrast to England, France and Italy were grasping, determined to pluck the last dollar out of American pockets. The emissaries they sent to the United States did not bring the latest technical information to spur aircraft development; they were salesmen, viewing America merely as a source of raw materials, manpower and dollars. The raw materials were to be imported into the homeland and converted to arms, and then sold back at a profit. Manpower from America was to be funneled directly into existing Allied units, to reinforce and refresh them with new blood. Technology developed by the Allies was withheld so that the United States would continue to have to purchase finished aircraft, often rejects from French frontline service such as the Dorand AR 2 and the Nieuport 28. The shortsightedness backfired, and ultimately only English designs entered mass production in the United States.

In a manner that would repeat itself over the years, a handful of young men were left to form the spear tip of combat, backed by the rubber shaft of an organizational fiasco. In both arenas, Benny Foulois and Billy Mitchell would wage interpersonal warfare on a colossal scale, stage-managing America's convulsive leap into aircraft production and then squabbling like two Chicago bootleggers over turf rights in the European air war.

PRODUCTION PROGRAM: DEBACLE OR TRIUMPH?

An insider on the General Staff since 1914, Billy Mitchell convinced himself that air power was the only path around the stalemate on the Western Front. To gain credibility in the area of expertise he was appropriating, he learned to fly at his own expense, then wangled his way to Europe in March 1917. He was in Spain when war was declared, and immediately responded to the sounds of the guns in France.

In Paris, Mitchell made his own arrangements for an office to control aviation, and began compiling lists of material that would be needed. His preparation purportedly became the basis for the famous telegram from the French Premier, Alexander Ribot, to the American government, which called for 4,500 airplanes, 5,000 pilots, and 50,000 mechanics to be at the front in 1918. Ribot also asked for additional 2,000 airplanes and 4,000 engines of "the latest type" a month, for the use of the Allies. All told, with the required trainers, Ribot asked for 22,625 airplanes to be delivered thirteen months later—only 273 times the total of the previous year's production.

Woodrow Wilson approved the request, as did the Army and Navy Technical Board, and most importantly, the American press and public. It did not matter that it was a fantasy proposal, with no basis in reality in terms of resources, production facilities, or anything else. *La Belle France* had asked, and an America flushed with pro-Allied patriotic fervor would respond.

A question unasked by both Mitchell and Ribot was exactly which types of aircraft were to be produced. To find out, an Aeronautical Commission headed by Major Raynal C. Bolling, in civil life a senior attorney for U.S. Steel, was sent to Europe in June 1917. The Bolling Commission's report would form the doctrinal and technical foundation for creating the American Expeditionary Force Air Service.

Bolling was well served. With him he had Captain Virginius E. Clark, an irascible engineering genius whose eccentricity would blossom over the years, and Foulois's assistant, Edgar Gorrell, a tactician and historian who was to become the youngest colonel in the U.S. Army at the age of twenty-seven. Beset by the parochial requests of their Allied counterparts, they used their best judgment to devise a formula for the balance of types—37.5 percent fighters, 37.5 percent night bombers, and 25 percent day bombers—and also recommended six aircraft designs for production in the United States.

It was quickly apparent to Bolling and his group that no matter what aircraft was selected from the existing stock for production, it would inevitably be obsolete the following year when (and if) it arrived from American production lines. But there was no alternative—the United States did not have the industrial capacity to develop its own aircraft, and there was no way to build European aircraft that had not yet appeared.

THE REAL DECISION

Although it was not perceived for many years, the real decision taken then was to produce obsolete Allied types immediately in order to build a production capacity while simultaneously developing advanced American types for delivery in 1919. The achievement of these formidable goals is too often overlooked.

The Bolling Commission's recommendations were reviewed and changed over time, and by September 1917, when contracts were let, only nine months remained before the Ribot deadline. The Dayton-Wright Airplane Company was to build 2,000 de Havillands and the Fisher Body Company 3,000. Curtiss, expanding continuously as it built JN-4 trainers, was given a colossal order for 3,000 Spad single-seat and 1,000 Bristol two-seat fighters. The Standard Aircraft Company, like Curtiss a builder of trainers, was authorized to build 500 Caproni three-engine biplane and triplane bombers.

It was an impossible task, compounded by the insistence that the just-developing American Liberty engine be used to power as many types as possible. Several crashes proved that the Liberty was too heavy and powerful for the

Bristol, and it was decided to obtain the Spads in France, so both contracts were canceled. The Italians proved to be impossible to deal with, refusing to furnish all the necessary drawings and prohibiting any changes without approval from Sr. Caproni himself, resulting not only in contract cancellation, but considerable ill will on both sides.

As a counterpoint to the endless troubles in selecting and producing airframes, the American engineers did make tremendous progress in the most difficult area of all, the design of a powerful new engine.

THE BULLY LIBERTY ENGINE

The Liberty engine has been surrounded by myths since its inception, the most enduring of which was that it was designed from scratch over a weekend by rapacious charter members of the military-industrial complex. It was also alleged to be too heavy for all uses, unreliable and expensive to operate, as well as an inordinate user of oil. The facts are so different that the Liberty story is almost a paradigm of the controversy surrounding World War I aviation production.

The design of the Liberty engine began on May 29, 1917, in Washington, D.C., in the Willard Hotel suite of Colonel Edwin Deeds, who would later be charged with heinous conflict-of-interest crimes but absolved of them by the Secretary of War, Newton D. Baker. Deeds had brought together veteran "engine guys" Jesse G. Vincent and Elbert J. Hall, both of whom already had ideas that would be incorporated in the Liberty. Vincent was in the process of designing a new 240-horsepower aero engine at Packard, while Hall was creating a 450-horsepower engine for his own Hall-Scott firm. Deeds, president of Delco, and S. D. Waldon, vice president at Packard, were both members of the Aircraft Production Board, and were determined not to let the United States fall into the absurd logistic tangle France and England were creating by building scores of different types of engines. They wanted a U.S. standardized aircraft engine, one built in four-, six-, eight- and twelve-cylinder types, with a range of 100 to 400 horsepower.

The companies Hall and Vincent represented had invested hundreds of thousands of dollars in the development of engines. They threw the knowledge and designs already in progress on the table as a *pro bono* starting point, and they then solicited ideas and information from every knowledgeable source in Washington, including the French Military Mission, the Society of Automotive Engineers, and the Bureau of Standards. The basic Hall-Scott/Packard ideas were synthesized with ideas gained from an analysis of the German Mercedes engine. The design that emerged, though marred by some shortcomings, especially excessive vibration, would ultimately prove itself.

Two days later, on May 31, their concepts were approved. By June 4, complete layouts had been made. On June 5 the Packard Company agreed to finance the program until the government could provide reimbursement. The first twelve-cylinder Liberty passed its fifty-hour continuous-run test on August 25, and on August 29, 1917, exactly three months after the door to Deeds's hotel suite had closed on Vincent and Hall, the Liberty engine made its first flight. By October 1918 Liberty engines were being produced at the rate of 46,000 a year, and the Allied nations were clamoring for them. (For various reasons, the four-, six- and eight-cylinder versions had all fallen by the wayside.)

With a retrospective stretch of the imagination, one might say that if the Liberty engine had been the only result of the $640 million appropriation, it would not have been a bad bargain, for the big twelve-cylinder engine was to power most of the heavier U.S. aircraft for the next ten years. Then it soldiered on as the power plant for everything from rum-running boats and Hollywood wind machines to 6,500 English tanks in World War II.

But the appropriation provided far more. Its first and most demanding task was the establishment of forty-one flying schools (sixteen abroad), twenty-eight mechanics schools, and a dozen other specialty schools. It created an entire aircraft industry where none had existed before. By 1918 there were indigenous manufacturers of airplanes, engines, instruments, electrical systems, magnetos, bombsights, bomb racks, fuels, propellers, tires, helmets, oxygen systems, pyrotechnics, fabric, dope, flying clothes, goggles, cameras, lubricants, and every other necessary material, raw and finished. In Dayton, Ohio, at McCook Field (graced by a sign warning pilots, "This Field Is Small—Use It All"), a surprisingly sophisticated engineering establishment sprang up, one from which all of today's Air Force engineering and test centers are derived.

THE LIBERTY PLANE

The two principal aircraft produced in America were the legendary Curtiss JN-4 Jenny and the de Havilland DH-4 Liberty Plane. More than 6,000 of the Jenny and its developments were built, and they became the standard U.S. trainer. Eventually, 4,846 Liberty planes were delivered, with orders for another 7,502 canceled.

Once the design had been chosen, the production effort on the American-built DH-4 moved as swiftly as that of the Liberty engine itself. On August 14, 1917, the newly formed Dayton-Wright Airplane Company was selected to build the DH-4. Some drawings were available, as was a sample of a complete British-built DH-4, less engine and other service equipment.

Dayton-Wright launched into production by creating drawings for 35,330 components, including 2,608 wood and 1,665 sheet-metal parts. In every case, dimensions had to be converted from English to American standards, and the whole system of building altered from the British "fits" to American "tolerances." Nonetheless, the first American-built DH-4 was sub-

stantially complete by September 1917 and made its first flight on October 29, seventy-six days after the go-ahead.

Thus, two brand-new projects, the Liberty engine and the American DH-4, were brought together in an amazingly short time. Their subsequent joint progress to the front would be tortuous. Production difficulties ensued almost immediately, as inevitable changes were introduced, and Dayton-Wright made the usual public relations gaffes that are almost implicit in a new production airplane. Eager to honor their pledge to get aircraft en route to France prior to January 1, 1918, they rushed an example out the door to a railroad car on December 31, 1917. After they had touted their success, it became known that the plane had been held up in port for weeks. Adding insult to injury, the freighter transporting it was sunk by a German U-boat, so it never reached France at all.

At about the same time the aviation industry came under attack from a

The very first American de Havilland DH-4, powered by the number four model Liberty engine. For many years it was presumed that this was a British-built aircraft, but the restoration by the craftsmen of the National Air and Space Museum's Garber Facility proved that the aircraft was entirely American-built. Early prototypes were rarely preserved; this is a unique example.

remarkable source. Gutzon Borglum, the sculptor immortalized by his monumental Mount Rushmore figures, took it upon himself to be the Ralph Nader of World War I aircraft production; he launched a series of ludicrous charges at the major figures in aircraft production. His principal target was Colonel Deeds, whom he portrayed as a profiteering pro-German whose real name was Deitz.

Armed by an innocuous letter from President Wilson, which he construed as a charter to investigate the entire aircraft program, Borglum used the *New York World* to trumpet his charges. It soon developed that Borglum, an official of the Ku Klux Klan, was furious that an aircraft of his own design had not been approved for production. Borglum claimed that his never-built "fish-type" aircraft would not only lay waste to Germany, but that he would use it to land in Berlin, capture the Kaiser, and end the war.

Borglum was the screwball lead-in to what became a postwar witch-hunt. On November 11, 1918, there were only forty-five American squadrons at the Western Front, with 740 airplanes, 767 pilots, 481 observers, and 23 aerial gunners. Applauded at the time, these numbers were derided the following year when an extensive congressional investigation into the "billion-dollar blunder" of the aircraft program began. Fueled by indignant editorials and the skewed testimony of industry gadflies like the eccentric inventor J. V. Martin, the politicians had a field day castigating the men who had done the only thing possible, using the existing American industrial automotive infrastructure as the basis for an aviation industry.

Harassed and on the defensive, the industry failed to convince the public of the magnitude of its accomplishments, even though it had achieved much. One of the greatest successes was the result of the Army's Spruce Production Division, a homefront operation that had both military and industrial impact. The Allied aircraft industry desperately needed Sitka spruce to build its airplanes, for the wood was light, strong, and easy to work. But Sitka spruce grew in isolated groves spread throughout the forests of the Northwest. A Spruce Production Division, under Colonel Brice P. Disque, sent almost 30,000 "spruce soldiers" into the forests to build sixty military camps, construct scores of roads and bridges, build thirteen railways, and increase spruce production by 1,000 percent. In the process, they pacified both the giant lumber companies and the always-grumbling, sometimes-sabotaging International Workers of the World, the "Wobblies." So involved did the Spruce Production Division become that it was not finally liquidated until twenty-eight years later.

Another triumph was the creation of modern U.S.-designed airplanes. By the time the furor over the aircraft program broke, there were already flying examples of what the Air Service of the American Expeditionary Force would have used in France. These included the Martin GMB, a twin-engine bomber comparable to the famous German Gotha that had raided London. Working with the French Captain LePere, McCook Field developed the Packard-LePere observation plane, greatly superior to the DH-4, and used after the war for

both test work and record setting. Several fighters were coming on line, including the Thomas-Morse MB-3, which was the first standard U.S fighter after the war, and the Orenco D, a sleek biplane. Grover Loening had developed the M-8, a radical two-place monoplane that he, for one, considered far superior to the Bristol fighter. And in the process, the authorities had weeded out calamities like the lethal, wing-shedding Christmas Bullet, the bulky J. V. Martin Cruising Bomber, and the Borglum "Fish."

The hue and cry from Congress and the press was beneficial, for it would force the services to do better planning for the next war to end all wars. The mistakes of the 1917–1918 production program may be evident to the sage historian looking back from the vantage point of seventy years. They were not so obvious to the workers struggling to pull a new industry together overnight in the midst of a world war.

INTERNECINE WARFARE

The homefront effort divided into two well-defined tracks. The first, the production of airplanes, engines, and aeronautical material, has been discussed; the second was the recruitment, selection, and training of personnel. Both were monumental tasks, and both succeeded surprisingly well, given the conditions of their creation; yet both have been criticized for not achieving more, sooner.

The creation of both the Air Service, American Expeditionary Force, overseas, and what ultimately came to be called the Division of Military Aeronautics in the United States, resembled nothing more than two drunken barn raisings. In both cases, the only commodity freely available was bosses; everything else was in short supply.

At home, the situation eventually stabilized and made progress in spite of the disorganization at the top, for as in any good large organization, natural leaders at the lower levels used pragmatic means to get the job done. They succeeded beyond any reasonable expectations, drawing on their College Park experience and opening thirty-five flying schools within the first year. Officers who had served as lieutenants for years suddenly found themselves colonels, setting up entire training camps. Aided by some veteran sergeants and totally willing communities, they performed miracles, particularly in the South, where flying weather was better. Sleepy towns soon played host to swelling hordes of Army recruits, sweating in their choke-collar uniforms and puttee leggings. Modeled after Canadian flying schools, the camps sprang to life with the apparent rapidity of time-lapse photography. First there would be rows of tents and open latrines, followed by temporary hangars and maintenance buildings built of wood and tar paper. Social matters followed suit. Relations between town and camp would be formal at first, but soon there would be dances, romances, marriages, and babies, not always in that sequence.

From today's perspective, the most unusual aspect of the national patriotic convulsion was the enthusiasm with which the great universities embraced the training programs. There may have been divisions within the academic community in 1917, but they were not obvious, and ground schools for training aviators were welcomed on prestigious campuses. The NACA, predecessor of NASA, arranged for a meeting on April 30, 1917, with representatives of America's six best-known scientific schools.

A scheme was devised almost on the spot for a large-scale primary flying training effort, calling for eight weeks of "ground school" courses at Cornell, Ohio State, MIT, and the universities of Texas, Illinois, and California. Incredibly, on July 14 the first classes were graduated, setting the tempo for the education program, which would continue throughout the war. Later, ground schools were established at Princeton and Georgia Tech.

Volunteers swarmed in. Sixty-six examining boards received 38,770 applicants for flying school by November 1918; of these, 18,004 were eliminated for physical reasons. Ultimately, 14,835 flying cadets passed ground school to be sent to newly established flying schools in the United States, Canada, England, France, and Italy.

The irreducible length of even minimum training meant that there was a year-long delay before the first American squadron would be deployed at the front. The 1st Aero Squadron, the same unit that Foulois had led against the Mexicans, arrived in France on September 3, 1917. There it was equipped with French airplanes—Dorands, Spad XIs, and Salmson biplanes, with their unusual water-cooled radial engines—and was trained as a Corps Observation squadron. It reached the front on April 8, 1918, a year and two days after America's entry into the war.

The other squadrons eventually arrived, stiffened by Yank veterans of the

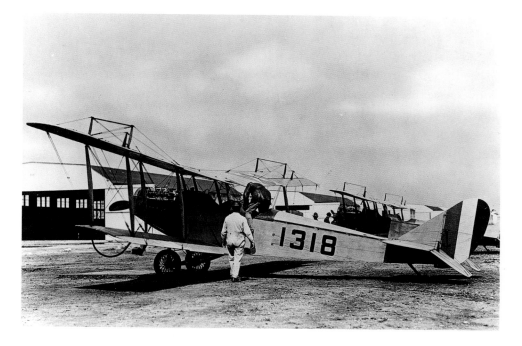

The Jenny—the name evokes not only the First World War, but also the era of barnstorming that followed. The name derives from the fact that it was a merger of the Curtiss J and N designs. The Jenny was the United States' most significant contribution to World War I aviation, for 95 percent of U.S. and Canadian pilots learned to fly in it. More than 6,000 were built, and perhaps a dozen are still flying, pleasing airshow crowds.

British and French air forces, but manned primarily by flyers who had just experienced the agonizingly slow training provided by the French. Initially, 100 flying cadets were sent overseas each month. By January 1, 1918, there were 1,060 cadets in Europe still awaiting training, living under primitive conditions.

The most ambitious flying school, at Issoudon, became an immense complex of sixteen airfields. It was commanded for a time by Lieutenant Quentin Roosevelt, who was soon to lose his life in combat. Issoudon was only a sea of mud when the first cadets arrived, To their dismay their hands were applied to shovels rather than joysticks. Worse, there were some almost unbearable irritations for those who had been the first to arrive. Having done well in their U.S. ground schools, the "cream of the crop" had been sent to France early for flight training. The French lacked planes, instructors, and method for the task, and the cadets found themselves freezing in makeshift barracks, assigned alternately to construction work on hangars or to close-order drill. They were sunk in boredom, often going for a month without baths, and forced to eke out their rations with an occasional omelet in town. They were still waiting, buck privates doing latrine duties, when, with the irony typical of war, the "slow guys," their erstwhile classmates from the States, arrived. The agony was that they came as commissioned officers, strutting first lieutenants charged with inspecting the quarters and demanding to be saluted! It almost caused a riot.

Despite all the problems, preliminary flying training began. When in full operation, Issoudon averaged 500 to 600 hours of instructional flying time a day, while its shops turned out 20 repaired airplanes and 100 engines a week. Other fields were quickly opened, some for specialized training such as the bombardment school at Clermont-Ferrand and the gunnery school at St. Jean-de-Monts. In a similar way, a logistics buildup began with the Air Service Production Center at Romorantin, which assembled aircraft shipped in neatly packed crates from the United States. It would ultimately have fifty acres of covered floor space, with 12,000 men operating it. The increase in its operations can be traced in terms of Liberty planes. The first arrived on May 11, 1918; by November 11, 1,087 had been assembled and 543 sent to the front.

By July 1918 preliminary training had been completed and the cadets were preparing for combat flying training. An egalitarian element was added when exceptional enlisted men from the American squadrons were nominated for pilot training. However, the intense training generated heavy casualties, as many as one a week; the cadets became hardened to pallbearer duty.

The cadets sent to Italian flying schools complained that they had the worst of the bargain, for the Italian training planes were antiquated and ill-maintained, but eventually the Italians graduated 406 pilots from the preliminary course, and 131 from the bombardment course, including a future mayor of New York City, the Little Flower, Fiorello La Guardia.

Despite the delays and the difficulties, the overseas training scheme proved to be the most effective solution to getting American pilots to the front, for building the flying training schools in the United States took longer than had been anticipated. In the end, not one wholly American-trained pursuit or observation pilot, and only eight such bombing pilots, reached the front before November 11, 1918. Ultimately, a total of 10,000 pilots had been trained, but at the Armistice they were still in the pipeline, waiting to get to France.

THE AMERICANS IN COMBAT

A squadron of American volunteers, the *Escadrille Américaine*, was formed in April 1916. Many of the founders were already veterans. The brothers Kiffin and Paul Rockwell, pioneer flyer William Thaw, Victor Chapman, the incorrigible Bert Hall, and Raoul Lufbery, for example, had enlisted to fight in the French Foreign Legion at the outbreak of war in 1914. Over the next two years their ranks were augmented by others, including Norman Prince and Frazier Curtis, who had already learned to fly in the United States but who did their first fighting as foot soldiers in the trenches, and still others, like James McConnell, who was a volunteer ambulance driver.

The idea for an American volunteer unit had many fathers, but the two leaders were Thaw and Prince, who joined forces to sell the French on the concept. Seeing both military and propaganda value, but aware that the U.S. government frowned on the idea, the French moved slowly, admitting many of the men into French squadrons as either pilots or observers.

After intolerable delay, the French finally issued an order on April 18, 1916, for Captain George Thenault to take command of the *Escadrille Américaine*, N. (Nieuport) 124. (It did not become the Lafayette Escadrille until five months later, after a heated protest from the German ambassador in Washington about the apparent American sanction of the French cause.) Six Nieuport 11 fighters arrived in May; they were delightful to fly and not as fragile as they appeared. The unit flew its first patrol on May 13, and Kiffin Rockwell scored the first victory on May 18, shooting down a German L.V.G. observation plane.

The popular image of the Lafayette Escadrille is that of young aristocratic idealists like the Rockwells, Thaw, and Chapman, all wishing to save the world for democracy. The truth was somewhat different. Bert Hall was a young rogue; Robert Soubiran, a tough race-car driver; Paul Pavleka, a sailor and inveterate rover; and Raoul Lufbery, the future seventeen-victory ace, a mechanic. Yet aristocrat or roughneck, their faces and their letters reflected how they aged in combat. They became acutely aware of the need for more powerful engines, more armament, better training, and greater numbers, an awareness they were unable to communicate to the United States. So removed from reality was the U.S. Army that in two intelligence reports made on the Escadrille, the only conclusion drawn was that the pilots might be useful in case of war with Mexico!

In almost two years of service, the thirty-eight pilots who were officially on the rolls of the Escadrille scored fifty-seven confirmed victories and suffered nine deaths. As a tactical unit the Escadrille was only marginally successful, but as a propaganda device it was without parallel. With its handsome young pilots, an American Indian-head squadron insignia, and two lion mascots, Whisky and Soda, the Lafayette Escadrille was unbeatable press, crystallizing public opinion positively for France just as the sinking of the *Lusitania* had worked negatively for Germany. (There were ultimately 209 Americans who served with the French in what became known collectively as the "Lafayette Flying Corps," a membership that became so prestigious after the war that the French received at least 4,000 bogus claims for membership, most of which added insult to injury by claiming to be from *founding* members of the Escadrille.) On December 17, 1917, all of the members of the Escadrille were released from French service.

It was said of Gervais Raoul Lufbery, the most famous member of the Lafayette Escadrille and the first American to become an ace, that he flew, fought, and died for revenge. A major in the Air Service, AEF, he stands here in front of his Nieuport 28. The Nieuport was one of the fastest fighters at the front, but it had grave structural and engineering flaws.

The great-great-grandson of Edmond Charles "Citizen" Genet, first Minister of the French Republic to the United States, Corporal Edmond Genet would become the first American airman to die after the United States had entered the war. He deserted from the U.S. Navy to join the French Foreign Legion, fought as an infantryman, and became the twentieth volunteer for the Lafayette Escadrille. He crashed to his death on April 16, 1917, while on patrol with Lufbery.

FLYING FOR ENGLAND

More Americans served as individuals in various Royal Flying Corps squadrons than with the French, and they collectively scored more victories with less fanfare. An initial U.S. recruitment of 210 flying cadets was sent to England for training, beginning on September 4, 1917, with the arrival of fifty-three cadets and one officer at the British School of Military Aeronautics at Oxford. Eventually, 542 men received training in England; of these, 216 pilots were sent as pilots to Royal Air Force squadrons or to the U.S. 17th and 148th squadrons, which were completely equipped and trained by the RAF. Ninety-six others went directly from British schools to American squadrons. Of the top sixteen American aces, eleven got some or all of their victories flying for the RAF.

The environment was ideal for the Americans, for the RAF leadership tolerated both extra privileges and slackened discipline for its pilots, who had but one chance in two to survive a year at the front. It was a rough attempt to assuage the guilt of heavy losses caused by tactical mishandling.

The British training produced some of the most colorful heroes of the war, including Elliot White Springs, who was among the first cadets to reach England. He achieved four victories flying with No. 85 Squadron, RAF, then he transferred to the 148th, essentially an RAF squadron manned by American pilots, where he continued to fly Camels. The irrepressibly good-natured Springs, a twelve-victory ace, introduced the British to mint juleps and American-style practical jokes and found that they responded rather more favorably to the former. Later he wrote *War Birds,* one of the two best novels of

In-flight photos of World War I aircraft are relatively rare; this one captures a Sopwith Camel in a climb, its rotary engine trailing a castor-oil cloud of exhaust. The Camel was less streamlined than the Albatros, but it was lighter, and far more maneuverable. Technically, the Camel was a dead end: the rotary engine would appear in a few more types, but it was nearing the upper level of its development.

World War I air combat, the other being V. M. Yeates's *Winged Victory*. *War Birds* was a mildly disguised rendering of Springs's own experiences and the diary of John McGavock Grider, who had fallen in combat.

Also serving with the RAF was the second-ranking American ace, Lieutenant William Lambert, who scored twenty-two victories—nineteen airplanes and three balloons. He had joined the Royal Flying Corps in 1916, flying with the famed No. 24 Squadron. A genial, modest-mannered man, Lambert returned to service with the U.S. Army Air Forces in World War II, retiring in 1954 as a lieutenant colonel, his great achievements almost unknown to the public.

When the Americans transferred from the Royal Air Force, which was formed from the Royal Flying Corps and the Royal Naval Air Service on April 1, 1918, to the Air Service of the AEF, they were given the same sort of bureaucratic treatment that their comrades serving with the French had received. A veteran of combat with the RAF's No. 40 Squadron, Captain Reed Landis volunteered for service with the AEF, only to find himself ordered back to flying school, where he was assigned to a second-lieutenant instructor. Landis boarded a train, went to Paris, and demanded to resign and go back to the RAF, saying, "I've shot down twelve Germans and now you give me a second lieutenant to teach me to fly. What kind of an army is this?" (Reed's official score was ten, but he may have had unconfirmed victories.)

PROBLEMS OF COMMAND

The command structure of the Air Service, American Expeditionary Forces, underwent a bewildering series of changes, primarily because of the open hostility between Billy Mitchell and Benny Foulois. Mitchell had been the first to France, and with his command of the language, flamboyant personality, and total disregard for procedures, had achieved much, particularly in terms of understanding with the French. Foulois, who really had not expected to go beyond the exalted rank of major, arrived in France as a brigadier general, outranking Mitchell, whom he considered an amateur, a man "without one minute of flying time as a rated Army pilot"; the confusion he found in France only confirmed his opinion. For his part, Mitchell regarded Foulois, now Chief of Air Service, AEF, and his entire 112-man staff as grossly incompetent, and proceeded to say so to anyone who would listen.

Their animosity brought no credit to either man, and the Air Service suffered from it. Of the two, Foulois was both the most vicious and most generous. He evicted Mitchell from his office, and sabotaged him with adverse reports to Pershing. Later he relented, recognizing Mitchell's talent and recommending that he be placed in command of the combat elements of the AEF. Pershing, with enough to do to protect himself from his Allies, much less the Germans, solved the problem in good Army fashion by bringing in General Mason Patrick over both their heads as Chief of the Air Service. Patrick did not know anything about aviation, but was a quick study who knew how to command.

The tragedy is that the two men's personalities were perfectly complementary, if they had had the wit and will to work together. Foulois was a book man, anxious to set up the necessary training, logistics, and supply. Mitchell was anxious to employ aircraft en masse in strategic operations. He was a charismatic visionary, wanting to close with the Germans behind their lines in great aerial pincers movements, or by dropping thousands of parachutists to seize Metz and hold it. They were wonderful dreams, but only that—and this was to be Mitchell's curse, for his grasp for air power would always exceed the technical reach available to him. Yet far from being futile, his quixotic efforts would provide essential inspiration for Army flyers for the next twenty years. In essence, Mitchell considered himself air power's Messiah, when in truth he was its John the Baptist.

Despite the squabbling at upper echelons, the burgeoning armament program forced American aviation into France, plane by plane, flyer by flyer. On February 18, 1918, the pilots of the Lafayette Escadrille became the nucleus of the new 103d Aero Squadron, the first of the Air Service, AEF. Aristocratic Major William Thaw, war-weary but determined, was the commander, and the 103d operated as a part of the French Groupe de Combat 21, with three French squadrons. This began an excruciatingly slow buildup of forces that began to accelerate only in the late spring of 1918. By July 1, there were thirteen American squadrons at the front; five months later the number had grown to forty-five.

The first all-American pursuit unit—pilots, mechanics, and support staff —to reach the front was the 95th Aero Squadron, which arrived in February 1918, without any aircraft. It would be joined by the 94th, 27th, and 147th Aero Squadrons to form the 1st Pursuit Group. The 95th began operations on March 15, flying patrols with unarmed Nieuport 28s. It was a foolish gesture, speaking to the American desire to take part in "the big show." It also illustrates how the romantic image of fighter-versus-fighter combat would appeal to desperate journalists. They were forbidden to write about the holocaust of the trenches, where only the brutality of noncommissioned officers enabled officers—who should have known better—to keep the men fighting. For the *poilu,* the Tommy, the *landser,* death was probable if you fought; it was certain if you fled, for the court-martials were merciless.

Thus the combat far above the bloody trenches became mythically portrayed as athletic contests where young men sparred gallantly. It was thrilling to read about and the odds were always sporting. The Allies outnumbered the Germans in total numbers, but the latter could choose to accept or not accept battle over their own lines. The Germans preferred to "have the customers come to the shop" and quite wisely tried to fight only when they felt they held the tactical advantages of height, wind, and position. The tactics worked; by the end of the war, the Germans had shot down two aircraft for every plane that they had lost.

WAR IN THE AIR

The image of the "knightly joust" of aerial combat was first popularized by propaganda, later by the memoirs of the aces, and still later by pulp novels. Yet the most influential myth shaper was Howard Hughes's film *Hell's Angels* and all the many subsequent films using its outtakes. The long, balletic dog-fight sequence in *Hell's Angels* shows dozens of aircraft swirling in apparent close proximity, with close-ups of one-on-one encounters between Holly-wood's stereotype of determined, round-goggled Allies and grim, slant-goggled Germans.

Unfortunately, the film was inaccurate. Relatively few battles took place in which dozens of airplanes were engaged simultaneously over an extended period of time, and when they did they were much remarked upon. Instead, the combats tended to be short, sharp engagements. Two flights of aircraft would spar for position until a decision to engage was made. Then there would be a diving attack, a swirl of combat, and quick disengagement. The ideal situation sought by the great aces was cold-blooded murder, the attacker stalking and executing his victim in a surprise attack.

FIRST BLOOD FOR THE 1ST PURSUIT GROUP

The initial victories of the 1st Pursuit Group were typical of the often acciden-tal nature of combat. The 1st flew fast, maneuverable Nieuport N28C-1s, which were flawed by two dramatically dangerous design problems. The first was a tendency for the vibrating Gnome rotary engines to crack the copper fuel lines, causing the Nieuports to burst into flames in the air, a catastrophic situa-tion for the parachuteless pilots. The second was for the fabric of the upper wing to rip away in a steep dive, causing an immediate loss of lift and structural damage. The French had rejected the airplane for frontline service, but there was a three-month wait for Spad production, and the Americans had to take what they could get. Yet the Nieuport was not without its advantages. It was far easier to maintain than the Spads, and probably made life easier for the fledg-ling mechanics of the Air Service.

On their very first day of operations, April 14, 1918, at Toul, southeast of Verdun, two young first lieutenants of the soon-to-be famous 94th Aero Squadron were on alert. Alan Winslow and Douglas Campbell sat in a tent playing cards, their planes armed at last with one machine gun apiece, waiting nearby. A call signaled that there were German aircraft in the vicinity. As soon as they took off, Winslow ran into a German Albatros D Va blundering across the end of the field in search of its own aerodrome. The startled Albatros pilot

The U.S. Air Service, AEF, procured 705 Salmson 2-A.2 observation planes from the French. Powered by a 270-horsepower Salmson water-cooled radial engine, the 2-A.2 generally outperformed the more powerful de Havilland DH-4, and was greatly preferred by crews who flew both aircraft.

A leading race-car driver, the top American ace, and later the dynamic leader of Eastern Airlines, Captain Edward Rickenbacker smiles over the top wing of his Spad XIII. The French Spad, with its all-wood construction and wings of thin airfoil section, represents the peak of the first generation of World War I fighter technology. Its most famous opposite number, Fokker D VII, was a technological leap forward, setting the stage for the next generation of fighters.

One of the most dangerous jobs in the war was attacking enemy observation balloons, because they were protected by heavy anti-aircraft emplacements and constant fighter patrols. Lieutenant Frank Luke specialized in "balloon busting," but his fearless tactics led to his death in combat. The Spad XIII was good for balloon work: it picked up great speed in a dive and had the structural strength to withstand the pullout.

The Albatros D III was aesthetically one of the most beautiful fighters of the war. In the hands of famous aces like von Richthofen, it established complete aerial superiority for Germany in the early months of 1917. The Albatros was well streamlined, but when its designers copied the Nieuport's V-strut bracing of the biplane wings, they also copied a fatal design error. In a dive, both aircraft could have their lower wings first twisted, then torn away.

fired, Winslow climbed, then stall-turned to come down on the German fighter's tail, spraying it with a long burst. The enemy crashed in a field near Winslow's airdrome. In the meantime, Campbell had shot down his own adversary, a Pfalz D III. Both Americans were back on the ground less than five minutes after they took off, each with a victory, the first for an all-American unit. It was sensational good fortune for Winslow and Campbell, and a morale-building tonic for the Americans, especially Campbell's enlisted mechanic, who pounded him on the back saying, "That's the stuff, Lieutenant, old kid."

(It should be noted that the first member of the U.S. Air Service to score an aerial victory was First Lieutenant Stephen W. Thompson, an aerial observer on a familiarization flight in a Breguet bomber of the French Day Bombardment Group No. 5. Thompson shot down an Albatros D III on February 5, 1918.)

The American forces had been introduced to battle in the quiet Toul sector, where they were opposed by two German Jagdstaffeln of acknowledged unaggressiveness. But the American Army and Air Service were thrown into the maelstrom of the last German drive of 1918. The fresh, young, strapping American soldiers prompted von Hindenburg to say later that the American infantry had won the war. By July 1918 the complexion of the war changed drastically. The 1st Pursuit Group began operations in the Marne sector, where the enemy opposition was both strong and aggressive, with a numerical superiority sometimes reaching four to one. The American flyers were now based too far from the front for the range of their aircraft, lacked adequate transportation and communications, and were making the transition from Nieuports to Spads. Billy Mitchell was now commander of the 1st Air Brigade, consisting of the 1st Pursuit Group and 1st Corps Observation Group. The Brigade fought for control of the air over Château-Thierry against the veterans of the German air force, equipped with increasing numbers of the best fighter of World War I, the new Fokker D VII.

EYES IN THE SKY

The mission of the Corps Observation Group was complex, performing visual and photographic reconnaissance to monitor the Germans for five miles behind their lines. In addition it did *reglage*, or fire control, reporting where artillery fire hit so batteries could adjust their aim. And it was occasionally tasked for ground attack, a role for which it was unsuited. In the process its planes were escorted both by pursuit aircraft and by other observation planes as a protective flight. The 1st Pursuit Group's mission was to protect Allied reconnaissance aircraft and destroy their German counterparts. They soon discovered a truth that had to be discovered again several times during World War II: pursuit planes could not operate effectively in close escort—they had to be able to range free to gain the initiative over enemy fighters.

Fuel tanks in World War I aircraft were simply sheet metal, usually located immediately between the pilot and the engine. When punctured, fuel was either pumped out under pressure or siphoned into a mist; the first spark would ignite it. This is a French Nieuport, seen from the German two-seater that shot it down.

A reproduction of the famous Nieuport fighter,
with the markings of Lieutenant Charles
Nungesser, a French ace with forty-five victories.
A long series of fighters—the 17, 21, 23, 24,
and 27—were used by many French and British
aces. The Nieuport 17 reached the front in March
1916 and quickly established its superiority over
existing German fighters.

ABOVE:

Not exceptionally attractive aesthetically, the Breguet Type 14 was used by sixteen U.S. units and was extremely popular with the crews flying it. The Breguet is an extemely significant aircraft structurally, for it was built entirely of aluminum, except for wooden wing ribs, the fairings, and the fabric covering. One feature regarded as particularly desirable by American crews was a provision to jettison the fuel in case of fire in the air. The Breguet was continued in production after the end of the war; ultimately more than 8,000 were built.

LEFT:

A Spad XIII restored at the magnificent Air Force Museum in Dayton, Ohio. The Spad was powered by a 220-horsepower Hispano-Suiza engine of advanced design and notorious unreliability. It has been reported that at times 50 percent or more of the Spads were out of commission because of engine difficulties.

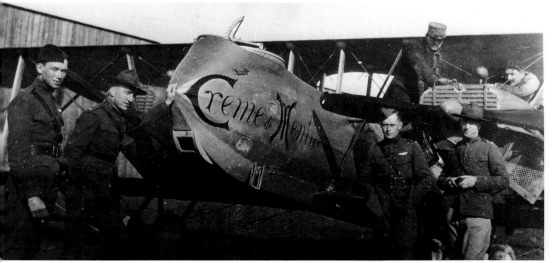

The French developed several twin-engine reconnaissance bombers, including this elegant Caudron R.11, powered by two 220-horsepower Hispano-Suiza engines, and armed with five machine guns. It is March 1918; the jaunty fellow in the campaign hat leaning against the nose is Lieutenant Edward Rickenbacker, before he had gained fame as an ace.

For the first two weeks of the battle of Château-Thierry, enemy opposition was fortunately light, for confusion reigned on the American side. There simply had not been time to train the air crews or the troops they worked with on the ground in the intricate details of their task. Mitchell was at his meddling worst, continually tying up the telephone lines all day long with questions and orders, further muddling the already tangled command structure. But by July 15 the substitution of direct daily personal contact between air and ground officers had gone a long way to make up the deficiencies in communication. In addition, the Allied counteroffensive quickened the pace of the battle, with visual reconnaissance suddenly becoming far more important than photographic reconnaissance because of the time lag in processing film and making prints.

It was not an easy task. The Germans had maintained control of the air from the start by concentrating their most aggressive fighter units in the area. They mauled the green U.S. flyers, killing three dozen pilots of the 1st Pursuit Group. The Americans endured, learning their trade as they protected Allied observation planes and attacked those of the enemy. In the process the prototype of a new breed of pure American hero, the fighter pilot, emerged in the person of Raoul Lufbery.

Born of an American father and French mother, Lufbery became an itinerant adventurer, gaining his American citizenship as an enlisted man in the U.S. Army in the Philippines. He traveled on to India, becoming a mechanic for a French pilot, Marc Pourpe. Their friendship led to Lufbery's becoming an ace, for after Pourpe joined the French air service he was killed in an accident. Lufbery blamed the Germans and swore that he would avenge him.

An excellent marksman, Lufbery was not a good pilot initially and, like the German ace von Richthofen, only squeaked through his flying training. Once trained and assigned to the *Escadrille Américaine*, Lufbery combined his mechanical skills, marksmanship, and sullen hatred of the Germans to score five victories and become the first American ace, on October 12, 1916. A loner, he was reckless in attack and indifferent to confirmation of his victories.

Assigned to a desk when commissioned a major in the U.S. Air Service, Lufbery fought his way to the 94th Aero Squadron, where he led the fledgling pilots on their first patrols. But he had brought his personal pitcher to the well too often, and on May 19, 1918, Lufbery attacked a German Rumpler two-seater. The gunner's return fire set his plane ablaze, and, as he had always said he would, Lufbery leaped to his death from his burning Nieuport. Officially credited with seventeen victories, some sources say that he had as many as seventy kills at the time of his death.

Lufbery was but the first of a series of heroes whose names still illuminate American aviation history. The most famous of all was Captain Eddie (Edward) Rickenbacker, the redoubtable race-car driver turned General Staff chauffeur turned ace. The same suspicion of all things German that caused America to call sauerkraut "Liberty cabbage" and dachshunds "Liberty dogs"

The common denominator of the cruel air war was the pilots who waged it—patriotic young men on both sides who loved flying. Whenever possible, a captured enemy pilot was entertained by his opposite numbers. Behind this group of aces from Jagdstaffel 10 is the Fokker D VII, the best fighter plane of World War I. Note the excellent personal equipment worn by the German flyers, even at a late stage of the war.

Members of Flying Section No. 62 at Doberitz pose in front of two German two-seaters, the L.V.G. at the left and the Roland Walfisch (Whale). Germany was unable to develop engines as powerful as those used by the Allies. Consequently, it was forced to tailor its aircraft to specific missions—reconnaissance, ground attack, or air combat. The Roland was one of the most unusual, with its semi-monocoque (hollow shell) construction. The designer eliminated some drag by attaching the wings directly to the top and bottom of the deep fuselage. The L.V.G., probably a C-IV, has a rare eight-cylinder in-line Mercedes engine—more powerful than the standard six, but less reliable because of crankshaft problems.

forced Rickenbacker to change the spelling of his name from its original Richenbacher. At twenty-seven, he had been considered a little old to become a combat pilot, but he persisted and was eventually assigned to the 94th. There, Rickenbacker later wrote, everything he knew he learned from Raoul Lufbery. Rickenbacker was at first the odd man out, too old, too plebeian, and too

serious for the taste of many. His knowledge of mechanics enabled him to keep his Spad XIII and its guns in better shape than those of most of his comrades, and eventually his seriousness of purpose led him to be selected by his squadron mates as commander.

Rickenbacker, whose time at the front was cut short by several weeks when he was sidelined with a severe mastoid operation, went on to become the leading American Ace of Aces with twenty-six victories, and was awarded the Medal of Honor.

The 1st Pursuit Group was replete with colorful aces. Frank Luke, Jr., was a sort of aerial James Dean, a rebel with a cause. He despised regulations and liked shooting down balloons, the most dangerous target on the front because of the way they were protected by heavy antiaircraft guns. During his brief career he ran Rickenbacker a close race, and eventually wound up credited with twenty-one victories, most of them balloons. The last ten days of his life were filled with spectacular fights. On September 18, he shot down two balloons and three airplanes in ten minutes, but lost his wingman and good friend, Lieutenant Joe Wehner, in the process. He scored again on September 26, and his new wingman was shot down. After being grounded

by his commanding officer for recklessness and lack of discipline, Luke took off anyway, dropping a note to the American balloon headquarters at Souilly, telling them to watch three "Hun" balloons on the Meuse.

He shot down the first one without incident, was wounded destroying the second, and was forced to land after he brought the third one down in flames. After strafing a line of German troops on the way down, he crash-landed at the edge of a village. Surrounded, he refused to surrender and fired with his .45 caliber pistol until he was shot dead. If Luke had returned alive, he probably would have been court-martialed. Instead he was posthumously awarded the Medal of Honor and ultimately had not one, but two, flying fields named after him, the first in Hawaii, the second in his native Arizona.

There were other famous aces: Elliot Springs, Harold E. Hartney, George Vaughn, James Norman Hall of *Mutiny on the Bounty* fame, Field Kindley, Reed Landis, and Ray Brooks. They are all gone now. Brooks, a kindly, vibrant man, the last survivor, died at the age of ninety-five in 1991. But equally important as the aces were the mostly anonymous pilots and mechanics whose smiling faces peer out of squadron photographs of the time. The aces scored the victories and garnered the laurels, but they could not have done so without the sup-

The Nieuport 28, one of the most aesthetically pleasing aircraft of the war, was hampered by technical difficulties that were ultimately easily solved. Here Roy Grinnell portrays the beautifully marked Nieuport of Lieutenant Douglas Campbell, who scored the second victory for an American unit.

The irrepressible Captain Ray Brooks, the last surviving American World War I ace, and a close friend of the author. Ray was a six-victory ace and a wonderful human being. He died in 1991 after a full life of many contributions to aviation. His Spad XIII, Smith IV, is on exhibit at the National Air and Space Museum.

OPPOSITE TOP:
Interest in World War I aircraft has increased dramatically as many accurate reproductions have been built in recent years. The master craftsman Jim Appelby built this Fokker E III "Eindecker" exactly to original specifications. The E III was used by such aces as Lieutenants Oswald Boelcke and Max Immelmann. Although it did not have an exceptional performance, the E III had a great technical innovation—a machine gun synchronized to shoot through the spinning propeller. The plane wreaked havoc on the Western Front, reducing enemy aircraft to "Fokker fodder" in a tabloid phrase of the time.

OPPOSITE BOTTOM:
The Fokker D VII, shown here in a reproduction, was the first of a new generation of fighters. Its thick, almost cantilever wings and steel-tube fuselage would be adopted by designers in almost every country. In the United States, fighters from both Boeing and Curtiss reflected the Fokker inspiration. Not particularly fast, it was said that the D VII made aces out of good pilots and good pilots out of bad ones.

port of hundreds of air-crew and thousands of ground-support personnel who made it possible.

Even more anonymous were the hard-pressed veterans of the bombing and observation squadrons. Even though their mission was considered by the military on both sides to be by far the most important, they received less attention from the press and public right from the start. Part of the problem was the nature of the mission—the two-place airplanes were not intended to engage in one-on-one combat, the reporter's favorite. Another part was the fact that individuals were not as easy to pick out. The pilot and observer operated as a team, and as such were half as interesting as the lone fighter pilot. And a third part was that the inadequate airplanes they flew were dull by comparison to the wasplike fighters.

Of the two missions, observation and bombardment, the former was far more important and effective. Using French-supplied Dorand, Breguet, and Salmson aircraft, as well as the de Havilland DH-4, U.S. airmen quickly became proficient in registering artillery fire and in reconnaissance. On photographic missions, the pilot would fly straight and level while the observer got down on his hands and knees in the rear cockpit to operate the 52-centimeter (20-inch) focal-length lens, changing the film magazine after each shot. The camera's nose extended through the floor, and the top was suspended in a frame that used Ping-Pong balls as shock absorbers. The observer would look through a glass in the cockpit floor, kicking the rudder or using reins attached to his arms to let the pilot know if he was drifting off course. When an enemy attacked, the observer left the camera to grab his machine guns.

The observation planes were not without a sting, and cumbersome two-place Spad XIs and Salmson 2-A2s mixed it up with German fighters. In an October 7, 1918, mission, pilot Lieutenant William Erwin and Lieutenant Arthur Easterbrook flew for two hours, had five encounters with a total of eight enemy airplanes, and shot down two of them. Easterbrook was shot through the thumb, gaining both a Purple Heart and an Oak Leaf Cluster to add to his Distinguished Service Cross.

Just as fifty years later in the Vietnam War, a victory was awarded to both pilot and observer in a two-seater aircraft. Many years later the Air Force retroactively revised the policy, and credited the victory as shared. But under the original system, Erwin wound up with eight victories and Easterbrook five. Two DH-4 observers, Captain Leonard C. Hammond of the 91st, and Lieutenant Byrne H. Baucom of the 1st, had six kills each. These were the top scorers in Corps Observation.

The bombardment mission was more difficult, both because of the weight of the bombs and the fact that bombsights and bombing techniques were primitive. Losses were high, for while German fighters might elect to avoid combat with Allied pursuits, they had to attack the bombers and observation planes that threatened their troops. Of the two, the observation planes

OPPOSITE TOP:

The Standard E-I, designed as a fighter in 1917, was immediately recognized by Air Service authorities as inadequate for use on the Western Front, and was redesignated as an advanced trainer. In appearance an amalgam of the Sopwith Camel, Spad, and Nieuport designs, the E-1 was reportedly pleasant to fly. This is an original aircraft, lovingly restored by the Air Force Museum.

OPPOSITE BOTTOM:

Still lacking the synchronizing mechanism that made the Fokker E III such a formidable opponent, the Royal Aircraft Factory created the F.E. 8, with a pusher engine. The pilot could fire his single Lewis gun forward without interference from the propeller. This is a reproduction from Cole Palen's world-famous Rhinebeck (New York) Aerodrome, where World War I in the air is fought each weekend through the summer, to the delight of thousands.

ABOVE:

Another of Palen's amazing reproductions is this Siemens-Schuckert D III, one of the best, yet least-known, German fighters. It was flown in 1918 by several famous aces, including Rudolph Berthold and Ernst Udet. The D III had a tremendous rate of climb and was very strong. It possessed one of the most ingenious engines of the war, an eleven-cylinder Siemens-Halske SH III, in which the crankshaft rotated in one direction at 900 rpm while the cylinders rotated in the reverse direction at the same rate, producing an actual engine speed of 1,800 rpm. This minimized the torque, although it did make cooling difficult.

Another of the great builders of exact reproductions of World War I aircraft is Carl Swanson, whose gorgeous Spad XIII is shown in flight. Everything is reproduced exactly—color, markings, fittings, materials. Only rarely are concessions made to modernity by the installation of brakes or tailwheels.

Used only in small numbers by the Air Service, AEF, the Morane Saulnier parasol monoplanes were fast but considered tricky to fly. Nonetheless, the firm persisted with the concept well into the 1930s. This is an original example, restored to flying condition.

Made internationally famous again many decades after the war by the machinations of the Charles Schulz character Snoopy, the Fokker Dr 1 triplane was the type of aircraft in which the Red Baron, Manfred von Richthofen, was shot down. The Dr 1 was quite slow, but had a terrific rate of climb and was wonderfully maneuverable. Its concept was revolutionary—the span was reduced, but the wing area maintained by the use of three surfaces. The wings were actually cantilever, but small wing struts were added in order to dampen vibration. Like many Fokker products, it had initial quality-control problems, and only 320 entered service.

The peak of fighter aircraft design was reached with the Fokker D VIII, a highly streamlined cantilever-winged parasol fighter. At a time when enemy fighter aircraft were powered by engines of 250 horsepower, the D VIII had only a 110-horsepower Oberursel rotary engine. Yet its clean design made it competitive in all aspects, particularly speed—it could attain 127 mph. When the original models of the aircraft (then designated E V) reached the front, the familiar Fokker quality-control problems emerged and three crashed due to wing failure. When production resumed the war was almost over, and only a few reached frontline squadrons.

Aircraft, by their very nature, take on a different aspect when in flight; here a reproduction Nieuport "Bebe" assumes a vitality that speaks to its very personality. The flying characteristics of World War I aircraft are vastly different from those of modern light planes, and present-day pilots who would fly them must be extraordinarily careful during the familiarization process.

For the first decade after the Wright brothers, it was enough for a designer simply to have his aircraft fly. The Curtiss JN-4 marks one of the first steps beyond that period, for it was designed to be a workhorse, able to withstand the rigor of training one ham-handed student after another.

fared better for they were lighter, and not as bound to a line of attack as were the bombers.

The bomber crews suffered brutal losses, flying the longest and most dangerous missions, often in ill-suited aircraft. The 96th Aero Squadron was the first bomber squadron to arrive in France, and the first to have bombing as its sole mission. It flew its first mission on June 12 in the excellent Breguet 14B2 bombers provided by the French, and then ran into a string of bad luck that would haunt it until the Armistice. On July 10, the 96th's commanding officer, Major Harry Brown, led a flight of six Breguets on a bombing mission to Conflans. The weather closed in, blanking out the ground beneath them, and a high wind blew the formation off course into Germany. All six aircraft landed at Coblenz and were captured. The embarrassment of the Air Service was compounded by the report of a probably apocryphal message from the Germans thanking the U.S. for the aircraft and asking what they should do with Major Brown.

There were few further losses for the squadron until the start of the Saint-Mihiel offensive on September 12. In just four days, the squadron was crippled by the loss of fourteen aircraft and sixteen pilots and observers.

The other units in the First Day Bombardment Group, the 11th and 20th Aero Squadrons, were equipped with U.S.-built Liberty planes. When fully loaded with bombs, the de Havillands had to fly low and slow, making them attractive targets for the German fighters. The position of the vulnerable fuel tank between pilot and observer inhibited crew coordination in an attack. Maintenance was difficult on the de Havilland, and the in-commission rate was low.

Yet the Americans were eager to fight, a future Hollywood motion-picture producer, Captain Merian C. Cooper, among them. Cooper, perhaps later best known for *King Kong*, was shot down on the 20th Aero Squadron's blackest day, September 26, when it lost five aircraft and ten crew members. Sixteen DH-4s had left the field at Amanty on mission to Dun-sur-Meuse. They were jumped by six Fokker D VIIs, their black fuselages marked with white bands. After a long running battle in which his observer, Lieutenant Edmund C. Leonard, was severely wounded, Cooper's DH-4 burst into flame. Believing Leonard to be dead, Cooper climbed from the cockpit, intending to leap like Lufbery, without a parachute, from his burning plane. As he struggled to get out, he saw that Leonard was alive. Cooper returned to his cockpit and managed to extinguish the flames, then made a forced landing. Both men survived as prisoners of war, and Cooper went on to cofound the Kosciuszko Squadron in Poland in 1919.

The tragedy of the bombing effort was that the weight of bombs being carried was inadequate to do more than annoy the Germans. Altogether about 138 tons of bombs were dropped in 150 attacks. Despite losses that kept them short of replacements, the American bombing units pressed on in the face of the heavy German fighter defenses, creating a tradition that persists to this day that no bomber mission can be turned back by enemy opposition.

MEDAL OF HONOR

The observation squadrons created their own traditions when a DH-4 crew from the 50th Aero Squadron won two of the four Medals of Honor awarded to World War I flyers. Lieutenants Harold E. Goettler and Erwin R. Bleckley of the 50th Aero Squadron were tasked to locate and drop supplies to the immortal "Lost Battalion," which was neither lost nor a battalion, but the remnants of the 308th Infantry Regiment, surrounded in a ravine in the Argonne forest. After getting badly shot up while locating the troops, the two men returned to their base on the afternoon of October 5 to pick up supplies to drop to them. As the big DH-4 lumbered along the ravine on its return trip, German machine gunners cut it to pieces, wounding both men. Goettler was killed in the crash landing, and Bleckley died a little while later. It was heroism typical of the time—inexperienced young men, in slow and vulnerable aircraft, taking the battle to the enemy.

MITCHELL AT SAINT-MIHIEL

While each day extracted similar heroism from the crews, Billy Mitchell, who functioned better at a conceptual level than as a commander in the field, was preoccupied with his larger vision of air power. His first intoxicating taste of directing large-scale operations was in July 1918, when he personally observed German troops pouring across a bridgehead at the Marne. Fearful that there was not sufficient strength to halt the Germans, he orchestrated a large-scale operation with the British, sending five RAF squadrons and the 1st Pursuit Group against the main German base at Fere-en-Tardenois. His claims for the raid are probably exaggerated, for the Germans were at the end of their offensive tether, but the attack served as the prelude to Saint-Mihiel, where he reached the pinnacle of his combat career. In this, as in so much he did during and after the war, and through no fault of his own, the portent was greater than the content.

In September 1918, the Germans were already beaten militarily by the battering of five years of war, and demoralized by the apparently endless stream of fresh American troops. More important, they were defeated politically by the Allies' clever if deceitful handling of President Wilson's fourteen points, wanting to believe in an arrangement that would be denied them. General John J. Pershing, commander of the AEF, was anxious to demonstrate his troops' ability in battle, and marshaled American strength for the largest U.S. operation since the Civil War, the Saint-Mihiel offensive, a drive intended to pinch off the horseshoe-shaped salient west of Verdun.

Mitchell commanded the largest force of aircraft yet to be employed in a

The famous Hat-in-the-Ring insignia of the 94th Aero Squadron graces this Nieuport 28 reproduction. The clean, streamlined look of the Nieuport was obtained by the use of fairing and stringers, covered with fabric.

The Albatros D Va was of advanced, semi-monocoque construction in which birch plywood was molded to form a streamlined shape. Restoration of this example was one of the most difficult projects ever undertaken by the craftsmen of the National Air and Space Museum's Garber Facility, for the structure had deteriorated over the years. Although obsolete, the Albatros continued to serve in frontline units until the end of the war.

At some point in the process, an aircraft undergoing restoration is usually completely assembled prior to being covered, to make sure that everything fits. This provides an opportunity to photograph the inner beauty of the structure. This is the first de Havilland DH-4 built in the United States, by Dayton-Wright.

Cole Palen's Albatros D Va reproduction in flight, authentic even down to the trail of exhaust smoke from its engine. Palen, who has brought World War I aviation to thousands as a labor of love, worked for years under the utmost difficulty, at one time living almost exclusively on peanut butter as he slaved to bring his idea of the re-creation of a World War I aerodrome to fruition. Now, rightly, he basks in international acclaim for his achievements.

Another view of the Carl Swanson Spad XIII in flight. Aircraft markings varied from country to country, as did camouflaging. The Germans used a lozenge-pattern camouflage fabric extensively, but also allowed wide discretion to their pilots for individual markings, as in the case of the nearly all-red aircraft of von Richthofen. The French tended to use standardized camouflage patterns, which varied over time; the English kept to an almost chocolate brown color for the latter part of the war.

For reasons of reliability and availability, reproductions of most World War I aircraft that used rotary engines are replaced with more modern radial types. In the rotary engine, the propeller was affixed to the cylinders, which rotated around a stationary crankshaft. In the radial, the cylinders are fixed, and the propeller is affixed to the rotating crankshaft. This Fokker Dr 1 reproduction has a radial engine, which makes it easier to fly.

Enamored of airplanes, the enthusiast sometimes finds it difficult to remember that all air forces of every nation depend upon the enlisted man to keep them flying. Here noted historian Fred Johnsen has captured the stripes of a Signal Corps corporal, in tribute to enlisted men everywhere.

single operation, 1,476 airplanes and 20 balloons from 101 different U.S., French, Italian, and British squadrons. His planning was tremendously detailed, and he insisted on the employment of brigade-sized units—400 airplanes at a time—to attack each side of the salient alternately.

The offensive began on September 12, but the weather was so bad that few missions were flown by the slightly less than 1,000 airplanes that were in commission. Despite having already decided upon withdrawal, the Germans resisted with their usual skill, but the American surge took many prisoners. To slow down the advance, the Germans threw in fresh, aggressive squadrons who took a terrible toll of the American bombing and observation planes, the losses forcing some squadrons out of action.

Later analysis shows Mitchell's efforts to have been premature. He did prove that large numbers of aircraft could be employed effectively, but his efforts would have been better spent in assuring that his crews were properly trained and equipped. In vivid contrast, one war later General Curtis E. LeMay would take painstaking efforts to ensure that his airmen were rigorously trained so that they could survive in combat. Mitchell undoubtedly grasped the larger picture of air power, but it was a picture painted with the blood of barely trained airmen flying still not fully developed aircraft.

As the war wrapped up, American strength and proficiency grew, and so did casualties. May 1918 had been the worst month, with 8 of 34 pilots killed for a 23.5 percent casualty rate. By October, when there were 270 pursuit pilots at the front, there were 34 casualties for a rate of 13.6 percent. The losses were unacceptable by later standards; at the time they were endured as part of the learning process.

LIGHTER-THAN-AIR COMBAT

An unsung group who had fought a long and difficult war were the members of the American Balloon Service, one of the most successful elements of the Air Service. The pioneer balloonist Frank Lahm had arrived in Paris to find nothing being done about organizing balloon squadrons. Colonel Lahm went right to work, purchasing equipment from the French and arranging for a school at Cuperly and for cooperation with artillery schools. Later, Colonel de Forest Chandler took over command of the balloon units. In much the same way as the pilots, American balloon observers were first trained by the French, then employed in French units to learn their trade. The Second Balloon Company went into action at the front on February 23, 1918, beginning a buildup that resulted in thirty-five companies in France at the end of the war, seventeen serving at the front. The first twenty balloons came from the French, followed by 265 balloons from the U.S. Forty-eight balloons were lost at the front, thirty-five by aerial attack, twelve by shell fire, and one by the cable breaking from unknown causes. Another thirty-five were scrapped for "fair wear and tear."

Observation balloons were cumbersome to handle. They required massive crews, and filling and lofting them involved lots of standing around and waiting.

The balloons were naturally called sausages, because of their shape. Balloon observers had important work, under difficult conditions. If attacked, they immediately bailed out, because the hydrogen-filled balloons could explode instantaneously.

The Caquot, Type R, captive observation balloons were large but fragile; 93 feet long and 28 feet in diameter, they were made primarily of rubberized cotton cloth. Stout cables, affixed to an electric or gas driven winch, connected them to the ground. A typical balloon company had six officers and 132 men; four of the officers were trained as observers.

It was tough work operating a balloon company, and tougher still to do the observation from a swaying kite or sausage-style balloon. The mission was similar to that of the observation planes—registering artillery fire and visual reconnaissance. The experienced balloon observer had some advantages. He could rise to an altitude of up to 5,000 feet, and was positioned in a familiar area, with two-way telephonic contact to the ground. But there were disadvantages, too. Balloons were the favorite targets of long-range guns and fighter aircraft. The two observers worked in a car suspended a few feet below 37,500 cubic feet of hydrogen; if a fighter plane's bullet struck the envelope, they had only twenty seconds to leap from their basket, descending to ground in their parachutes. Although the attacks were numerous, only one man was killed, when the falling balloon set his parachute on fire. Some became quite hardened to the process, one man making four emergency jumps in a single day, another leaping three times in four hours.

The excellent service the balloons provided the Army was reflected in the original postwar projections for strength: balloon units were supposed to have almost the same number of personnel as the aircraft units.

At war's end all of the squadrons at the front, both heavier and lighter than air, were at last beginning to be manned by well-seasoned pilots and observers. The names of those who would be famous in the next war were found there, and at home as well. George C. Marshall and Henry H. "Hap" Arnold would have much preferred fighting assignments, but their apprenticeships in Washington prepared them for vastly larger commands in the future. Their tasks would be made easier by men such as Frank Hunter, Edward Curtis, and Carl Spaatz, who scored their victories on the Western Front in World War I and went on to hold high positions in World War II.

During World War I the lifespan of an
aircraft type was extremely short. An aircraft might be in service only a few months
before being replaced by a new type. Now
aircraft serve for decades. The four-jet
Lockheed C-141, first flown on December
17, 1963, will remain a mainstay of the
new Air Mobility Command for many
years to come.

Camouflage was used for deception during
World War I, and the Germans even tried
their own version of stealth with aircraft
covered in transparent Cellon material.
But neither in-flight refueling nor true
stealth capability, here demonstrated by a
McDonnell Douglas KC-10 tanker and a
Lockheed F-117A Stealth fighter, could
even have been imagined at the time.

CHAPTER THREE
The Trying Years of the Golden Age 1919-1939

The years 1919 to 1939 were the Golden Age of Flight, as aircraft shed their functional gawkiness and became sculptural works of art. New records were set almost daily, and the newspapers courted colorful celebrities. Jimmy Doolittle could light up a room with a smile, or a company with an idea, and was equally at home in the classroom or on the race course. The famous transatlantic flight of cool and precise Charles Lindbergh came at exactly the right moment to lift a jazz-mad country to a higher level; few noticed that the flight also established a new benchmark for engine reliability and performance. The brave, ineffably sad Amelia Earhart was perceived as Lindbergh's perfect counterpart. And although all were heroic, there was a raffish, gut-tickling element too, best exemplified by the snoot-cocking daredevil Douglas "Wrong-Way" Corrigan.

Immediately after the Great War of 1914–1918, the Air Service's golden age was enlivened by a circus atmosphere, with air shows being provided by every base at the drop of a hat. Casualties and expense soon put an end to this, and years of record breaking mixed with public service in forest and border patrols, crop-dusting experiments, and relief missions ensued. The Army still permitted participation in the major air races and it thrilled the crowds with lovely fighters like the Curtiss P-6Es in their Snow Owl livery. But more than anything, it was a time of tremendous stress, with low budgets and unconscionably high casualty rates. Flying was a terribly dangerous profession. Fortunately, the fledgling service had a secret for survival.

In the files of the magnificent Air Force Museum at Wright-Patterson AFB, Ohio, is a hand-drawn map of officers' quarters at Maxwell Field, Alabama, circa 1937, showing who lived where. The names are a litany of heroes, record setters, future generals, and, all too often, those for whom Air Force bases were named posthumously in their honor. Circled around the Maxwell Officers Club were the modest homes of Major Claire Chennault, future leader of the Flying Tigers, and Major Ira Eaker, future commander of the Eighth Air Force. There were also such luminaries as Lieutenant Colonel Herbert A. Dargue, Lieutenant Colonel Harold H. George, Major

The Curtiss P-6E had a top speed of 198 mph. This famous photo shows a 17th Pursuit Squadron P-6E painted in the Snow Owl insignia. Despite its gorgeous appearance, the P-6E was only of average performance, and had structural problems that resulted in a high accident rate.

OPPOSITE:
The Loening amphibian had a long and useful life in all of the services, served many explorers and long-distance flyers. On December 21, 1926, the newly organized Army Air Corps sent five Loening OA-1As on a Pan-American goodwill flight, with stops in twenty-two nations. Three aircraft completed the 22,000-mile journey on April 23, 1927. Today the San Francisco may be seen in the Air Force Museum in Dayton, Ohio. Here it is captured in Douglas Smith's painting.

OPPOSITE LEFT:

Brigadier General William Mitchell, every inch the patrician. Mitchell and Charles Lindbergh are the only two airmen ever to receive the Medal of Honor in peacetime. The son of a senator, a commissioned officer at eighteen, Mitchell was the American air power visionary. One of his predictions was that some Sunday morning the Japanese would make a surprise attack on Pearl Harbor. Always twenty years in advance of his time, Mitchell continually called for air power achievements that were not yet possible, knowing that his very call would make them inevitable.

OPPOSITE RIGHT:

Mitchell's archenemy, who could easily have been his friend, Brigadier General Benjamin Foulois. Both men wanted the same thing: an independent air force capable of defending the country against all comers. Each despised the other's modus operandi, and they fought when they should have made common cause. In the end, both were dealt with shabbily by the service. Mitchell died in 1936, before his ideas were vindicated. Foulois died in 1967 at the age of eighty-seven, as stoutly convinced that he was correct about air power as he had been when he taught himself to fly in 1910.

Frederick I. Eglin, Major Millard F. Harmon, Major William E. Kepner, Captain Harry H. Halverson, and Lieutenant Haywood S. Hansell. Captain Benjamin W. Chidlaw lived in NCO quarters, and Lieutenant Carlisle I. Ferris, father of Keith, the famous aviation artist, lived in the still-sleepy city of Montgomery. It was as if Maxwell were an enormous petri dish of talent from which the virus of aviation genius would flow for the next fifty years.

The social life of the Air Corps was engaging in its simplicity, a strange mixture of frontier post and *Our Town.* Riffling through the files of the service journals of the period, one finds elements that reflect both a simpler time and common concerns of today. At San Antonio's Kelly Field, General and Mrs. Halstad Dorsey put on the play *Rosemary Shrub* in their home, with junior officers taking part, the proceeds going to the Chapel Fund. Horse shows were big, although one pathetic request by an Air Corps officer for permission to withdraw from the mandatory equitation classes on the basis of his fear of horses and the fact that he flew an airplane was summarily denied. And there was a vicious debate over whether the traditional neck-choking high collar should be abandoned as a uniform item in favor of a more modern roll collar.

It is almost shocking for a contemporary reader to find the open reflection of the less politically correct attitudes of the time; there are jocular references to gender and race that would today result in instant dismissal. But the service tried to take care of its own, rationing its small privileges as equitably as it could. Artist Keith Ferris recalls with pleasure the annual flight he could take with his father, a treat extended to wives, mothers, and children, but strangely forbidden to fathers of the pilots.

From this gentle milieu came the men who would hammer out doctrine as they broke record after record to establish a spirit that lives to this day. They were the secret of the survival of the tiny, impoverished Air Service; what it lacked in money and resources it made up for in brains and energy, mastering the emerging technology and overcoming the political brawls with which it entered the new age.

THE FEUD GOES ON

Although there may have been an armistice with the Germans, there was none between Billy Mitchell and Benny Foulois. The two men continued their battles for the next seven years, until Mitchell's extremist charges impaled him on the cold bureaucratic spear of Army regulations and he was court-martialed.

The peace had brought with it a precipitous drop in strength, the Air Service plunging from a peak of just over 195,000 officers and men in 1918 to hover around 10,000 for the next decade. Aircraft strength did not fall off quite so rapidly, because there were warehouses full of Jennies and DH-4s, disassembled so that as many as 68 planes could fit in a single hangar. Both types were more dangerous to fly with each passing year, but new airplanes were rare.

Over the next two decades, the U.S. Army Air Service (after July 2, 1926, the U.S. Army Air Corps), was hampered by budgets averaging $13 million a year, and could only fight a losing battle against obsolescence.

During this drawdown, which was to be repeated even more dramatically after World War II, Mitchell's and Foulois's roles remained roughly the same, even though their jobs changed dramatically. When Brigadier General Foulois returned to New York, he reverted to his previous rank of captain as soon as he stepped on shore. Promoted a few months later to major, Foulois pulled in his horns, and as a flyer-administrator tried to keep things going in an orderly way. Even more forceful and idea-laden than Mitchell in his dealings with the Army staff and with Congress, he was low-key and kept within channels, not exciting rancor at this time. That was to come later, after Mitchell had been disposed of. Mitchell, beloved of the press and bedecked with so many foreign decorations that he was called the "Prince of the Air," kept both his rank of brigadier general and the attention of the media. Sadly, even though the two men had adjacent offices, they never spoke.

Mitchell was appointed Director of Military Aeronautics, serving under the Director of the Air Service, Major General Charles T. Menoher, an

artillery man. The angry prophet of air power immediately began opposing Menoher's policies, wooing the public so that he could bend Congress, the Army, and the Navy to his will. In the process of making his incredible but too-often-fulfilled prophecies, he also made the bitter enemies who eventually did him in.

THE PHANTOM ARGUMENT

Mitchell's battles with the Navy brought him his greatest peacetime moment, when his bombers sent the tough old German battleship *Ostfriesland* to the bottom in July 1921. Fired with the idea of an independent Air Service, Mitchell repeatedly derided the role of the Navy in future warfare. He argued that funds for ships were a wasted investment in the past, and that spending for air power was the only rational choice for the future. His pointed attacks had maneuvered the Navy into accepting the challenge of determining whether or not airplanes could sink battleships. Mitchell picked the fight and then used all of his leadership skills to create the 1st Provisional Air Brigade, assemble the cream of the Air Service's airplanes and pilots, create new bombs (there were none big enough in the inventory), and carry out the tests successfully. It was a brilliant achievement, the repercussions of his 2,000-pound bombs echoing in the halls of Congress long after they had been stilled by the sea. Yet it had the unfortunate side effect of intoxicating Mitchell with the correctness, even the inviolability, of his views—a self-delusionary hubris that would lead first to his exile and then to his ouster. Ironically, his success would have greater immediate effect on the Navy than on the Air Service. The planning for more and larger aircraft carriers began almost immediately.

Mitchell's argument was a phantom. There should have been no doubt in anyone's mind that a sufficient weight of explosives, whether delivered by cannon, torpedo, bomb, or Railway Express, could sink a ship. He artfully argued that a fleet of aircraft was less expensive than a single battleship, obscuring the real questions of whether air force bombers could defeat an invading enemy fleet or bomb a potential enemy's homeland. They could not. The range of contemporary bombers was pitifully short, they lacked the capability to fly in poor weather, and they had precious little in the way of combat equipment—bombsights, radios, oxygen, and so on. The same was true for all air forces everywhere; the technology to do what Mitchell sought was simply not available. However, once again, the importance of Mitchell's work was not what he claimed *could* be done at the moment, but his creation of a mind-set that permitted the eventual development of equipment that *could* do what he claimed.

Mitchell's efforts kept the concept of air power on the front pages and forced the Army to devote more resources to it than it might otherwise have done. Without him, the Army might have cut the Air Service back to the level apocryphally suggested by President Coolidge—buying one airplane and taking turns using it. Mitchell was an intelligent man, and undoubtedly knew that many of the ideas he expounded in speeches and articles had been appropriated from Foulois and others on his staff. Despite being the nominal author of the manual of operations for the Air Service in 1918, one that emphasized that aviation was a supporting arm for the infantry, the flamboyant general had been much influenced by Sir Hugh Trenchard, father of the independent Royal Air Force. When he perceived after the war that the Army was not going to nurture the Air Service at the level he desired, Mitchell began advocating a Trenchard-style independent air force. His views were not shared by many of his colleagues. They knew there would never be enough money appropriated to set up the necessary support facilities for an independent service, not when there were idle Army facilities. The Air Service needed the Army for basing, logistic, and supply support. And, for much of the next decade, it bled the Army for personnel that could not be recruited.

Mitchell ignored his subordinates' views on independence, continuing to use the press to put forward his definition of air power and pressing for the establishment of a separate air force. His August 29, 1921, report on the bombing tests recommended sweeping changes in the War and Navy Departments, with a separate air force to be established for frontier and coastal defense. Air Service Director Menoher forwarded it to Secretary of War John W. Weeks, noting his disapproval. Things have not changed much in Washington: the story was leaked to the press and Menoher decided that either he or Mitchell had to resign. Unfortunately for Menoher, Weeks was afraid to cashier Mitchell before the next series of tests, and Menoher stepped aside. But instead of appointing Mitchell in his place, Weeks called on Mitchell's old boss, Major General Mason Patrick, who must have asked "Why me?" when the assignment came.

Patrick could handle Mitchell, letting him know who was Chief of the

Air Service and who was Assistant Chief. When Mitchell threatened to resign, Patrick took him by the arm to walk down to the Secretary of War for action. Mitchell backed off. But in 1923, when all of the bombing tests, including the sinking of the *Alabama*, had been completed, Weeks and Patrick recognized that Mitchell had antagonized everyone from President Coolidge down. Weeks declined to recommend Mitchell's reappointment as Assistant Chief of the Air Service, and Brigadier General James E. Fechet was named in his place. Mitchell reverted to his permanent rank of colonel with an assignment as Air Officer, 8th Corps Area, at Fort Sam Houston, Texas.

It was a nothing job. Never one to suffer in silence, Mitchell deliberately sought a court-martial. The Navy gave him the opportunity when in quick succession it lost a Hawaii-bound PN-9 patrol plane (later to be rescued) on August 31, 1925, and then on September 3, the dirigible *Shenandoah*. Mitchell called a press conference and issued a nine-page diatribe that charged the Navy and War Department with incompetence, criminal negligence, and almost treasonable administration.

President Calvin Coolidge moved with customary caution. He had charges preferred against Mitchell, but convened an investigating board headed

General Mitchell baited the U.S. Navy into testing his theories of bombers versus battleships. The tests went on intermittently from 1919 to 1923, always with tremendous public interest. Here spectacular phosphorous bombs shower the USS Alabama *in the last of the tests. These were intended to show how the ship's antiaircraft batteries would be disposed of. Later, 2,000-pound bombs would sink the old battleship.*

by Dwight W. Morrow to study how aircraft should be employed. It was a clever tactic, sequenced so that Mitchell would have a chance to put his considered recommendations on air power to the board as a serving officer, rather than as a martyr at his court-martial.

Curiously, Mitchell was at his worst before the Morrow Board, abandoning his infectious charm in the witness box and insisting on reading the rather turgid prose of his book, *Winged Defense.* It was as if he had suddenly realized that his strategy of seeking a court-martial was flawed and that he had created a denouement that he no longer wanted. Like the majority of the investigating boards that would proliferate over the years, the Morrow Board found that the Air Service was just that, a service to the infantry, and should not be an independent force.

The result of his court-martial was a foregone conclusion. Although there could be debate about Mitchell's ideas and his prophecies (including his prediction that the Japanese would attack Pearl Harbor one Sunday morning, and then take the Philippines), there was no debate about whether he had been insubordinate, or whether his conduct had not been "prejudicial to good order and military discipline."

Mitchell dragged the trial out for seven weeks, but the verdict was merciless. He was sentenced to suspension and forfeiture of all pay and allowances for five years. President Coolidge softened the sentence by granting him full subsistence and half pay, a meaningless gesture as Mitchell was independently wealthy. Tired and unwell, Mitchell resigned. He spent the next ten years until his death repeating his message in books and speeches, but he had lost his forum. Without the inspiration of his staff, he had few new ideas, and consequently had negligible impact; he died a prophet without honor. In 1947, recognition of his prescient contributions to the victory in World War II caused Congress to pass a special bill promoting him to major general, retroactive to the day of his death.

His court-martial might have had ruinous consequences, for the solid heart of the Air Service—loyalists like Hap Arnold, Carl Spaatz, Herbert Dargue, Bob Olds, William Gilmore, Horace Hickam, and others—stood up for him, testifying for him though they knew that it could well mean the end of their careers. It was a heroic showing of apolitical officers saying what they thought, careers be damned—a model for the military for all time.

Fortunately, the acrimony died with his court-martial, and the Army flyers turned their attention in full to what most had been doing all along: painstakingly developing the technology that would be required in the next war.

PLANNING THE FUTURE

During the years 1919 through 1939 there evolved almost inadvertently a five-track plan to achieve the aims of the air arm, with these elements:

1. Preserve the training base and be ready for expansion.
2. Create doctrine for pursuit, bombardment, and attack aircraft.
3. Develop logistic and supply expertise by vying for aviation records.
4. Preserve the base of the aviation industry by spreading contracts out as widely as possible.
5. Expand the Air Service's research and development capability.

By carefully matching personalities against the requirement, and by a clever management of funds, the Air Service was able to sustain itself, moving from the chaos caused by abrupt cutbacks after World War I to a position from which it could handle the tremendous expansion that would be required by World War II. In the process, the transition from wood and fabric biplanes to all-metal monoplanes was matched by more rigorous standards in training and performance.

1. PRESERVING THE TRAINING BASE

Preserving the training base and maintaining a cadre of first-class people who could manage an explosive expansion when the time came conformed to traditional Army thinking. Part of this effort was the creation of the Reserve and National Guard forces that would seventy years later become essential ingredients in today's Total Force concept. Of all the tracks, preserving the base for expansion was the most difficult. In the midst of the country's postwar boom economy, when the civilian 1920s were really roaring, the military 1920s were at a standstill; both were at a halt in the 1930s. Throughout the military, promotions were nonexistent, demotions were a distinct possibility, and pay was constant from 1922 to 1942. Security was no inducement to reenlist during boom times and although the Army posts managed a comfortable air of genteel poverty, men still had to support their wives and plan for their children's educations even as they pursued a hazardous profession.

Grim statistics showed that it was twenty times as hazardous to be an officer on flying duty as on ground duty, and Air Corps officers were encouraged to maintain the $10,000 life insurance policy the government offered. Between 1923 and 1932 there were 542 casualties from aircraft accidents. The average pay and allowances of an Air Corps pilot amounted to $394.18 a month; airline pilots at National Air Transport, a predecessor of today's United Airlines, earned an average of $650 a month.

Enlisted men were in even more difficult circumstances. A private drew a base pay of $21 a month; if he were promoted to specialist sixth class, it went to $24. A staff sergeant drew $72, and a technical sergeant $84. The problem became so acute that the Adjutant General put out a letter calling for the elimination of married enlisted men who could not support their dependents, and prohibition of marriage for lower-rated enlisted men. It was simply not in the cards—or the budget—for the Army to consider providing adequately for them, even though the turnover in trained personnel was costly, then as now.

The only genuine incentive for most men, officers or enlisted, was the adventure of flying. Ironically, civil aviation was booming; airlines were forming left and right, as were new manufacturing companies. Even the future five-star general of the Air Force, Henry "Hap" Arnold, was dropped back to captain after being jumped to colonel during the war. Depressed by his prospects and concerned that he was depriving his family of an adequate living, he had decided to accept an offer to become the president of the newly formed Pan American Airways at a considerable boost in salary. But his support for Billy Mitchell caused him to be exiled to a squadron commander's job at Fort Riley, so he reluctantly turned Pan Am down, feeling that he could not leave the service under fire.

Still another star, Jimmy Doolittle, remained a first lieutenant from 1920 until his resignation in 1930, even though during that time he had become the foremost test and racing pilot in the world, and the only one with a doctoral degree from MIT. But because the Air Corps did not have a separate promotion list, he was submerged in the rolls of the Army, too junior to expect promotion. Unable to support his family on a lieutenant's pay, he left for a senior position with Shell Oil and was lost to the Air Corps for ten years—but not, fortunately, to aviation.

Most of the key leaders stayed on, using obsolete equipment as well as they could, taking care of the enlisted men to the best of their ability, and hammering out a skeleton framework they could one day expand. They began the slow process of creating Air Corps doctrine, based initially on the lessons learned in World War I. Because service to the Army was the goal, observation

A Fourth of July open house at McCook Field, Dayton, Ohio, in 1924. McCook was the center of aeronautical development and the direct ancestor of most of the major R&D facilities in the United States today. Note the arrows pointed on the tops of the buildings—these gave the direction and heading to various cities.

and attack became the most important missions, with pursuit and bombardment falling behind.

2. CREATING THE DOCTRINE

The Army Air Service emerged from World War I with its missions and policies so firmly based on support of the infantry and artillery that the War Department decided that almost half of its strength was to be devoted to lighter-than-air observation balloons and airships for reconnaissance. The Air Service was thus placed in a difficult position, wishing to create doctrine for pursuit, bombardment, attack, and observation aircraft while still supporting the Army and justifying its own existence. But what it really wished to do was develop the technology to become a decisive independent arm.

The first element of doctrine to emerge was the result of the 1929 annual Air Corps maneuvers, which were analyzed closely by the thinkers at Langley Field's Air Corps Tactical School. There, First Lieutenant Kenneth N. Walker (later a brigadier general and Medal of Honor winner) propounded that a well-organized, well-flown air attack could not be stopped. The school even pinned numbers to its belief: bombing planes could accomplish their mission without pursuit escort if opposed by no more than twice their number in enemy planes. Unescorted attack planes were supposed to be able to fend off equal numbers of enemy fighters. This was incredible optimism, given that bombers of the time performed only slightly better than World War I Gothas, and if found by the fighters would surely be their victims. Yet it matched British thinking. Only a few years later, Prime Minister Stanley Baldwin would terrify England by pronouncing that "the bombers would always get through," thus enhancing the propaganda value of the threat from Germany's aerial rearmament. Many of the future Air Corps leaders were convinced of the same, among them Hap Arnold, Hugh Knerr, and Frank Andrews.

The naive belief in bombers grew not from their prowess, but from the

One of the tasks at McCook Field was testing captured German equipment. The Roland D VI, intact at the left, was an elegant-looking aircraft, with an unusual fuselage of lapped wood, much like the construction of small boat hulls of the time. It was quite maneuverable, and with a 116-mph top speed, relatively fast for a German fighter. At the right it is seen after a sudden fire on the ground.

By 1930, change was in the wind. Boeing had already built its Monomail, a low-wing, all-metal cantilever monoplane with a retractable landing gear. Its B-9 "Death Angel," seen here, was the next step forward. It was the first modern bomber, just as its civilian counterpart, the Boeing 247, was the first modern air transport. The B-9's performance revolutionized Air Corps thinking, but unfortunately for Boeing, Glenn Martin had a better aircraft under development.

Always a difficult man to deal with, Glenn Martin stoutly resisted the specifications that Wright Field was trying to impose upon him. However, over the course of three years he had to give in time after time; and the result was the beautiful Martin B-10/B-12 series of bombers. They had all the features of the Boeing B-9 plus a revolving gun turret and canopy-enclosed cockpits. The Norden bombsight was installed in the B-10 series, giving the Air Corps its first genuine approach to air power. Faster than existing fighters, reliable, and with an adequate range, the B-10s would soldier on to fight in World War II.

demonstrated inability of the fighters to first find and then catch them. Escaping fighters was not difficult during the day, for the sky is vast; at night, without radar to detect them, bombers could easily slip through. The belief was strengthened by the procurement of the first two modern bombers, the Boeing B-9 and Martin B-10. The Boeing presaged the Flying Fortress in construction, but it had inherent vibration problems and was not procured in quantity. There was an order, huge for the time, for forty-eight of the beautiful Martin B-10s, which were at least as much a product of the Wright Field development office as of the Martin Company. Wright Field had framed the specifications for a twin-engine, all-metal, retractable-gear monoplane, and

then had to browbeat Glenn Martin into producing what they wanted. Martin wanted to deliver what he knew how to build—a fabric-covered biplane.

The new bombers were faster than the contemporary fighters, which set in concrete the theory that unescorted bombing was the tactic of the future. It was to prove very costly in World War II. Claire Chennault railed against the idea, convinced that pursuit aviation was king, especially when used in concert with an early-warning system of his own devising. His intransigent opposition led first to his early retirement, and then to immortality leading the Flying Tigers in the Far East.

Fighter and attack aircraft lagged behind bombers, in part because sufficiently powerful engines were not yet available, but also because the big builders, like Curtiss and Douglas, tried to stretch their basic designs for as long as possible to keep their costs down. Thus, the Curtiss Hawk series, which began in 1923 with the XPW-8, was stretched out over the next fifteen years, the last production examples of the design going to China in 1938. In a similar way, the Curtiss Falcon observation and attack planes were only slowly changed over a long number of years, even though much more modern aircraft—the Northrop Alpha and the Boeing Monomail—had been developed commercially.

3. DEVELOPING LOGISTIC PROWESS THROUGH RECORD SETTING

The most colorful track was the development of logistic expertise in the continuous pursuit of aviation records. The public could be amused, Congress impressed, and the technology tested by going faster, farther, and higher. Enthusiasm was abetted by foreign competition. America might hold the speed record one week, France the next, England the next. National pride and political power soon came to be reflected in the number of flying records set.

The process began in 1919 when Lieutenant Colonel Rutherford L. Hartz and Lieutenant Ernest E. Harmon, with two master signal electricians, Jack Hardin and Jerry Dobias, flew a Martin bomber "Around the Rim," a circuit flight of the United States covering 9,823 miles. The trip took fourteen weeks and taught an important lesson: every record flight needed careful planning and the advanced placement of logistic and service teams.

Billy Mitchell fostered two major events in 1919. The first was a New York to Toronto race, with thirty Air Service planes of all types entered. It was won in a DH-4 by the "Flying Parson," Lieutenant Belvin W. Maynard, with an incredible 133.8 mph. The next event, in typically grandiose Mitchell style, was a New York to San Francisco race. The former commander of the 95th Aero Squadron, Lieutenant Colonel Harold E. Hartney, laid out the course through Buffalo, Cleveland, Chicago, Omaha, Cheyenne, Salt Lake City, and Reno, with twenty-nine control points.

Entry was easy. Any government plane or pilot with local command approval could enter, as long as his plane could reach 100 mph and was not modified in any way. There were seventy-four entrants, of whom sixty-one made it to the starting line, forty-six in New York and fifteen in San Francisco.

Mitchell's goal was not really to demonstrate cross-continent flying, but to establish a series of flying fields and awaken community interest. Advance teams went out to preposition oil, gasoline, and spare parts; rudimentary weather and communication facilities were established.

Bad weather, old airplanes, and poor piloting took their toll. Twenty-six airplanes reached San Francisco from New York, and seven reached New York from San Francisco. Of these, seventeen immediately started the round-trip back across the continent. The best time for a one-way trip was Lieutenant. Maynard's 3 days, 6 hours, 47 minutes; he also set the round-trip record of 9 days, 4 hours, 25 minutes.

The race proved that standard Air Service aircraft could be moved from coast to coast, but the cost was high: fifty-four accidents and seven fatalities. There was no great public outcry, but within the service some hard conclusions were drawn about training, maintenance, and the general suitability of the wartime DH-4.

The mass-race concept was soon supplanted by assaults on individual altitude, distance, and point-to-point records. On February 27, 1920, McCook Field's chief test pilot, Major Rudolph "Shorty" Schroeder, set a world's altitude record of 33,113 feet in a LePere biplane powered by a supercharged Liberty engine, one of the critical milestones on the trail to the fleets of supercharged World War II bombers and fighters. The tall, gangly Schroeder suf-

Much of the experimental work done at McCook Field would have an impact on World War II, especially the pioneering efforts of Sanford Moss in creating the turbosupercharger. Here a crew is hand-starting a Liberty engine at Pike's Peak, at an altitude of 14,109 feet. Without the supercharger, the engine would deliver only 230 horsepower; with the turbosupercharger installed, it produced 356 horsepower.

The LePere biplane is one of the aircraft that would have fought over France if the war had continued into 1919. Equipped with a Moss turbosupercharger, it set many altitude records in the postwar period. Standing in front of a supercharged Lepere, from the left are famous test pilot John A. Macready, Dr. Sanford Moss, Major George E. A. Hallett, "Mr. Engine" to the Air Service, and Adolph Berger of General Electric.

fered from hypoxia and cold, and plunged 25,000 feet before waking up in time to manage a landing at McCook. His ground crew found him almost helpless in the cockpit, his eyes frozen open from the intense cold. Such flights were not only for the records; they also tested oxygen equipment, propellers, flying clothing, and the human body.

The following year, Lieutenant William D. Coney flew a DH-4B from San Diego to Jacksonville in 22 hours, 27 minutes, only to crash to his death on the return flight. Coney's efforts set the stage for the next big leap, a nonstop transcontinental flight, the brainchild of Lieutenants Muir S. Fairchild and Oakley G. Kelly.

The two young men surveyed the world's aircraft, seeking one with the capability to make the flight, and selected a version of the Fokker F IV transport being built in Holland for the Air Service. Big and awkward-looking, the high-wing monoplane, designated the T-2, was powered by a Liberty engine.

The Air Service was not parochial. When it needed the best aircraft available for the proposed nonstop transcontinental flight, it went to Holland to the Fokker Aircraft Company to procure the T-2. Although not a handsome aircraft—few of the larger Fokkers were—the T-2 was highly efficient, and hangs today in the National Air and Space Museum.

Planning was extremely thorough for the several transcontinental attempts, including the testing and selection of the fuel that would be used. John Macready, at the left, and Oakley Kelly, at the right, were lieutenants destined for great flying achievements. The amount of fuel and oil carried by the T-2 is indicated by the barrels of gasoline and cans of oil.

First Lieutenant Ernest W. Dichman spearheaded the enormous amount of planning required for the flight. Extra tanks were installed to increase the T-2's fuel capacity to 752 gallons. Similar additions were made to the oil and water tankage. A set of dual controls was installed so that the two pilots could trade off during a flight made that much more fatiguing by the noise from the engine placed literally at the pilot's elbow.

Lieutenant Fairchild was injured in a crash before the flight and Lieutenant John A. Macready replaced him. A west-to-east attempt failed when the airplane was unable to climb over the Rocky Mountains with its heavy fuel load, and the two pilots elected instead to establish an unofficial new world's endurance record of 35 hours, 18 minutes, 30 seconds. A second attempt also failed; they got across the Rockies, but were forced down at Indianapolis because of engine problems.

Then, after setting an official endurance record of 36 hours, 4 minutes, 34 seconds, they attempted another transcontinental trip, this time from east to west. Barely scraping into the air at Roosevelt Field, Long Island, on May 2, 1923, the T-2 staggered along at treetop height until enough fuel was burned off to permit it to climb, foot by foot, to a safe altitude. By the time it reached the worst part of the route, at Tucumcari, New Mexico, the airplane was flying high. It landed in San Diego after 26 hours, 50 minutes, 38 seconds, a triumph of persistence as much as pilotage.

Just three months later, after several attempts, Lieutenants John P. Richter and Lowell H. Smith forecast the future by setting an endurance record of 37 hours, 15 minutes, in a de Havilland DH-4, using air-to-air refueling from another aircraft. The DH-4 tanker used a forty-foot hose routed through a hole in the fuselage floor to transfer fuel. A filling station nozzle on the hose was directed by hand into the tank opening on the receiving aircraft.

Impressive as these records were, they were homegrown and had not stirred public enthusiasm on a national basis. That was to come with the first round-the-world flight in 1924, in part because of the scope of the challenge, but more importantly because there was competition from Great Britain, France, Italy, and Argentina.

The discipline and planning that now characterized the Air Service contrasted sharply with the poorly planned and near-tragic efforts of their competitors, who, in addition to failure, had to endure everything from white ants devouring propellers to sharks attempting to devour the crews.

In contrast, and as an indication of General Mason Patrick's far-seeing leadership, the Air Service sent a survey team around the world in 1923 to help the State Department obtain transit rights, arrange no less than fifty-two landing places, and most important of all, establish well-equipped supply dumps. Unlike the battleship bombing controversy, the attempt produced interagency cooperation on a grand scale, with the U.S. Navy placing patrol vessels at

strategic places, the Bureau of Fisheries and the Coast Guard both moving men and equipment and standing by for emergencies, and the Signal Corps providing a meteorologist.

After careful analysis of available airplane designs, the Air Service picked the new Douglas Aircraft Company to build a prototype and four production aircraft, the Douglas World Cruisers, which launched a great aircraft company into five decades of uninterrupted success.

The mission was to fly in loose formation around the world, stopping for fuel and maintenance as required. As no one had accomplished the feat before, merely completing the trip would establish the initial records for speed and distance, which happened to last for many years.

Everyone wanted to fly the mission, and a rigorous pilot selection process winnowed the huge field of candidates down to just seven. From these, General Patrick picked four, letting each pilot select his own crewman. The lucky pioneers were Major Frederick L. Martin as Flight Leader, with Sergeant Alva L. Harvey; Lieutenant Leigh Wade with Sergeant Henry H. Ogden; Lieutenant Lowell H. Smith with Lieutenant Leslie P. Arnold; and Lieutenant Erik Nelson with Lieutenant John Harding.

Working at the Douglas plant in Santa Monica, today the site of the Museum of Flying, the crews tested their planes as they came off the assembly line, naming them for cities that corresponded roughly to the cardinal points on a compass. Martin selected the *Seattle*, Smith the *Chicago*, Wade the *Boston*, and Nelson the *New Orleans*.

Designed to use pontoons and wheels interchangeably, the World

Unkindly styled "Mitchell's Folly" by critics, the huge Witteman-Lewis XNBL-l (Experimental Night Bomber, Long Distance, Number One) was more familiarly called the Barling bomber after its designer, Walter Barling. Although it set many load-lifting records, the Barling's six engines, three wings, four rudders, and two elevators created more drag than performance.

The Verville-Sperry racer was extremely advanced technically, with a cantilever low wing and retractable landing gear. Its configuration is essentially no different from that of the Hawker Hurricane fighter of eleven years later, except for the open cockpit. Unfortunately, the methodical testing and improvement of aircraft had not matured as fast as the design, and the Verville-Sperry never realized its full potential. If a single year of intensive test work had been invested in it, the United States would have had a fighter with features a decade in advance of any other aircraft in the world.

Cruisers were big, tough airplanes, with an 80-mph cruise speed and a range of 800 miles. Six years of experience and a lot of experimentation had made the Liberty engines that powered them much more reliable than their wartime counterparts.

The flight started officially from Sand Point in Seattle on April 6, 1924; it ended there 175 days and 26,345 miles later, after an epic adventure that saw the pioneers lose two planes, use seventeen Liberty engines, and blaze a trail of friendship through twenty-nine countries.

The first plane had been lost early on, when Major Martin and Sergeant Harvey flew the *Seattle* into a mountain in the Aleutian peninsula. By a miracle, both survived, then walked for ten difficult days to safety in a native fishing village. Leigh Wade, a jovial daredevil test pilot destined to outlive all the others, had to force-land the *Boston* midway between the Orkneys and the Faroe Islands in the North Atlantic. He and Ogden were rescued by the USS *Richmond*, but their plane was lost when a cable snapped on the hoist lifting it aboard. Later, the prototype was named *Boston II* and brought to Nova Scotia, from where Wade and Ogden completed the trip.

As brilliant as the flying had been, the pilots freely acknowledged that the real achievement had been in the solid spadework of preparation and supply that enabled engines to be changed, pontoons replaced, and repairs made all across the world. Less than two decades later, the same sort of preparation would result in the thousands of airports, supply dumps, and aerial routes of the military airlift system, which not only helped win World War II but also laid the global foundation for postwar commercial aviation.

Journalist Lowell Thomas kept the public excited over the world flight, but the gut interest was always in raw, unadulterated speed. The Air Service, like the Navy and most of the air forces of the world, responded with an evolving series of new racing aircraft. Funding for a racing event was difficult to obtain from Congress, so it was customary to pass the race planes off as potential fighter prototypes. There was more than a little truth in this, for the ultimate benefit of racing was the forced development of ever more powerful engines. Then, as now, performance depended upon power, and engines were more costly and more difficult to develop than airframes.

There were many venues for speed records—a flight between any two cities can still qualify for establishing a record—but for the first ten years of the Golden Age the military used the Pulitzer Prize and the Schneider Trophy races to develop their engines and aircraft, and incidentally, to catch the public eye. The results were especially rewarding because the Americans came as upstarts to the speed arena, and left it with far more victories than any other nation.

The Army and Navy competed in both races, sharing the development of the Curtiss engine, propeller, and successive generations of racers. The process of improving engine and airframe design began with the McCook Field-designed

Verville VCR-I, which won the first Pulitzer at 156 mph. It continued in the increasingly sophisticated Curtiss racers that dominated both the Pulitzer and the Schneider Trophy races. These racers raised the world speed record on several occasions, the last time in a flight by Al Williams in 1923, at 267.16 mph.

4. PRESERVING THE INDUSTRIAL BASE

The fourth track of long-term Air Service development was less obvious at the time, although it should be familiar to us today, for exactly the same problem exists—the preservation of an industrial base in order to fight the next war. The Air Service undertook to preserve the infant aviation industry by the judi-

The Curtiss Aeroplane and Motor Company offered the XNBS-4 for night short-distance bombing. Although somewhat more advanced in design than the original Martin bomber from which it stemmed, its performance remained on a par with the World War I German Gotha.

Ground handling of fighter aircraft was still rather simple in 1929; the worker here nonchalantly supports a Curtiss XP-3A on his shoulder. This aircraft illustrates how Curtiss stretched its designs. The XP-3A was converted from a 1925 Curtiss P-1A by installing a Pratt & Whitney R-1340 radial engine and a rather handsome deep-chord NACA cowling. It was later reworked into the XP-21 in 1931 with another engine change.

Tony Fokker was famous for making airplanes in Germany during the First World War. It was obvious that his designs were needed in America, and he set up the Atlantic Aircraft Corporation in Trenton, New Jersey, to manufacture them. The basic Fokker F VIIA was produced as the Atlantic C-2, C-5, and C-7, for the American public was not quite ready to buy Fokker airplanes. A special wing, built in Holland, was installed on this, the "Bird of Paradise," in which Lieutenants Lester J. Maitland and Albert Hegenberger would fly from Oakland, California, to Honolulu, Hawaii, on June 1, 1927.

cious award of enough contracts to keep as many companies as possible in business. Annual budgets were so small that companies could not count on contracts, but they could count on Air Service procurement officers to spread the wealth as much as possible.

One effect of this careful largess was that engineers became migrant workers, following contracts from company to company. Thus the great Jack Northrop moved from Douglas to Lockheed to his own firm; James S. McDonnell went from Huff-Daland to Consolidated to Stout to Great Lakes to Martin before forming McDonnell Aircraft; his colleague Donavan Berlin began his commercial career at Douglas, polished the tools of his trade at Northrop creating experimental fighters, then moved to Curtiss to design what became the immortal P-40.

There was the usual fudging of funds. Few new aircraft could be procured, but there was money for maintenance and plenty of ancient Liberty planes to work with. Wartime experience with the DH-4 revealed some problems, the most serious of which was that the heavy fuel tank mounted behind the pilot would move forward in a crash, crushing him. The aft position of the DH-4's landing gear created a pronounced tendency to nose over, especially on soft or muddy ground. Some brave observers would routinely leave their cockpits and crawl aft, straddling the fuselage like a rodeo rider, to make the plane less nose-heavy.

The Air Service used the subterfuge of "maintenance money" to remedy these defects in a redesign called the DH-4B. Then, beginning in 1923, a program was started involving at least ten companies and Army depots to create the DH-4M (for Modernized). Boeing and the American Fokker division, Atlantic, used engines, hardware, wings, and tails of the old DH-4s, but built new fuselages that used welded steel-tube construction. The dollar values of the contracts were not great, but they permitted the companies to maintain skeleton work forces along with minimum engineering staffs.

5. FOSTERING RESEARCH AND DEVELOPMENT

The fifth and most important Air Service track was the expansion of the McCook Field research and development center into what ultimately fathered not only the gigantic Wright-Patterson Air Force Base complex, but all the associated research, development, and logistic facilities in the country. In addition, this effort spawned the leaders of the aviation industry with on-the-job training at its facilities. Those nurtured by the system include legendary leaders like Berlin, McDonnell, Donald Douglas, Virginius Clark, I. M. Laddon, Alfred Verville, Jean A. Roche, Sam D. Heron, Alexander Klemin, and many more. Research and development also provided industry with the HIAD, the *Handbook of Industrial Aircraft Design,* which was the beginning of a systematic system of specifications for military aircraft.

Later generations would decry all this as the establishment of what became known as the military-industrial complex. The truth was that military aviation was too demanding for an infant industry to deal with without close cooperation of the military itself. Conversely, industry was totally foreign to military men, who needed education and experience in how best to use it to the service's advantage.

A perfect example of this relationship is the way McCook Field worked with the Huff-Daland Aircraft Company. A tiny firm in upstate New York with a penchant for goofy names for its airplanes (one of the first was the *Dizzy Dog*), it had submitted the TA-2, an absurd-looking trainer with few redeeming

General Mitchell's enthusiasm for advanced airborne tactics led McCook's Engineering Division to design the GAX, which was built, reluctantly, by Boeing. A twin-Liberty-engine pusher triplane, the GAX was heavy, slow, and unmaneuverable. However, it forecast the future in terms of armament, being fitted with a 37mm cannon and four machine guns in the nose for ground attack. Here, test pilot Harold R. Harris can be seen in the cockpit, which he later likened to being inside a bass drum.

TOP AND MIDDLE:

An early example of the infamous work of the military-industrial complex. Huff-Daland had submitted a series of designs, all even more cluttered in appearance than this TA-2 trainer (at left). Lieutenant Harold R. Harris worked with the firm, and they came back with the very work-manlike AT-1 (middle), of which ten were procured. Huff-Daland became Keystone Aircraft in 1927, and was the principal supplier of bombers for a number of years.

American aircraft designations have repeated themselves over the years. This is the first B-1B—in this case the Huff-Daland XB-1B, a twin-engine derivative of the earlier single-engine XHB-1. While performance was good, the aircraft was bested in competition by the more advanced Curtiss B-2.

Racing was one means of attracting public support, especially when spiced by interservice rivalry. Ten aircraft entered the Merchant's Exchange of St. Louis Trophy Race on October 5, 1923, seven from the Army Air Service and three from the Navy. From the left, a series of Martin bombers, then a Fokker T-2; the last plane on the right is the rarely seen Navy Douglas DT-4, powered by a twelve-cylinder Wright engine. Overhead is one of the few Army lighter-than-air craft, the TC-7. A later architect of air power, First Lieutenant Harold Lee George, won the race in a Martin bomber at 114.28 mph.

characteristics. But the firm seemed to have some promising talent—Jim McDonnell for one—and a tall, gregarious Air Service test pilot named Lieutenant Harold R. Harris took them under his wing. Harris explained the HIAD, and showed them a captured Fokker D VII as an example of advanced construction. Huff-Daland went back to the drawing board and responded with a series of trainers that kept it in business. Ultimately Huff-Daland become Keystone Aircraft, and was the principal supplier of bombers to the Air Corps for many years.

In the course of time, similar nurturing would coax firms such as Bell, Consolidated, McDonnell, Hughes, and others into being. Inevitably, there were abuses of the system by individuals exploiting situations for personal gain. But in the aggregate, the integrity of both the service and the industry, morally stiffened by the abrasive forces of competition, kept things in check. No one was quicker to blow the whistle on suspected chicanery than a competitor who had just lost a contract.

As is usually the case in the workaday world, while public attention was focused on the racing planes, the grunt work of advancing the science of aviation was done almost anonymously in Dayton, Ohio. From McCook Field emerged a group of top-flight test pilots with a temperament, ability, and mystique to which the first groups of astronauts corresponded almost exactly. Less visible, but more important, was the systematic engineering development work being done. The breadth of the McCook and Wright Field experimentation was dazzling, ranging from research into metals, lubricants, and other materials all the way to the creation of design specifications for new aircraft. In between, development was fostered in fuels, propellers, parachutes, cameras, flying clothing, radios, instruments, navigation aids—the whole gamut of aviation, extending even to the "Radio Dog," a simulated land tank that could be controlled by radio from the air. A good example of the critical nature of the work is the creation of the reliable General Electric supercharger system that helped make our World War II fighters and bombers a success. The first efforts on a turbo-supercharger had been under the guidance of Dr. Sanford A. Moss at General Electric. Moss built on the work of French Professor Auguste C. E. Rateau and conducted tests at Pike's Peak, using a Liberty engine that had been carefully calibrated to deliver 350 horsepower at its home station, McCook Field. On top of Pike's Peak, it delivered only 230 horsepower. Moss's supercharger was an exhaust-gas-driven turbine that turned a compressor that packed more fuel-air mixture into the aircraft's engine, boosting its power. When the supercharger was installed, the Liberty delivered 365 horsepower at a 14,109-foot elevation.

The Army was convinced, and assigned the task of developing the GE supercharger as standard equipment to Lieutenant E. T. Jones, Opie Chenoweth, and A. L. Berger at McCook Field. The installations first made history with the altitude records set at McCook and on some of the Martin bombers Billy Mitchell used during the battleship sinkings. It would take another fifteen years of experimentation, but in World War II it was superchargers that lifted the B-17s and B-24s to altitudes that gave them a combat advantage, and superchargers that gave our fighters an edge.

Despite the minimal budgets, the contemporary efforts at McCook and at Wright Field were blessed with an inestimable advantage—virtually no interference in day-to-day matters from Congress. In the glorious days of the Golden Age, Congress had not yet grown the huge staffing tumor it has today, and did not second-guess every decision. Instead, it tended to applaud the achievements in weather and distance flying, in speed records, and in new models. Only when there was an obvious target, like the six-engine, three-winged Barling bomber, as overweight as it was overcost, did Congress take what are now routine cheap shots.

Of new designs, there were plenty. Between 1919 and 1923, the McCook Field engineers designed twenty-seven aircraft of all types. But by 1924, the drying up of experimental funds and vociferous objections by aircraft manufacturers to this threat to both their pocketbooks and their originality forced McCook to stop building its own ideas. It was for the best, for the incestuous nature of development at a government facility, where everyone was responding to the same regulations and the same thought processes, had already imposed a dreadful similarity on the McCook Field homegrown designs. They were almost uniformly ugly, and although usually possessing some innovation, were often not successful. McCook and, later, Wright Field were far more useful in framing specifications and letting commercial companies compete for contracts.

A serious crew of serious leaders. From the left, Sergeant Ray Hoe, Lieutenant Elwood Quesada, Lieutenant Harry Halverson, Captain Ira C. Eaker, and Major Carl Spaatz, the crew members on the Fokker Trimotor "Question Mark." Spaatz would become the first USAF Chief of Staff, after glorious roles in combat in both World War I and World War II. Quesada would lead the Ninth Air Force in Europe, be the first commander of the Tactical Air Command, then go on to a spectacular career in commerce. Eaker would head the Eighth Air Force, then the Twelfth, and finally become CEO of Hughes Aircraft and a world-famous military commentator. Halverson led the first raid on Ploesti, while Hoe had a distinguished military career of his own.

The ostensible object of the flight of the "Question Mark" in 1929 was to set an endurance record by refueling in flight. The real purpose was to determine the feasibilty of in-flight refueling as a tactical maneuver for bombers. The flight did both.

The techniques used then may be useful today. As in the 1920s, the threat of war seems diminished, the armed forces are being reduced in number, and the budget does not permit large production runs of new weaponry. The answer may again be to expand the reserves, extend aircraft service life, and try to build new prototypes while maintaining a production capacity that can be expanded quickly.

Accepting the results of the fifteen or so investigating boards of the period, the Air Service nonetheless edged its way toward autonomy, amid a welter of disputes. The War Department permitted the Army and Navy to squabble endlessly over who had responsibility for coast defense—a moot point, for neither could have defended against a determined enemy. Fortunately, there was no determined enemy at the time.

During the early years, the Air Service owed much to a man largely forgotten. General Mason Patrick, son of a Confederate surgeon and classmate of General John J. Pershing, was a grizzled veteran of the Mitchell wars who learned to fly at the age of fifty-nine. If Mitchell was air power's John the Baptist, then Patrick was its St. Paul for the manner in which he soothed Congress, managed legislation, and kept the Air Service functioning despite the lack of funds. Patrick wished the Air Service to become to the Army what the Marine Corps was to the Navy, a cohesive unit with its own mission and budget, reporting directly to the Secretary of War. The Morrow Board's adverse recommendations carried weight with Congress, however, and a compromise was reached. The Air Service was to become the Air Corps, with the implication that it was more than just a service organization to the Army, with a strik-

A Boeing P-12 equipped with a ring cowl that added a few miles per hour and improved cooling. Aircraft as rare as the P-12 are not flown often because of the attendant risk, but when they do fly, they gather crowds of fans to watch.

ing capability of its own. With the change in status came the authorization to carry out a desperately needed five-year expansion program, with a goal of having 1,800 serviceable planes by 1932.

Despite living a hand-to-mouth existence (its budget cuts averaged 40 percent every year), the Air Corps managed to make significant advances in logistics and training. By 1927, it had moved its research and development and logistics capabilities to Wright Field, and in 1930 opened the "West Point of the Air" at Randolph Field in San Antonio, even though there were funds to train only 150 cadets annually. A severe pilot shortage ensued, with most units being drastically understrength; each time a new unit prescribed in the expansion plan was created, the Air Corps had to reduce or shut down others. The lighter-than-air units, already in disfavor, suffered most.

FOULOIS ON TOP AT LAST

With more swash than Errol Flynn ever buckled, Jimmy Doolittle poses by the Laird Super-Solution in which he won the 1931 Bendix Trophy Race. Unwilling to remain a first lieutenant forever, Doolittle had left the Air Corps to carve out a career in industry and in racing. The little Laird biplane was symptomatic of the times—it was a civilian aircraft, faster than the best Army fighters.

The Air Corps enjoyed relative political peace from its inception in 1926 until 1934. When General Patrick retired in 1927, he was succeeded by his assistant, Brigadier General James Fechet, who gave Benjamin Foulois a series of top jobs. Four years later, Foulois, the former enlisted man who had twice made brigadier general without ever being a colonel, succeeded Fechet to become a major general commanding the Air Corps. With experience dating back to the Army's first dirigible and enriched by his contacts with foreign airmen, particularly in Germany, Foulois was convinced of the necessity of having long-range bombers.

The classic Stearman PT-13 primary trainer. Thousands trained in it all over the world. A rugged and forgiving aircraft, it still had to be flown, and it turned students into good pilots.

The technology of the B-9 and B-10 was scarcely in hand when the Air Corps planners began to reach even farther, setting specifications that resulted in the Boeing XB-15, a gigantic aircraft with five times the weight and more than twice the span of the B-10. Unfortunately, engine development lagged, and the four 1,000 horsepower Pratt & Whitney R-1830s were inadequate for the XB-15. But the research paid off in the smaller, faster B-17 derived from it.

By euphemistically stressing defense instead of offense, Foulois succeeded in making the long-range bomber and the concept of a General Headquarters (GHQ) Air Force palatable to both the War Department and Congress. The GHQ Air Force was designed to be a central striking force capable of defending the coasts and American overseas possessions, and was the first concrete step toward an independent air force. Then, in December 1933 Foulois gave the go-ahead for Project X, a superbomber with a range of 5,000 miles and a speed of 200 mph. Project X developed into the underpowered, unsuccessful Boeing XB-15, but more importantly it spawned the technology that led directly to the B-17.

The B-17, the fruit of the XB-15 research. World War II saw vast clouds of this bomber in the skies.

The honeymoon ended in 1934, when Foulois and the Air Corps were blindsided by a totally unexpected problem from the administration of President Franklin D. Roosevelt.

THE ARMY FLIES THE MAIL

In 1932 Fulton Lewis, a reporter and radio commentator, had begun to investigate the way the U.S. Post Office handled mail contracts under the auspices of Walter Brown, Herbert Hoover's Postmaster General. Brown had favored the larger airlines with the most financial backing, and had forced smaller airlines—often low bidders—either to merge with the larger airlines or to go out of business. (The scenario is not too different from the effects of the 1978 deregulation of airlines.) In classic Washington, D.C., style, Lewis's stories and the instinctive desire of one party to capitalize on any possible malfeasance on the part of the previous opposing administration led to the establishment of a Special Committee on Investigation of Air Mail and Ocean Mail Contracts in the U.S. Senate.

The results of the complex five-month-long investigation were given to the new Postmaster General, James A. Farley. He met with President Roosevelt on February 8, 1934, and asked for authorization to cancel the air mail contracts.

On the afternoon of February 9, General Foulois was called into the office of the Second Assistant Postmaster, Harllee Branch, and asked whether, if the President canceled all air mail contracts, the Air Corps could carry the mail and keep the system operating. In the course of the discussion, Foulois understood him to mean "operating" at a lower level of service—not the entire system, nor with the regularity of the airlines.

Foulois later stated that he thought for a moment, considering the fact that the Air Corps had little in the way of cargo aircraft and that its pilots had never flown regular schedules on instruments or at night. On the other hand, accepting the mission might mean some extra funds for training, parts, and planes. The clincher was that it was in the Air Corps tradition to accept whatever tasks were assigned. Foulois agreed to take it on, estimating that the Air Corps could be ready about ten days after a go-ahead. Somewhat naively, he had assumed that he'd have time for planning, training, and the stockpiling of necessary materials *before* the go-ahead. That was not to be the case. Roosevelt set the date for February 19.

There was an immediate vocal reaction from the business community, led by Charles Lindbergh of Pan American and Eddie Rickenbacker of Eastern Airlines. They knew, as Foulois did, that the airlines were operating 500 airplanes over 25,000 miles of routes, carrying 1,500 tons of mail a year. Where airline pilots had radios with adequate range and well-mounted instruments, and flew an average of 900 hours a year, the Army pilots had none of these things and flew only about 200 hours. Foulois had only about 250 planes available, almost all lacking adequate instrumentation, and in any case, most of his pilots were not instrument-trained. Disaster was predicted and tragedy ensued, abetted by the worst winter weather in years.

The Air Corps turned manfully to the job, trying to learn the routes, equipping the airplanes with instruments as fast as possible, and training the pilots. Two hundred officers and 374 enlisted men (the privates earning $21 a month) used about 148 planes to fly 16,000 miles of routes. Ten pilots died in accidents, only four of them while actually carrying the mail. The press leaped on each death, and the public furor temporarily forced Roosevelt on March 10 to cancel having the Air Corps carry the mail. After some intensive training, it resumed service on March 19 and soon was able to use the new Martin YB-10s with pilots who had been rushed through an instrument course at Wright Field. By June 1, when the airlines resumed service, the Air Corps was operating at a level of efficiency comparable to the airlines.

Although pilloried in the press and popularly regarded for years as having produced a fiasco, the Air Corps had in fact done a remarkably good job once it acquired a little experience at the task, logging 13,000 hours of flying time and carrying more than 750,000 pounds of mail. Shorted as usual by the bean counters who controlled the funds, men working in the field were not paid per diem and often had to scrounge food and shelter from the local citizenry.

The public outcry had some good effects. Skillfully deflecting blame from himself, Roosevelt released some Air Corps R&D funds that he had impounded, and even added an additional $7.5 million for new aircraft and instruments. More importantly, the experience pointed up the desperate need for

General Benjamin Foulois, Chief of the Air Corps, in front of a map of the Air Corps mail routes. Foulois was a fighter, not a diplomat, and despite all criticism he always maintained that the Air Corps did a remarkable job, and that the advantages that accrued from carrying the mail far outweighed the bad publicity.

The pursuit equivalent of the Martin B-10 was Boeing's Peashooter, the P-26. It was a transitional aircraft, the first of all-metal, low-wing construction, and the last with an open cockpit and fixed landing gear. Called "Old Limber Legs" by its pilots, who were unused to the close-set oleo gear, the P-26 was a handful on the ground, but delightful in the air. Some were on the ground at Pearl Harbor on December 7, 1941; others fought with the Philippine air force against Japanese Zero fighters over Luzon.

the Air Corps to provide adequate instrumentation and training. This would be invaluable preparation for World War II.

In response to all the difficulties, the Secretary of War appointed yet another investigative committee, headed by Newton D. Baker. Unlike most of the committees of the past, this one came forward with positive recommendations for more airplanes, more flying time, more training, and more practice bombs and ammunition. It also commended the Air Corps for the job it did carrying the mail, even though it had not been adequately trained or equipped for the job.

Still, congressmen were as eager for headlines in 1934 as they are today, and Benny Foulois, irritable and not articulate in testimony, became a favorite whipping boy. He had given what he considered to be a pep talk about the brave men flying the air mail; it was interpreted as the calloused indifference of the man who had authorized the "legalized murder" of the airmen. The hounds were loosed and he was saddled first with the entire responsibility for the "air mail fiasco," then charged personally with culpability for an Air Corps procurement system that had been in effect more than a decade and that had the approval of both the Judge Advocate General and the Assistant Secretary for War. These charges gave the coup de grace to Foulois's career, as controversial in many ways as Mitchell's had been. A week before his retirement, after thirty-seven years of service, he took a long solo flight in his personal Douglas O-38 command plane, getting in his flying time for the last time. In the pocket of his flying suit he carried a horseshoe good luck charm given him in 1912 by Corporal Frank Scott, the first enlisted man to die in an airplane crash. On the day Foulois left office, no one from the General Staff or from the War Department had dropped by or written a note. There was no parade, no decorations, no fly-bys, no eulogies at a farewell dinner. In the cruel tradition of the military, Foulois had served, Foulois was out of favor, and now Foulois was history. It would be another twenty years before it was recognized that his leadership had created the organization and the airplanes that would win World War II in the air. Benjamin Foulois had fostered the creation of the GHQ Air Force, the first precondition for an ultimately independent service, and he had staffed the Air Corps with great leaders. Some, like Horace Hickam and Oscar Westover, would lose their lives in crashes before they were put to the ultimate test of World War II. Others, like Frank Andrews, Hap Arnold, Ira Eaker, Elwood Quesada, and Carl Spaatz, would go on to make history.

TOWARD INDEPENDENCE: THE GHQ AIR FORCE

The July 18, 1934, report of the Baker Board had indicated its approval of the War Department's approach to the General Headquarters Air Force concept,

One of the most influential recruiting movies of all time was Bernie Lay's I Wanted Wings, *which starred Ray Milland, Bill Holden, and Wayne Morris, and introduced Virginia Mayo. This flight-line shot at Randolph Field was taken during the filming of the picture.*

The Douglas XB-19 was an exercise in gigantism. With its 212-foot wingspan and 160,000-pound gross weight, the XB-19 would be the largest land plane built in the United States until the advent of the Consolidated B-36. Like the XB-15, the XB-19 was hopelessly underpowered even though it had new Wright R-3350 engines of 2,200 horse-power each. Parked under its wing at March Field in standard public relations style of the period is a Curtiss P-40.

which offered the advantages of an independent air force while still preserving the unity of command. As a result, the Air Corps was well positioned in 1936 to begin a program of expansion that would suddenly become urgent as the dictatorships in Europe and Asia pursued a course toward war.

Lieutenant Colonel Frank M. Andrews had been given command of GHQ Air Force, with three pursuit, four bombardment, and two attack groups and four reconnaissance squadrons, about 1,000 planes in all. These units began to receive relatively modern aircraft—Boeing P-26 Peashooter fighters, Martin B-10 bombers, and Curtiss A-12 and Northrop A-17 attack planes. With them, for the first time, doctrine was created based not on Billy Mitchell's prophecies but on demonstrated experience in maneuvers in the field. The new

There was far more to the advance of technology than engines and airframes. Lieutenant Colonel Henry H. Arnold (standing, center) led a flight of ten Martin B-10s on a 1934 survey flight to Alaska, which garnered headlines across the country. A routine flight today, at the time there were few maps and fewer weather stations. Many of the landing strips were primitive, hacked out of the forest. Arnold was awarded the Mackay Trophy for the flight, and edged closer to leading the Air Corps.

The famous "Twin Beech," Model 18, was one of many civilian aircraft that were drafted into military work. It did yeoman service in a variety of designations including C-45. The all-metal, twin-engine aircraft remained in service for thirty years.

The next to last Air Corps observation plane, the North American O-47. A large, slow aircraft, its greatest contribution was preparing the North American Aircraft company for large wartime contracts.

The name Jack Northrop appears in the pedigree of many great aircraft. His development of the Northrop Alpha and Gamma led directly to the Northop A-17 attack planes, as well as to the Douglas SBD dive-bombers. The A-17A incorporated a retractable landing and entered service in 1937.

Like other air forces around the world, the Air Corps was unable to shed the Army's desire for observation aircraft to do reconnaissance and assist with artillery fire. This Douglas O-43 was one of twenty-four purchased in 1934. Elegant-looking, it was an obsolete design pursuing an obsolete mission. It was obvious to fighter pilots that the slow, ill-armed observation planes would not be able to live in the air over the front, but O-43s and similar craft continued to be purchased in relatively large quantities right up through 1939. Then a shift was made to lighter Piper Cub-like airplanes, the grasshoppers.

Among the more unusual Army aircraft of the period was the Sikorsky C-6A, the military version of the successful Sikorsky S-38 amphibian. It was more familiar in the flamboyantly marked versions used by Osa and Martin Johnson for exploration.

Chief of the Air Corps, Major General Oscar Westover, saw to it that the textbooks used in the Air Corps Tactical School were, with modification, promulgated as doctrine. In doing so, he conferred upon professional military education the prestige that Foulois had denied it.

By May 1937 the first seven of a service-test batch of thirteen Boeing YIB-17 aircraft were able to participate in joint Army-Navy maneuvers off the Pacific coast. The performance of the Boeings, with their supersecret Norden bombsights, was so sensational that the Air Corps wanted to adopt the type as the standard bomber. The War Department demurred, insisting that procuring 133 obsolete Douglas B-18s made more sense than buying 65 B-17s. Yet the B-17 opened up so many genuine possibilities that the Air Corps Tactical School could now openly advocate the bomber as an *offensive* weapon, abandoning the subterfuge of coastal defense, and stating that it could apply military force directly against an enemy homeland immediately upon the outbreak of war.

Pursuit aviation still had its advocates, too. Captain Gerald E. Brower called for supplementing the single-seat pursuit craft with larger long-range escort fighters, an idea that tempted many countries but was never successful. In the United States it led through two beautiful planes, the Consolidated P-30 and the exotic Bell YFM-I Airacuda, but the concept was an engineering dead end. A fighter big enough to carry the fuel for long-range escort could not compete with a smaller, more maneuverable interceptor. Claire Chennault

One of the most beautiful prewar aircraft was the Consolidated PB-2A, which had its genesis in the 1932 Detroit XP-900. A derivative of the Lockheed Sirius design, the two-place fighter was large but fast, and aerodynamically very advanced. In its final form, a General Electric turbosupercharger provided a top speed of 274 mph at 25,000 feet, far faster than any other fighter or bomber in the Air Corps. Fifty were purchased in 1935, but like all other two-seaters, they did not have the dogfighting capability of single-seaters, and proved to be a design dead end.

New bombers spurred pursuit development. On June 16, 1936, the new Seversky Aero Corporation won an order for 77 P-35 pursuit planes. The P-35, below, was modern looking with an enclosed cockpit, retractable gear, and a variable-pitch propeller, but it lacked armor, firepower, and self-sealing fuel tanks. Its top speed was only 281 mph and it was armed with only two .30 caliber machine guns. In comparison, on June 3, 1936, the Royal Air Force had ordered 600 Hawker Hurricanes, with a top speed of 315 mph, and 310 Supermarine Spitfires, which topped 347 mph. Both British fighters had eight-gun armament, for it had been realized that at modern combat speeds, aircraft would remain targets for only a few seconds. Yet, the P-35 fought nobly in the Philippines, and its design led to one of the great fighters of World War II, the Republic P-47. This shiny example belongs to the Headquarters Squadron of the 1st Pursuit Group at Selfridge Field, Michigan.

117

TOP:

The Curtiss P-36. Angered because they lost the 1936 fighter competition to the upstart Seversky P-35, Curtiss came back in July 1937 to win the largest fighter contract awarded since World War I. The Air Corps purchased 210 of the new P-36s for a total price of $4,113,500. Although still not comparable technically to the latest European fighters, the P-36 was a strong step in the right direction. France would buy the airplane in quantity, and it would do well in combat against the German Messerschmitts.

MIDDLE:

The North American BT-14 was another excellent trainer. It prepared students for the more advanced North American AT-6, the most famous trainer of World War II.

BOTTOM:

Tight formation in a flight of North American BT-14s, a scene from Bernie Lay's great film I Wanted Wings. *In general, American pilots had the best weather, facilities, and airplanes for training, and went into combat with the most hours of flying time compared with pilots from other nations.*

OPPOSITE TOP:

A trainer that did great service at the primary flying schools was the Fairchild PT-19. A classic Fairchild, powered by an in-line Ranger engine, the PT-19 was relatively docile up to its limits—beyond them it could turn into a handful.

OPPOSITE BOTTOM:

Randolph Field in 1941. What an inspiration shots like these were to aspiring young pilots: line of North American BT-9s, instructor in the back seat, eager cadet in the front.

An intermediate step from the Curtiss P-36 to the P-40, this Curtiss YP-37 was one of the most handsome aircraft of the time. The long nose, with the cockpit set far aft, gave it a distinctive look that made it the delight of modelers. Visibility was poor, however, and while the YP-37 was fast at 331 mph, it did not offer development promise; only thirteen were purchased.

As crucial as the development of new aircraft was, the training of pilots was even more critical, for the established Air Corps flying schools had a maximum capacity of about 1,500 a year. The Civilian Pilot Training Program proved to be the answer, and by 1944 pilots were being trained at the rate of 100,000 a year. Here the aviation cadets line up in front of Ryan PT-22s, a radial engine development of the classic Ryan ST.

The United States military buildup had been handicapped by the Depression and the traditional isolationist sentiment of the country. However, the imperative needs of England and France led to orders for U.S. aircraft, which greatly strengthened the American industry. One program, the Douglas DB-7, led directly to a series of excellent combat aircraft, including the Douglas P-70, used as an interim night-fighter and a trainer.

still insisted that the pursuit plane was king, and went beyond aerial tactics to devise aircraft warning and control services using visual aircraft observers with radio and telephone communication lines, ideas later easily adapted to radar equipment. And although the "unescorted bomber" theorists maintained an advantage, the controversy forced the development of three famous fighters, the Curtiss P-40, Lockheed P-38, and Bell P-39.

ROOSEVELT'S BOMBSHELL

Then President Roosevelt dropped a bombshell that turned the entire situation around. He had watched Germany blackmail England and France with air power at Munich. On November 14, 1938, the President announced that airplanes, not ground forces (and although he didn't say so, not naval forces), were the only implements of war that would influence Hitler's decision process. He called for an Army air force of 20,000 planes and an annual production capacity of 24,000 aircraft, about six times that existing at the time. The numbers were reduced over time because of political considerations and the intransigence of the War Department, but eventually the Air Corps was authorized to more than double its strength to 5,500. No less than 3,251 new planes were to be purchased, and there were small orders for airplanes whose names would become legend in just a few years: 16 Consolidated B-24s, 183 North American B-25s, 201 Martin B-26s, and a single Republic P-47. These air-

The Vultee Aircraft Corporation literally
bristled with ideas, among them the concept
of building a family of aircraft—trainers,
attack planes, and fighters—that would use
basic common components. Vultee succeeded
only with the trainers, especially with the
BT-15, beloved and bemoaned as the Vultee
Vibrator. With its low-wing, all-metal construction and powerful engine it was quite
an advance over biplane trainers.

Designers followed contracts in the days
before World War II. After helping develop
a beautiful series of Northrop fighters,
Donavon R. Berlin went to Curtiss, where
he designed first the P-36 and then the
immortal P-40. Berlin always maintained
that had he been permitted to develop the
P-40 as he had planned that it would have
been a superior aircraft to the North
American P-51. Here a restored P-40
flies over the Wisconsin countryside.

A step on the road to the glorious Douglas
C-47 is this C-39. The C-39 used a
DC-2 fuselage with a DC-3 tail and
outer wings. Thirty-six were built.

OPPOSITE:
As the country edged toward World War II,
two companies that one day would be giants
were struggling to stay alive. In 1938, few
people would have bet that Boeing and
Lockheed would be prospering in the
1990s, any more than they would have
imagined aircraft like those seen here, the
Lockheed F-117A Stealth fighter and the
workhorse Boeing KC-135 tanker.

There are endless arguments about flying restored World War II aircraft. Some feel that they are in such short supply now that they should be retired to museums for safekeeping. But when one sees and hears, and quite literally feels the passage overhead of the Confederate Air Force's Boeing B-17, one understands the argument for keeping them flying.

planes did not yet have nicknames, but the public and the enemy would soon become familiar with them as the *Liberator, Mitchell, Marauder,* and *Thunderbolt.*

It was very late in the game. When World War II began on September 3, 1939, the U.S. Army Air Corps possessed only about a dozen B-17s and a handful of Curtiss P-36 and Seversky P-35 fighters. No one knew that the country would have a two-year grace period, until December 7, 1941. In the interim, British and French military purchasing commissions would breathe

new life into our aviation industry, spreading its base, introducing new ideas, and poising it for the greatest industrial expansion in history, a fitting finish for a Golden Age. It would be the beginning of the end to social problems that had never been examined by the services, as the demands for personnel opened the gates to women and to blacks as never before. Segregation by race and gender would still be the order of the day, but it was a crack in the dam of custom that would over a too-long period erupt into a flood of equal opportunity.

The Eighth Air Force's first raid on Europe was flown by six American crews using Douglas Boston IIIs provided by the RAF's No. 226 Squadron. Here artist Nixon Galloway depicts Captain Charles C. Kegelman's flak-damaged Boston struggling to stay aloft for the flight back to England. Kegelman succeeded and was awarded the United States' second-highest decoration for bravery, the Distinguished Service Cross.

CHAPTER FOUR

The Challenge of the Century 1940–1945

As important as President Roosevelt's November 1938 call for an air force powerful enough to deter Hitler was the flood of contracts for military hardware from France, England, and China, an injection of economic adrenaline that spurred the most massive industrial growth in the history of the world. It was obvious that this growth would bring a corresponding increase in American air power; it was less obvious that it would inevitably lead to the independent air force for which General Billy Mitchell and his followers had fought so long and so hard.

From America's current position as the only superpower, it is difficult to remember that before World War II the public and Congress vehemently opposed Roosevelt's call for the United States to become the arsenal of democracy. Even in 1939, an influential congressman would ask the Chief of the Air Corps "who [sic] we were going to fight." A little later, Congress passed the absolutely critical extension of the draft by only one vote.

BOTTOM, LEFT TO RIGHT:
A series of photographs evoking World War II, created by the Air Force Association.

Families all across America heard the news of Pearl Harbor on "table model" radios like this. Soon after, ration coupons became essential requirements for shopping.

Cigarettes were almost an item of government issue during the war years; Hershey candy bars were even harder to get.

The map and currency were from a flier's escape kit; the Life *magazine cover features Major General Ira Eaker.*

PLANES FOR THE ALLIES

The post-World War I reversion to isolationism had resulted in a series of neutrality laws forbidding trade with belligerent powers. Roosevelt skillfully saw to it that these were modified after Poland fell to Germany. By November 1939 he had pushed through Congress a new "cash and carry" law that permitted the warring powers to purchase arms in the United States for cash, and carry the goods home in their own ships. Although the wording of the law was neutral in content, it was effectively pro-Allies in intent, for the Germans had neither cash nor ships to carry arms in.

As great as American domestic needs were, the needs of the Allied powers were even greater. In the 1920s France was the possessor of the world's largest, most efficient air force; by 1938 it had a only a small, obsolete fleet of aircraft. Even worse, its personnel situation was deplorable, with overage and undertrained pilots and ground crews. The recently nationalized French aviation industry was in disarray. In desperation, a French Purchasing Commission came to order more than 1,000 Curtiss H-75s (the export version of the P-36 pursuit plane) and 270 Douglas DB-7 twin-engine light bombers. The British Purchasing Commission had an open checkbook, seeking to buy virtually every modern type in production. By the end of 1939, France and England had ordered more than 2,500 airplanes worth $400 million from the United States, revitalizing the American aviation industry and poising it for a quantum leap into true mass production on a scale never before envisaged. Both France and England soon exhausted their available funds, and in what has been called "the most unsordid act," President Roosevelt engineered the Lend-Lease Act of March 11, 1941.

After twenty years of fighting for tiny contracts, the new production orders were of an incomprehensible magnitude, but the companies turned to the task with imagination and skill. Lockheed had learned of the visit of the British Purchasing Commission only five days before its arrival, yet working at full speed under Kelly Johnson's leadership, had a full-scale wooden mockup of a bomber version of their twin-engine Electra transport ready for inspection. A few months later, it received an order for $25 million, by far the largest in its history, and a whirlwind start to what would become a total production of 2,941 Hudson bombers.

North American had sizable orders for trainers and its B-25 bomber, but when England asked it to produce Curtiss Model 87s (the P-40D equivalent), it demurred, campaigning instead to manufacture a new fighter of its own design. The British gave reluctant agreement, and in an amazing 120-day peri-

Mustangs like this first saw service in World War II and were then considered obsolete—only to see service again in Korea. Bathed in oil, this P-51 was able to make a safe emergency landing in Japan in 1949. Harry White was the pilot.

od, Dutch Kindelberger, Lee Atwood, Ray Rice, Edgar Schmued, and the North American team produced the prototype of the fighter that would become famous as the P-51 Mustang.

PREPARING FOR BATTLE

The war was a test of production capacity; it was even more a test of resilience, courage, and fighting skill. For the United States, World War II began with the December 7, 1941, Japanese bombing raid on Pearl Harbor, and ended with the U.S. atomic bombing raid on Nagasaki on August 9, 1945. The introduction of the nuclear weapon provided an impenitent Japanese government with a grisly way out of its previous boasts of a fight to the death, forestalling an invasion and undoubtedly saving thousands of American and millions of Japanese lives.

In the less than four-year period between the two raids, the United States Army Air Forces grew from strength to strength, achieving utter air superiority in every theater. After long months of slow buildup and hard fighting, it destroyed the Luftwaffe and brought the war to virtually every city in Germany. Curiously, these great victories were achieved almost precisely as planned by four junior Air Corps officers during nine days in the fall of 1941.

This small group of planners, whose work is discussed below, typifies the essential conceptual difference in the way the air forces of the United States and those of its enemies operated. The U.S. planning team envisioned the true scale of the war from the start, conceiving of an unprecedented aerial effort to support not only the combat aircraft, but all of the necessary ancillary services including supply, repair, training, and construction. Most importantly,

Perhaps the most famous biplane trainer of World War II, the Stearman PT-17 Kaydet was used for decades by dozens of countries around the world, first as a primary trainer, then as a crop duster. While not technologically advanced, the PT-17 was a sturdy aircraft, one that demanded that the student fly it at all times—consequently it was a good trainer. More than 10,000 were built; most were actually Boeing Model 75s, built after Boeing had acquired the Stearman firm. Nonetheless the plane is always referred to as a Stearman.

An image that is a public affairs officer's dream: three powerful Republic P-47Ns in formation, glittering silver in the sun. Affectionately called the "Jug" in reference to its rotund shape, the P-47 was the harbinger of a significant change in American thinking about fighters. Configured as a fighter-bomber, it had a maximum gross weight of 20,700 pounds, almost three times that of the 7,500-pound Messerschmitt Bf 109G that opposed it. Its huge size was necessary to carry sufficient fuel for penetration missions, and the munitions for extensive fighting. Although huge for its class, the P-47's heavy firepower and diving ability made it a formidable opponent in a dogfight.

it also provided for replacements, something the Japanese and Germans virtually ignored. It was remarkable that young officers who had grown up in an impoverished force that never exceeded 800 operational aircraft could have the vision to plan for a hundredfold expansion to an armada of 80,000 planes. In the 1930s we were as much a captive of the media as we are today, and we imputed to the enemy a monolithic strength and an unwarranted planning discipline and genius. Aware as we were of the bumbling of our democracy, with its provincial Congress at odds with the President, it seemed to us that the totalitarian states must surely run things more efficiently.

The facts were far different. Germany and Japan were both essentially smash-and-grab bandits whose policies and planning were based on either bullying neighbors into submission or resorting to what the Nazis called *blitzkrieg*—lightning war—short campaigns that their limited economies could sustain. Germany's aircraft production, portrayed as so formidable before the war, soon lagged well behind that of both the United States and England. And even after Albert Speer provided the production genius to spur aircraft production to record heights—4,300 fighters were built in October 1944—the Germans were incapable of expanding the other necessary elements to use them efficiently, for they lacked fuel, training planes, and pilots.

On the other side of the world, the Japanese planned a war as stylized as a Kabuki play, scripting a sneak attack for the beginning and a craven U.S. public demanding peace at any price for the end. Japan planned for the war it wanted to fight, not for the war it would have to fight. Sundered by political and military rivalries, each faction tied to controlling industrial cartels, Japan developed separate small air forces for its army and navy. The pilots, particularly in the navy, were well trained and very experienced, capable of extracting the utmost from their aircraft, which were deliberately designed to sacrifice safety and durability for performance. Japan's fatal error in believing America would have no taste for a long war was compounded by its utter inability to perceive the scale of the war the Americans would wage. Even as the Americans were already planning on producing 100,000 pilots a year, the Japanese navy typically graduated 2,000 pilots annually, weeding out all but the very best in a training program of sadistic discipline. After the Battle of Midway, when the truth was brought home that it lacked the resources to compete, Japan began to use human lives as substitutes for adequate equipment, a process that led inevitably to the kamikaze tactic of the pilot crashing his bomb-laden plane directly into the target. The difference in capacity is evident by a casual glance at comparative strengths. In January 1943 the Japanese had about 3,200 frontline aircraft against 3,500 U.S. aircraft of roughly equivalent quality. By July 1945 the Japanese strength had risen only to 4,100, opposed by almost 22,000 American aircraft of a far higher standard of quality, flown by superbly trained pilots. And even late in the war, when the Japanese were clearly unable to cope with the vast numbers being deployed by the United States, their two services still refused to cooperate effectively. Like the Germans, both services consumed their training base by throwing instructors into combat.

A fascinating phenomenon of the 1970s and 1980s was the resurgence of interest in the airplanes of the World War II. Aircraft like this beautiful Curtiss P-40 were restored to better-than-new condition and flown at air shows around the country.

ABOVE:
A Boeing B-17G built by Vega, Lockheed's subsidiary company. After March 1944, U.S. bombers were no longer covered with camouflage paint, saving several hundred pounds and lowering drag. The USAAF bought 8,680 B-17Gs, which featured a chin turret mounting two 0.50-inch machine guns. It also had improved turbo-superchargers that boosted the service ceiling to 35,000 feet.

LEFT:
The Wright brothers could not have envisaged a production scene like this. Neither did Boeing when it first launched its B-17 program in 1934. Produced in quantity by Boeing, Lockheed, and Douglas—12,731 were built—the average cost of a B-17G was $238,329.

It was not that either enemy lacked military men of genius. In Japan, Admiral Yamamoto Isoroku understood full well America's ultimate strength, but was overruled, and Commander Minoru Genda was an amazingly talented tactician. In Germany, young officers like Werner Moelders, Adolf Galland, and Hajo Hermann were extraordinarily capable. Yet the totalitarian system of each country would not allow its effective people to function as the American system did. Their influence on strategic planning was almost nil; instead, they had to attempt to salvage what they could from an impossible situation. It was perhaps worse in Germany, where although Adolf Hitler had no genuine understanding of either the potential or the limitations of strategic air power, his unrealistic demands were inevitably endorsed by the sycophantic Hermann Goering. The fundamental flaw for both Japan and Germany was that they were fatally tied to the concept of air power as a service to ground or naval forces, rather than as a strategic entity. They clung to the very idea that U.S. air power advocates had disavowed.

General H. H. Arnold had survived his exile for supporting Billy Mitchell and worked his way to becoming Chief of the Air Corps on the basis of energy, personality, and an uncanny ability to work well with both superiors and subordinates. His genius for picking the right men for the job was never more ably demonstrated than when he selected four officers who were both thinkers and fighters, and who had worked together at the Air Corps Tactical School, to create the concept of American strategic air war. With his typical political finesse, Arnold managed to persuade the already overworked War Department to allow his group—the Air War Plans Division—to plan all the air requirements, rather than to work as a subcommittee on the Army's overall plan. With this action Arnold also provided the single most important step toward an independent air force.

The Air War Plans Division, AWPD, was headed by ruggedly handsome Lieutenant Colonel Harold Lee George. A bomber pilot in the First World War and a veteran of Mitchell's battleship bombing, the quick-witted, amusing George (who one day would become mayor of Beverly Hills, California) had pioneered new tactics in the Boeing B-17. On his staff were three eager, aggressive, yet thoughtful, young officers, the kind preferred by the Army Chief of Staff, General George C. Marshall. They included future Medal of Honor winner Lieutenant Colonel Kenneth Walker; Major Laurence S. Kuter, to become the youngest general in the Army at the age of thirty-six; and Major Haywood S. "Possum" Hansell. Their names were virtually unknown to the public then, but all would become general officers.

The group had a solid foundation for their plan. Arnold had already created a Strategic Air Intelligence section, which had gathered the information that enabled them to compile a list of targets in Germany, primarily the electric power grids, the transportation system, and the petroleum system. The defeat of the Luftwaffe was not considered possible to achieve in the near term—

bombers were simply going to have to fight their way through without any escort fighters.

Ultimately, 154 select targets were pinpointed, along with many secondary targets to use as alternates when the weather was difficult. Ironically, much of the target data was based on information that had been provided by the Germans to U.S. banks in their pursuit of loans to finance their booming war industries. The AWPD proceeded on the existing assumptions established by the ABC-1 (air base construction) conferences held with the British, and upon Rainbow 5, the overall war plan that envisioned the United States and Great Britain at war with Germany, Italy, and Japan. Both ABC-1 and Rainbow 5 assumed that Germany was the primary enemy and had to be dealt with first.

The essence of the AWPD approach was not to consider matching the enemy plane for plane, the time-honored method of measuring strength, but instead to make a revolutionary evaluation of the total target system to determine the most critical elements. The planners then estimated how many tons of bombs would be required to destroy those targets. Many factors went into the

The peak of piston-engine fighter development during World War II was attained in the North American P-51D Mustang. No other fighter had its combination of speed, range, maneuverability, and firepower. Its ability to escort bombers to Berlin and beyond was the death knell for the Luftwaffe. Designed to British specifications, and later powered by a Packard-built Rolls Royce Merlin engine, the Mustang nonetheless epitomized the American fighter philosophy of taking the war to the enemy and beating him on his home ground.

More people have probably seen this particular Lockheed P-38 than any other example. Veteran airman Lefty Gardner has been touring the country with it for years, flying it both in air races and in air shows. A consummate aerobatic pilot, Gardner puts his P-38L through a series of elegant maneuvers that leaves the crowds cheering.

calculation, for the tonnage was based on the probable accuracy (peacetime bombing-range errors multiplied by a factor of 2.25), weather (five bombing days per month), percentage of aborts, enemy opposition, dispersion of the targets, and other considerations. Insofar as possible, the attacks were to be made on military targets only; civilian population centers were *not* to be objects of the attacks, even though it was recognized that there would inevitably be collateral damage to them.

Once the targets and the tonnage were defined, the planners backed into the astounding number and types of aircraft that would be required, considering their capabilities in range, bomb load, and other tactical factors, and assessing their production-schedule availability.

They did not stop there, but went on to determine requirements for production capacity, combat loss, and replacement and training. They even planned for the possible loss of bases in England by calling for construction of the gigantic Consolidated B-36, which would not in fact appear until after the war. They estimated a combat loss rate of 25 percent a month, which amounted to an attrition rate of 2,133 aircraft a month, 25,596 annually. This meant losing almost half of the operational force each year, a number many times the size the total size of the Air Corps they had grown up in. It was a very tough bullet to bite, and an estimate that fortunately proved to be pessimistic, but its acceptance as a measure of risk was also a measure of the determination of the American command.

The target for beginning full-scale strategic air operations against Germany was set for twenty-one months after the outbreak of war. The completed plan envisioned 251 combat groups, with 105,467 aircraft and a personnel strength of 2,164,916—figures that are remarkably close to the actual 1945 peak.

General George C. Marshall approved the plan and personally shepherded it through the War Department's bureaucratic maze, with a goal of obtaining presidential approval. Two events intervened. The first was on December 4, 1941, when the *Chicago Herald Tribune* printed the entire plan in facsimile, a security breach that rocked both the United States and Great Britain and seemed to scuttle all chances for AWDP-1's approval. (Later the leak was attributed to Harry Hopkins, who must have felt that it would prepare the country psychologically for war.) The second occurred three days later, when the attack on Pearl Harbor effectively put AWPD-1 (and its subsequent upward modifications) into action.

A TRULY NATIONAL FORCE

It's Tommy this, and Tommy that, an'
"Chuck 'im out the brute!"
But it's "Saviour of his country," when
the guns begin to shoot.

Prior to World War II, Rudyard Kipling's poem "Tommy" was as true of American forces as it was of the British. Service life was incomprehensible to the great mass of Americans; there was simply nothing to recommend it. The pay was low, advancement slow, posts isolated, and prestige nonexistent. (After World War II another writer, James Jones, would limn the classic picture of the "lifer" during the prewar period in *From Here to Eternity.*)

It was, of course, an unfair characterization. Some men were meant to be soldiers, and they and their families derived a considerable satisfaction from military life. But even within the Army, the members of the flying branch were considered a little offbeat, pursuing a terribly dangerous career with little future. Flyers constituted 8 percent of the Army officer corps, and accounted for 54 percent of its casualties, statistics that were served up almost annually in the continuing fight for flight pay.

Things changed forever with the rapid buildup in preparation for World

War II. After years of scrambling to retain a force of a few thousand officers, the Air Corps (named the U.S. Army Air Forces after June 20, 1941) now had to reach out to the public and bring in masses of candidates from every walk of life to fly the airplanes and man the ground organizations that supported them. The service moved statistically from a very small, skewed sample to the center of the population's bell curve, and it has remained there ever since, the United States in microcosm.

This sudden expansion was a metaphor for the awakening of the sleeping giant of American industrial strength, for just as the best and brightest flocked to serve in the "Air Corps," as most people continued to call it, so did the products the USAAF required elicit the best from the American public. The demand for materials and goods extended from aluminum to zirconium, as the need for qualified personnel ranged from construction workers to physicians. All of the latent production capacity was brought to bear through the creation of new factories, new products, and new workers. From the malaise of a ten-year depression there sprang within two years a complex industrial system unlike any the world had ever seen. Where once jobs had been scarce, now it was manpower that was needed, and barriers to women and minority groups began to be lowered—not everywhere and not always equitably, but lowered nevertheless.

The industrial growth was staggering. In five years, 296,901 aircraft, 71,060 ships, and 86,388 tanks would be produced, and these were simply the most visible weapons, the products of factories that had also to be built, work-

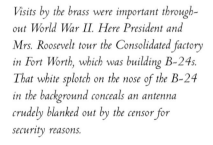

Visits by the brass were important throughout World War II. Here President and Mrs. Roosevelt tour the Consolidated factory in Fort Worth, which was building B-24s. That white splotch on the nose of the B-24 in the background conceals an antenna crudely blanked out by the censor for security reasons.

ers who had to be trained, raw materials that had to be obtained. As a suggestion of the breadth of the effort is the fact that, working at top speed, it still took an average of thirty-four months between the time a new factory was started and the first new aircraft rolled out. In calendar terms, a factory started on December 7, 1941, would not be operating until March 1944.

The small cadre of military personnel on duty in the immediate prewar years managed the expansion with full regard for military discipline and tradition, even though extremely unorthodox measures were taken. In 1938 Air Force Chief Hap Arnold characteristically put himself out on a limb to solve the pilot-training crisis. At a time when Randolph Field was turning out about 750 pilots a year, the wartime demand was projected at 100,000 annually. Arnold called together the leading owners of civilian flying schools around the country and told them that he wanted them—on faith—to believe that he could push through a training-program budget that would pay them a flat fee for every pilot graduated, and a lesser one for each cadet washed out.

The contractors, long starved by the depression, demurred at first, because even the basic startup costs for barracks, mess halls, and runways would cost them at least $200,000, an enormous sum then, especially for people who were just breaking even on their current operations. Arnold asked them to borrow the money until he could get an appropriation, an act that, if not illegal, was at least fraught with personal risk. Purely on their faith in him, the contractors agreed, and the framework was laid for the largest pilot-training program in history.

General George C. Marshall, the Army Chief of Staff, engaged in animated conversation with Donald W. Douglas. While not an airman himself, Marshall understood air power. Perhaps even more important, he knew how to pick the fliers who could wield air power when they had the resources. The aircraft on the production line behind is a Boeing B-17 being built in the Douglas plant. It was not a one-way street; Boeing also built Douglas A-20Cs.

Arnold used the same approach with manufacturers, cajoling, inspir-ing, browbeating, doing whatever was necessary to get them to commit their funds on faith. In the process he used a technique he had refined: telling pilot-training contractors that he had more planes than pilots, and manufacturers that he had more pilots than planes.

It was with the same sort of gambler's vision that he launched the cre-ation of overseas air routes. Beginning modestly with the Air Corps Ferrying Command flying bombers to England, the concept was soon expanded into an unprecedented transportation system. Spurred by a 26,000-mile round-the-world survey trip in a Consolidated B-24 by Colonel Caleb V. Haynes and Major Curtis E. LeMay and by the acquisition of islands in the Pacific, the overseas air routes became the foundation for the global network of airports and facilities that continue to serve the world today.

PREVIEW OF WAR

Just as the Lafayette Escadrille had brought public sentiment to the Allied side in the First World War, so was there a surge of sentiment in the Second. At least twelve U.S. pilots fought for the Royal Air Force during the Battle of Britain, and they scored at least fifteen victories. Their presence was never acknowledged because they were breaking U.S. law, with potential fines of up to $20,000 and ten years in prison, along with a loss of citizenship. One man, Pilot Officer Carl Davis, was unofficially the first American ace of the war, gaining eleven and a half victories.

The first ace, officially, was William R. Dunn, who flew with the Eagle Squadron, the first of three.

The Eagle squadrons provided a legal way for Americans to participate in the air war. In Canada, the Empire's Ace of Aces, Air Vice Marshal Billy Bishop, had asked the famous American aviation artist Clayton Knight, himself a veteran flyer of World War I, to set up an organization to screen potential applicants for the RAF. An interview process was set up and by the time of Pearl Harbor, more than 50,000 applications had been reviewed and 6,700 American pilots made eligible for service with either the RAF or the Royal Canadian Air Force. In England, a wealthy American sportsman, Charles Sweeny, complemented Bishop's effort with a similar campaign for the estab-lishment of the unit, named the Eagle Squadron. The first three men joined the Eagle Squadron in September 1940 at Church Fenton, 180 miles north of London. The three—Vernon Keough, Andrew Mamedoff, and Eugene Tobin—had escaped from France, where they had intended to fly with the now defunct Armée de l'Air. They joined 609 Squadron, where they saw action and achieved victories, and so were potent leavening for the new unit.

The Eagles got their first aircraft—Hawker Hurricanes—on November 7, 1940, and by August 1, 1941, all three Eagle squadrons, Nos. 71, 121, and

In nine months of combat, Robert S. Johnson became the fourth-ranking USAAF ace, scoring twenty-seven victories with the 61st Fighter Squadron and rising from second lieutenant to captain in the process. His mount was the rugged eight-gun P-47

123, were in action. After conducting fighter sweeps over France, they went on to fly in the defense of Malta and to participate in the tough battles of North Africa. In their time of combat, the Eagle squadrons scored seventy-three victories.

When the United States entered the war, the Eagle squadrons became the nucleus of the Eighth Air Force's 4th Fighter Group, the top-scoring USAAF fighter group of the war. Not all the pilots transferred; some remained with the RAF. But those who did came proudly, wearing their U.S. wings on the left, their RAF wings on the right.

SUPPORT IN ASIA

On the other side of the world, unusual political considerations combined to vindicate the ideas of the "pursuit maverick," Claire Chennault, who since 1937 had served as a special adviser to the Chinese Air Force. Having secured permission from Generalissimo Chiang Kai-shek, Chennault went to Washington to convince the President and his staff of the need to stiffen the Chinese Air Force with a group of American volunteers, in the spirit of the Lafayette Escadrille. Ordinarily such a proposal would have fallen on deaf ears, but the desperate need to defend the Burma Road and keep China in the war was abetted by a sophisticated lobbying group with intimate contacts at the highest levels of both governments.

Able to offer adventure and financial reward to U.S. military pilots on active duty, Chennault secured agreement to place the volunteers on inactive duty, with no loss in seniority. There were soon 100 pilots and 200 ground-crew personnel ready to go, along with 100 P-40B Tomahawks, obsolete fighters allocated to Sweden but redirected to Rangoon.

Chennault had rightly demanded that the American Volunteer Group—immortalized as the "Flying Tigers"—go into action fully trained as a unit, with a standard system for the replacement of personnel and aircraft. Instead, the pressures of war diverted interest, and he had to fight with what he had, committing smaller units to the point defense of Chinese cities and the Burma Road. Nonetheless, when his pilots entered combat on December 20, 1941, they proved Chennault's theories. The P-40s they flew were less maneuverable than the Kawasaki Ki-43 Oscars opposing them, but Chennault's tactics were superior. The P-40s were very effective against the lightly armed Japanese bombers, and in the course of time proved to be useful in the ground-attack role. But more than anything else, the Flying Tigers established an ascendancy over their opponents, proved that the seemingly unstoppable Japanese were in fact beatable, and gave heart to the Chinese and inspiration to the USAAF. The American Volunteer Group passed into legend when it was integrated into the USAAF on July 4, 1942. By then it claimed almost 300 victories against the loss of fifty planes and nine pilots. Some have subsequently questioned the number of victories, but while there was undoubtedly some confusion and exaggeration, the Flying Tigers' great contribution, like that of the Eagle squadrons, was to be at the point of combat first, and to achieve victories at a time when the American public was learning only of defeats.

THE PLUNGE INTO COMBAT

In 1941 the United States Army Air Forces were led by a group of warriors who had trained for two decades in their specialties. They were champing at the bit to show what they could do, and suddenly they were called upon to fulfill their oaths. After starving for equipment for years, these men were now given the means to combat two loathsome enemies, Nazi Germany and militaristic Japan, both openly intent on world domination. At the time of Pearl Harbor, Germany had already conquered Poland, Norway, Holland, Denmark, Belgium, Luxembourg, France, Yugoslavia, and Greece; it had apparently defeated Russia, and had a stranglehold on the British in Africa. The Japanese empire, already exploiting Korea ruthlessly, had raped large areas of China as surely as its troops had raped the women of Nanking, and would soon conquer all of Indochina, the Philippines, the Dutch East Indies, and many places in between. Australia was threatened, and it seemed possible that there could be a linkage of the Axis forces in India.

It is not easy to remember how serious were the times or how deep

One of the greatest passenger transports of all time, the Lockheed Constellation made its first flight on January 9, 1943, at Burbank, California, as the C-69, the largest and fastest USAAF transport. The elegantly streamlined C-69 was extremely advanced, using Wright R-3350 engines similar to those in the B-29, and featuring a pressurized cabin to carry sixty-four passengers in comfort. Later variants of the design were EC-121s, used during the Vietnam War. The last of these aircraft served with the Air Force Reserve through 1978—a thirty-five-year career.

America's patriotic fervor. After the war Major General Haywood Hansell said, "My military bosses and my associates and I were consumed with one overpowering purpose: how to win the war with assurance and fewest American casualties. We had little concern for what happened afterward."

Just getting into combat was difficult. The Japanese sneak attack came before America was prepared, and it diverted attention from the original plans to deal with Germany first. But the defeat at Pearl Harbor had positive repercussions as well, sweeping aside all dissent against involvement in the war, and totally mobilizing the American economy. Even the most hidebound of isolationists, Senator Burton Wheeler of Montana, allowed that we now had to "lick hell out of them."

THE STRUGGLE IN THE EAST—DEBACLE AND RIPOSTE

The Japanese attack on Pearl Harbor on December 7, 1941, was a tactical masterpiece. It was based in part on their study of the success of British Swordfish torpedo planes against the Italians at Taranto, but stemmed primarily from their philosophy of using a relatively small, highly elite force of intensely trained professionals. The parallel attack on the Philippines, while not so dramatic, was even more effective, achieving its principal objective by destroying the USAAF forces on the ground.

U.S. Army Air Forces losses in Hawaii were high. Out of a total strength of 231 planes, 64 were totally destroyed and only 79 remained usable. To make guarding them easier against possible acts of sabotage, the planes had been marshaled closely together—into a perfect target. Caught napping despite a radar

warning, the Army flew about forty sorties during the attack; ten victories were claimed. A total of twenty-nine Japanese planes failed to make it back to their carriers, although rough seas damaged a further fifty on landing, a cheap price for so great a victory.

The day was studded with individual heroism. Pilots dressed in everything from pajamas to dinner jackets jumped into the sparkling new fighters that had been so long in coming—Curtiss P-36s and P-40s—and threw themselves upon the enemy wherever they could find him. Twelve unarmed and vulnerable B-17s completing a 2,400-mile flight from the States arrived in the middle of the battle; one was destroyed and three were badly damaged.

The Japanese never intended to invade Pearl Harbor. They wished to destroy the battleships and aircraft carriers stationed there to protect their flank for their conquest of Southeast Asia. But they were determined to invade the Philippines as soon as they had established air superiority. The battle was conducted on a scale considered suitable by the Japanese. They knew that the Americans had about 153 modern fighters, P-35s and P-40s, and thirty-five B-17s, with about another 100 obsolete types. Against these less than 300 aircraft, Japan marshaled a combined force of 422 aircraft, including 186 fighters and 189 bombers.

USAAF units in the Philippines went on alert immediately after the report of the Pearl Harbor attack about 0300 local time on December 8 (0800 on December 7 in Hawaii, on the other side of the International Date Line). Patrols were established and the sole operational SCR 270 radar set was manned and operating.

Weather delayed the Japanese attack on Clark Field on Luzon until about

The calm before the storm—one of the Doolittle-raid aircraft is shown on a practice flight in Texas, just weeks before the famous April 16, 1942, mission. This North American B-25B, 02-297, was flown by Major John A. Hilger, Doolittle's second in comamand. Hilger and his crew bombed Nagoya, then flew on to China, where they bailed out successfully. The B-25 Mitchell was beloved by its crews because it was rugged and easy to fly.

noon, some nine hours after the initial warning. Still it caught the American bomber force on the ground and destroyed half of it. The precious assets, wheedled out of Congress and flown with such effort to reinforce the Philippines, went up in flames, squandered by the indecision of the U.S. commanders on the scene. Instead of launching a headlong B-17 attack on Japanese bases in Formosa, they chose instead to wait for reconnaissance reports. By tragic coincidence, not only were the bombers crowded into a convenient target on the ground, but at the very moment the Japanese strike force from Formosa arrived the Curtiss P-40s were coming to Clark Field to refuel. Low on fuel, lightly armed, they were no match for the attackers.

It must have seemed incredible to the small Japanese force that eight hours after the war started there could still be so juicy a target ripe for picking. The Mitsubishi bombers—twenty-six G3Ms and twenty-seven G4Ms—were not very effective, but the thirty-six A6M Zero fighters came down to ground level to strafe the American forces.

With this first attack, Japan had destroyed half of the Far East Air Force's strength—eighteen B-17s, fifty-five P-40s, and another fifty miscellaneous aircraft—and eliminated any hopes that an invasion of the Philippines could be forestalled. The Americans continued to battle bravely in the following months, but the B-17s were expended in penny-packet attacks against invasion beachheads until the battered remnants were withdrawn to Australia. The P-40s and P-35s were whittled down to the point that they were withdrawn from offensive operations and dedicated solely to reconnaissance.

The defense of the Philippines continued until May, morale kept high rumors of reinforcement and by individual acts of heroism like those by the commander of the 17th Pursuit Squadron, First Lieutenant Boyd "Buzz" Wagner, who shot down four enemy aircraft on one mission on December 13 and went on to become the first USAAF ace of the war. Eventually the overwhelming Japanese strength ground the American and Filipino defenders down, and they suurendered the rocky green island fortress of Corregidor on May 6.

Despite the tragic events in the Philippines, the war in the Pacific had already taken an upturn with two separate events, the second famous, the first virtually forgotten. The first was a raid in response to a request from Major General Jonathan M. Wainwright, who had been left in command of American forces in the Philippines when General Douglas MacArthur was ordered by Washington to leave. Wainright asked for a bombing attack that would lift the Japanese blockade long enough to ship supplies from Cebu to beleaguered Corregidor, the strategic American stronghold in Manila Bay. Led by General Ralph Royce, on the morning of April 11, 1942, three B-17s and ten B-25s took off from Darwin for a secret strip on Mindanao. From there they made attacks for the next two days, protected by a mixed bag of six battered fighters. The results were not startling, but the morale boost was great, as the bombers returned to Australia with forty-four U.S. and Filipino officers and civilians.

The second event was one of the most famous raids of World War II, and the first attack on the mainland of Japan. It astonished the world for it came when the Japanese and most Americans believed that American strength had been reduced to nothing in the Pacific. It was a bravura performance, planned and executed by Lieutenant Colonel James H. "Jimmy" Doolittle. Sixteen B-25s were launched from the carrier *Hornet* on April 18 to hit Tokyo, Yokosuka, Nagoya, Osaka, and Kobe. There was no hope that extensive damage could be done; the raid was a symbol to raise American spirits, and a sign to the Japanese that they were vulnerable. Although all sixteen aircraft were lost—and Lieutenant Colonel Doolittle expected to be court-martialed—the daylight raid did everything expected for both countries. The United States rejoiced in having won a round against the rampaging Japanese, and Doolittle was promoted to brigadier general and awarded the Medal of Honor. In Japan, despite propaganda disclaimers, a chill swept across both civil and military leaders as they became aware that their country was not invulnerable, a sense reinforced by the standoff battle of the Coral Sea.

SLOW BEGINNINGS IN EUROPE

In Europe, the USAAF was to begin slowly, stumble briefly through a hard learning process against the veterans of the Luftwaffe, and ultimately grow to overwhelming strength in all areas. Curiously, its doctrinal backbone came from an unlikely source, General Bernard L. Montgomery of the British Eighth Army. Not known for flexibility himself, Montgomery had written that the greatest asset of air power was flexibility, that it should not be frittered away in individual packets for individual army commanders, but instead should be centrally controlled by an air officer who maintained close association with the ground commander. It was a formula that would be adopted by Brigadier General Carl Spaatz, Commanding General of U.S. Army Air Forces in Europe, and become, in essence, the USAAF's Declaration of Independence.

The European air offensive started on a minor key. The first U.S. bombing attack in Europe was carried out by the Halverson Project, a group of twenty-three brand-new Consolidated B-24D bombers originally intended to operate out of bases in China against Japan. The Doolittle raid had spurred a Japanese offensive that captured proposed U.S. landing fields in China, and Colonel Harry A. Halverson's detachment was ordered held up en route. In the first use of the B-24 in combat, and the first experience in battle for the crews, the unit was diverted to mount an attack on the Romanian oil fields at Ploesti. Thirteen B-24s took off singly from Egypt to bomb through an overcast at dawn on June 12, 1942. Twelve of the planes got their bombs on the target. The return trip was hazardous: four B-24s were interned in Turkey, and one crash-landed. The damage to the oil fields was light, but it was the first blow

OPPOSITE TOP:

The famous Lockheed P-38 Lightning was one of the most distinctive and technologically advanced aircraft of the war. Among its engineering advances were the tricycle landing gear; butt-jointed, flush-riveted sheet metal in its external surfaces; and the use of twin turbosupercharged engines. The P-38 reached its peak in the Pacific, where the two engines provided a measure of safety over the long reaches of the ocean. Beloved by its pilots, it was respected by the enemy. The Germans called it der Gabelschwanz Teufel—"the fork-tailed devil" — *while the Japanese pictograph represented it as "two planes, one pilot."*

at a target system of vital importance to Germany, and it was the first mission of a unit that would become famous later as the Ninth Air Force.

But it was the Eighth Air Force that was to become the mightiest aerial force in the history of warfare, despite a buildup that was both agonizingly slow and often diluted. The Eighth Air Force began with the arrival in England on February 21, 1942, of a DC-3 carrying seven USAAF officers, led by Brigadier General Ira Eaker. The Eighth would grow steadily until it had achieved the complete destruction of Nazi Germany, a task accomplished in concert with the RAF Bomber Command and the other Allied forces.

General Eaker was perhaps the perfect person for the job. A longtime friend of Carl "Tooey" Spaatz, the beloved leader Air Force Chief Arnold regarded as his deputy commander, Eaker was a brilliant planner and administrator, and though soft-spoken was extremely articulate. His first speech in England, often quoted, typified his modesty and courtesy and captured the hearts of the English. Invited to dinner by the mayor of High Wycombe, Eaker went with great reluctance and a promise there would not be any speeches. The mayor kept the promise at the dinner, but then dragged Eaker across the street to a building where 2,000 people were waiting. The mayor spoke for a quarter of an hour, and then introduced Eaker, who said only, "We won't do much talking until we've done more fighting. After we've gone, we hope you'll be glad we came." It was a masterpiece, and it reflected perfectly the attitude with which Spaatz and Eaker invested the Eighth Air Force.

The two men's tasks were Herculean. Spaatz had to supervise the overall

Each American heavy bomber carried a crew of ten men, none more valuable nor more vulnerable than the gunners who manned the various ball turrets. Here an unidentified gunner, wearing the latest in electrically heated flying suits, wiggles into position in the belly turret on the underside of the fuselage.

More Consolidated B-24 Liberators were built during World War II than any other American aircraft, a total of 18,432. Although the B-24 never caught the public's fancy as the Flying Fortress did, it was well liked by its crews. More modern in concept than the B-17, with its tricycle landing gear and Davis wing, the B-24 was also designed for easier service. Production expanded so swiftly that new aircraft were often taken immediately to storage to await the routine postproduction modifications.

As the air war intensified, the armament of American bombers was increased. From the B-24G on, all Liberators had a four-gun forward turret to meet incoming fighters. Here a silver B-24 emerges wounded from a cloud of antiaircraft fire. The Davis wing, with its long width-to-chord ratio, gave the Liberator its superior range.

growth of the force in Europe, and was soon tasked with the leadership of the North African and then the Mediterranean theaters. Responsibility for the Eighth shifted to Eaker in December 1942. One year later, he had 185,000 men and 4,000 airplanes at his disposal. By June 1944 his force had grown to 400,000 men and 8,000 airplanes. He had to build 43 airfields, each with 165 barracks, hangars, mess halls, and all the impedimenta of a bomber base, plus another 40 major facilities for depots, storage, and training. As all of this mass of men and material was being gathered, it simultaneously had to be whipped into shape for battle. And it had to have its mission defined.

A CRISIS FOR DAYLIGHT BOMBING

Royal Air Force experiments with daylight bombing had been disastrous; the German fighter forces devastated the bombers. The RAF then resorted to night bombing of military targets, with lower loss rates but wholly inadequate results. Because of difficulties with weather, antiaircraft fire, navigation, and bombing equipment, only about 10 percent of the bombs fell within five miles of their intended targets. Yet in 1942, when Russia was already demanding a second front, England had no means of striking at Germany except by bombing. The result was a decision by RAF Bomber Command to turn to area bombing, the indiscriminate destruction of German urban areas to "dehouse" (the preferred euphemism for slaughter) the German civilian population and break its morale,

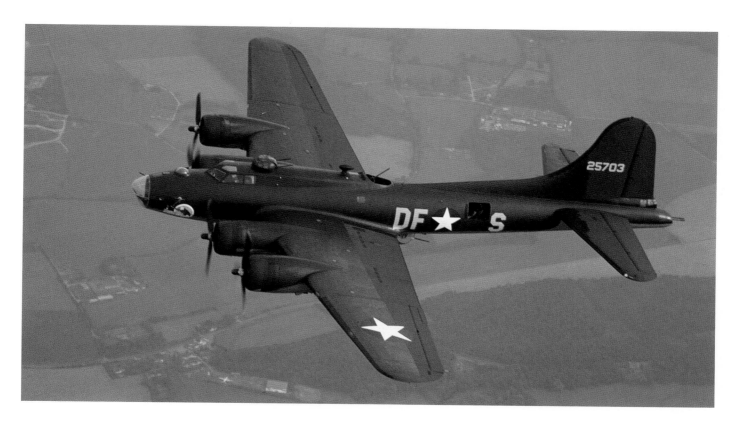

the dream since the 1920s, when Guilio Douhet, the Italian prophet of air power, had first put forth his theories.

Unable to bomb by day themselves, the RAF was certain that the fledgling USAAF could not. And they were not impressed by the Flying Fortress, having experimented with a few B-17Cs earlier, only to reject them as unsuitable for the European war zone.

The entire USAAF strategic concept was based on precision daylight bombing, using the B-17s, the newer B-24s, and the Norden bombsight. Eaker argued that the B-17s could not operate effectively at night. In the course of 1942, Winston Churchill, prodded by complaints from his staff, would come to have grave doubts about daylight bombing, and try to pressure the United States to join the RAF's night area-bombing strategy.

Eaker's position was unenviable. It was a primary, perhaps war-winning, characteristic of American commanders not to let feelings of personal friendship get in the way of the need for results, although Eaker's compassion occasionally interfered with this philosophy. The film *Twelve O'Clock High*, written by Bernie Lay, one of Eaker's original staff of seven, portrays with great accuracy a typical instance of American discipline, which was meted out swiftly to combat commanders and staff members who did not measure up.

Arnold, Spaatz, and Eaker had served together for more than two decades. They admired, respected and liked each other, Eaker considering Arnold a "nonconformist genius." Pressured himself by both General Marshall

One reason the Boeing B-17 was so popular with the public was its sheer beauty, unusual in so large an aircraft. Even late in the war, when its lines had been encumbered with chin turrets and other guns, it was still an elegant aircraft. Like the B-24, it survived because it was fitted with the turbo-superchargers whose development had begun twenty years before at at McCook Field. Without them it would have had to fly at lower altitudes, where it would have been far more vulnerable to antiaircraft and fighters.

and President Roosevelt, Arnold's insistent demand for performance from the Eighth Air Force was both unrelenting and unrealistic. A three-way managerial wrestling match evolved, with the taciturn, mordantly humored Spaatz acting as a shock absorber for Arnold's complaints and Eaker's always courteous but not always compliant replies. The subject that divided them was that of aircraft allocation. Even as America's productive capacity soared, there were still never enough aircraft to go around, especially when political considerations overrode military strategy, as in the decision to invade North Africa.

Such was the case when, over Eaker's objections, the Eighth was forced prematurely into combat on July 4, 1942. With six Douglas A-20s borrowed from the RAF's 226 Squadron, American crews of the 15th Bombardment Squadron (light) raided four Luftwaffe fields near the coast of Holland. Two planes were lost and the bombing accuracy was bad. But it was a propaganda triumph heralding the beginning of two long, hard struggles, one against the Germans, the other against the pressure of events within Eaker's own service.

Five weeks later, on August 17, the first B-17 raid took place against the rail yards at Rouen, in northern France. Eaker had to leave a sickbed (he had suffered twenty-seven hornet stings the day before) to fly as an observer on the attack by twelve B-17s of the 97th Bomb Group. The bombing was good and the group sustained no losses, although it is indicative of the rigor of the campaign that of the 111 men who flew on this first mission, 31 would later be posted as killed or missing in subsequent raids.

It was an auspicious start, but the Eighth Air Force's strength would build far more slowly than anticipated, due to diversions to the Pacific, and then, in massive quantities, to Operation Torch, the invasion of North Africa. An entirely new air force, the Twelfth, was carved from the Eighth. Jimmy

OPPOSITE TOP:
First put into production as the DB-7 for France, the Douglas A-20 played an important role in every theater of the war, in attack, light bomber, reconnaissance, intruder, and night-fighter roles. The A-20 was particularly devastating to the Japanese in its low-level attack role, dropping parachute-retarded bombs with instantaneous fuses that wiped out aircraft and troop concentrations with equal facility. A total of 7,385 of the type were built, and it laid the groundwork for the even more advanced Douglas A-26 that was to follow.

OPPOSITE BOTTOM:
The heavy bombers—B-17s, B-24s, and B-29s—garnered the majority of the headlines, but the medium bombers did their hard work every day, striking behind enemy lines at altitudes where flak was the thickest. Here Martin B-26 Marauders take out a railroad bridge over the Rhône River at Arles, in southern France. The B-26 had a rocky start, but went on to become the bomber with the best survival record.

World War II Navy fighters are sought by warbird enthusiasts, and the Vought F-4U Corsair is as popular, if not as numerous, as the P-51 Mustang. Here a Corsair flies in formation with a Parrish Curtiss P-40, resplendent in faded desert camouflage that the sunlight is turning pink.

Doolittle, now a major general, had come to Europe to serve in the Eighth, and was given the Twelfth to command in support of Torch.

At the same time, the British became increasingly critical, charging that the Eighth had not bombed any targets outside the range of RAF fighter escort. The British complaints had particular sting. Since revitalization of the Bomber Command by Air Marshall Arthur "Bomber" Harris, the RAF was regularly sending hundreds of planes, and sometimes as many as a thousand, against targets deep in Germany. (Curiously enough, Harris himself stalwartly supported Eaker's efforts.) When 1943 began, the Eighth had flown only twenty-three bomber missions, most against submarine-pen installations in France, none into Germany.

Eaker, blocked by circumstances from proving his point in the air, did so with words, convincing Winston Churchill at the Casablanca conference in January 1943 that daylight precision bombing was the proper role for the USAAF, so that in conjunction with Bomber Command, Nazi Germany could be bombed "around the clock." The phrase intrigued Churchill, who "rolled the words off his tongue as if they were tasty morsels."

With Churchill's approval, the USAAF planners created Operation Pointblank, the Combined Bomber Offensive that would ultimately destroy Germany, even though the bulk of its effort came after the invasion of Europe, rather than before, as the air war planners had desired.

Two separate endeavors in August 1943 showed how desperately long-range escort fighters were needed to secure air superiority over Europe if daylight bombing were to continue. Both missions were fairly successful, but both were tragically costly.

The first was a follow-up strike at the most important source of German petroleum, the oil refinery at Ploesti in Romania. Two groups of the Ninth Air Force and three borrowed from the Eighth, 177 B-24s in all, conducted a low-level mission across the Mediterranean. A series of critical navigation mistakes and an alert German defense resulted in the loss of fifty-four aircraft, more than 30 percent of the force. The damage to Ploesti was severe, but as the Allies were to learn, the Germans were expert in repairing damage, especially when there were no subsequent attacks.

Even bloodier were raids on Schweinfurt and Regensburg, intended to cripple Germany by destroying its ball-bearing industry. As soon as the escorting P-47s reached the limit of their fuel supplies and had to leave, the Luftwaffe began a sustained attack, destroying 24 of the 146 bombers attacking Regensburg. The force attacking Schweinfurt was delayed three and a half hours by weather, giving the Germans time to rest and refuel. This time they destroyed 36 of 230 attackers, and damaged many more.

Sixty bombers and 600 men had been lost, and although the ball-bearing plants had been mauled, they were not destroyed. Despite the evident German air superiority, the Eighth persisted, with dire results. In three missions—

Bremen, Gdynia-Danzig, and Muenster—88 bombers were lost in less than three days. Yet the Eighth marshaled its resolve to attack Schweinfurt again on October 14. The results were even worse—60 of 291 B-17s were shot down, a catastrophic 20 percent loss rate. Four months elapsed before the Eighth attempted a long-range penetration of Germany, and in that period a series of shifts in emphasis and leadership ensued. Eaker was sent to Italy to assume command of the Twelfth Air Force, and Doolittle was brought in to command the Eighth. General Arnold sent a message stating that the enemy air force had to be destroyed "wherever you find them, in the air, on the ground, and in the factories." Fortunately, Arnold's instructions were backed up by the long-awaited arrival of the war's best piston-engine fighter, the North American P-51 Mustang. Although the range of the P-47s and P-38s had been extended by means of larger auxiliary tanks that could be jettisoned when emptied, it was not until the P-51s that the bombers could be escorted all the way to Berlin and beyond.

On February 20, 1944, Doolittle launched a series of massive raids, hundreds of bombers escorted by hundreds of fighters, to attack German aircraft factories. In five days known later as "The Big Week," the Eighth and

Even though 15,683 Republic P-47s were built, only a handful remain in the world; of those, only a few are still flying. When World War II ended, the USAAF designated the Mustang as the standard piston-engine fighter, and the Thunderbolts were either salvaged or sent to Reserve and National Guard outfits. They were soon replaced by Mustangs, and most were cut up for scrap. The majority of surviving Thrunderbolts were sold to foreign air forces, and then purchased years later by enthusiasts.

One of the world's greatest racing pilots, David Price, flies "Cottonmouth," a gorgeously restored P-51D, for pleasure. The streamlined fuselage of the Mustang is possible because of the small frontal area of its liquid-cooled Merlin engine and very refined cooling system. The technology leading to this sleek combination began with the Curtiss pursuits of the late 1920s, when Prestone coolants were introduced and radiators were reduced in size.

Fifteenth air forces flew 3,800 sorties against a dozen factories and regained undisputed air superiority. The next month, the Eighth sent bombers and fighters over Berlin for the first time. It was a clear signal to knowledgeable Germans that the war was lost, even though the Luftwaffe defended Berlin fiercely, destroying sixty-nine bombers, the most the Eighth had lost in a single attack.

Almost simultaneous with the arrival of the long-range Mustangs was the installation of H2X, the U.S. version of the British H2S radar bombing system, which for the first time permitted bombing even when weather obscured the target. It was far from precision—bombing the radar sets were crude and the crews were inexperienced in their use—but it increased the number of attacks the Eighth Air Force could launch.

The remainder of the bombing campaign would be long and hard. Although the Luftwaffe would occasionally be able to muster enough strength to attack in force, it never came near regaining air superiority, not even when it finally brought its "wonder weapon" jets into action.

THE MEDITERRANEAN THEATER

The success of the U.S. fighters over Europe, particularly after D-day, the massive invasion of Normandy on June 6, 1944, can be attributed to the training

ABOVE:

A restored Douglas A-26, the "Spirit of Waco," at the Confederate Air Force Airshow in 1983. The A-26 Invader entered World War II in the fall of 1944. With a top speed over 370 mph, and carrying as many as fourteen forward-firing .50 caliber machine guns, it was a formidable opponent. The A-26 would become the mainstay of night interdiction during the Korean conflict, and then serve again in the Vietnam War.

LEFT:

Waco CG-4A gliders landing on September 18, 1944, in Operation Market Garden, the abortive airborne invasion of Holland. C-47s towed 904 gliders into carrying the American 82d and 101st Airborne divisions into battle. Glider pilots needed skill and courage to handle their passive craft.

General Billy Mitchell would have been proud to know that his name was applied to so valiant a warplane as the North American B-25. More than 11,000 of the twin-engine bombers were built, and they first gained fame in Doolittle's raid on Tokyo. These B-25Cs of the 340th Bomb Group are taking off from Hergla, Tunisia, for a strike against the Germans in Sicily. The insignia is unusual—the standard 1942–43 white star in a blue circle, but surrounded by a yellow ring in the fashion of the RAF. Stable and forgiving, the B-25 was a lovely airplane to fly.

and experience gained in the Mediterranean campaign. Working in unprecedented harmony with their RAF colleagues, the American air commanders quickly learned the technique of air-to-ground warfare. Carl Spaatz commanded the North African Air Force, and quickly grasped the importance of controlling and concentrating airpower. His quiet, sharp manner intrigued Air Vice Marshall Arthur Coningham, the Commander in Chief of the North African Tactical Air Force, and created a remarkable harmony between the two services. Taking his lead from Coningham, Spaatz soon molded the offensive spirit of USAAF tactical doctrine, which persists to this day.

The scale of the fighting in the Mediterranean theater was always smaller than that in Europe, but never less fierce. The U.S. invasion of North Africa on November 8, 1942, had been met by token French resistance, and then ran into a series of weather and logistic delays that handicapped the Allied air arm in fighting against the German aircraft. The latter operated from prepared fields. Within weeks, however, the relatively green American forces, alongside the RAF, drove the German and Italian air forces from the skies.

One memorable mission was the "Palm Sunday Massacre" on April 18. The enemy had run a large convoy of Junkers Ju 52 transports into Tunisia. Flying back at low level, with an escort of Italian Macchi MC-202s and German Bf 109 and 110 fighters, the transports were attacked by an Allied force of four P-40 squadrons, three from the 57th Group and one from the 324th, with a top cover of RAF Spitfires. More than fifty of the hapless three-engine Ju 52s were shot down, along with sixteen of the escort fighters, against a loss of seven Allied fighters.

With the skies secured, the Allied air forces turned to a ground support role, flying as many as 2,000 sorties a day until the huge German North Africa force of 270,000 men surrendered. The success in North Africa was followed by Operation Corkscrew, the aerial conquest of Pantelleria, an Italian fortress island that blocked access to Sicily. More than 1,000 operational aircraft were available to Spaatz, including A-36s (the attack version of the Mustang), A-20s, B-17s, B-25s, B-26s, P-38s, P-40s, and RAF Wellingtons, Bostons,

The Curtiss P-40 was one of the great workhorses of World War II. While often dismissed as technically inferior to the best enemy fighters, the P-40 had the great quality of being available when needed, and it served well in every theater of war. This P-40F of the 79th Fighter Group bakes in the Middle East sun in Egypt in early 1943. The P-40F used the Packard Merlin V-1650 engine, and had a top speed of 364 mph at 20,000 feet. Most of its fighting in Africa, however, was at ground level, strafing the Afrika Corps.

Beneath lowering clouds over the North African desert, Captain Lester L. Blount treats an Arab child while the father looks on with hope and trust. Scenes like this have been repeated in every war in which the United States has participated.

and Baltimores. On May 18, 100 sorties a day were launched against the island, building later in the month so that by June 6, at the end of phase one of the offensive, 1,700 sorties had dropped 1,300 tons of bombs.

By the time of the climactic phase two assault on June 10, 6,200 tons had been dropped in 5,285 sorties, and as Allied amphibious forces streamed toward the shore, a white flag was run up. Pantelleria had surrendered to the air attack; the only ground casualty suffered by the invading forces was a British Tommy who was bitten by a local jackass.

Similar overwhelming force would be applied to the conquest of Sicily, where weeks could pass before Allied ground troops would see an enemy plane. The loss of Sicily drove Benito Mussolini from power, and the Italians secretly surrendered to the Allies. Still capable of quick reaction, German forces swiftly occupied Italy and prepared for its defense. After initial hard fighting at Salerno, the Allies established an air superiority that was maintained for the rest of the war.

The Luftwaffe, drained while defending the Eastern Front and Hitler's much vaunted "Fortress Europe," was able to mount only about thirty sorties a day on the Italian Front. The new Mediterranean Allied Air Forces, headed by General Eaker, began Operation Strangle, a systematic interdiction of enemy supply lines in Italy. The 280 combat squadrons of the MAAF flew thousands of sorties against roads, bridges, railroads, and tunnels, cutting German resupply to a trickle of trucks at night. The success of the Allied fighters was enhanced by the widespread use of mobile forward air controllers known as

"Rover Joes," a development that would be refined again for use in Overlord, the D-day invasion of Europe, and then prove itself in later wars in Korea and Vietnam.

FROM D-DAY TO V-E DAY

General Lewis Brereton, an old war-horse who had commanded the 12th Aero Squadron at the front in 1918 and was at Clark Field in the Philippines when the Japanese attacked, was Commander of the Ninth Air Force. His right-hand man was a pioneer airman, the short, dark-haired, personable Brigadier General Elwood R. "Pete" Quesada. With medium bombers, fighter-bombers, and troop carriers, the Ninth became the world's largest tactical air force. Its destruction of all avenues of transportation—roads, railroads, and canals—brought Germany's production to a halt as the network of widely dispersed subcontractors could no longer get their parts to assembly sites.

Although occasional sharp fights could still erupt, the Allied air forces had established complete air superiority over Europe. The D-day invasion was made possible by the isolation of the beaches by 6,700 tons of bombs directed against railways, roads, canals, and airfields. Even during these major efforts, the Eighth Air Force continued operations over Germany, bleeding the enemy fighter forces down. On D-day, the Eighth and Ninth air forces flew 8,722 sorties, while the RAF flew 5,676. Against this torrent of fire, the Germans were able to throw only a handful of attacks.

The flexibility of air power was demonstrated by the rapid switching of targets. Fighters and medium bombers ranged over the invasion area and on into Germany, destroying anything that moved, while heavy bombers would be occasionally diverted to lay a tactical bomb carpet, as in saturation bombing at Saint-Lô. Perhaps the most brilliant example of flexibility was during the breakout from Normandy, when Lieutenant General George S. Patton asked that the XIX Tactical Air Command protect his left flank as he wheeled toward the German border. It did so gladly; Allied control of the air was so well established that troop carriers and gliders were then able to effectively supply the fast-moving tank columns.

The air effort over Germany continued even as the Allies pushed forward in France. During the five months from May to September 1944, 230,000 tons of bombs were dropped by the Eighth Air Force alone, the beginning level of effort necessary to demonstrate true air power, given the technology of the time. Fighter opposition was sporadic. The Luftwaffe had been reduced to a handful of veterans of superlative skill and many young, ill-trained pilots who often did not survive their first combat missions. The Germans began employing their Messerschmitt Me 262 jet fighter in small numbers, but the new weapon never became the threat it was perceived as being.

In late 1944, with its petroleum supplies destroyed, Germany found itself

Unquestionably the greatest technical achievement in World War II fighters was the Messerschmitt Me 262, as represented by this beautifully restored example at the National Air and Space Museum. Powered by two Junkers Jumo 004 engines, it was 120 mph faster than the Mustang, and packed enormous firepower. The Germans managed to build more than 1,300 of these superb aircraft, but were able to commit only about 300 to combat operations. If the German engineers had concentrated on the metallurgy necessary for jet engines in 1940 and 1941, the Me 262 could probably have been introduced in quantity in 1943, and the air war over Germany would have been even bloodier. The 262 could not have changed the outcome of the war, but probably would have prolonged it long enough so that the first atom bomb would have been dropped on Berlin, rather than on Hiroshima.

well equipped with planes but without fuel to train pilots or mount defensive sorties. Occasionally, by husbanding supplies, the Luftwaffe could still mount a major attack, which they did on November 4, and again on New Year's Day, 1945. But for the most part the air arm that had spearheaded Nazi conquests was a spent force. However, the story was quite different with the antiaircraft defenses, which intensified as German territory was compressed by the Russians from the east and the Allies from the west. In July, when the struggle for air superiority was long over, the U.S. Eighth and Fifteenth air forces still lost a total of 642 planes, an average of 20 a day.

By the spring of 1945, German opposition was shattered, and the strategic bombing campaign was curtailed because so few worthwhile targets remained. The leaders of the USAAF had seen their plans partially fulfilled, but it had still been necessary for the Army to invade and conduct an intensive ground campaign. Even so, the Germans, from Adolf Speer down to the lowliest infantryman, attributed the Allied victory to air power. Anyone flying over the hollowed shells of cities, hundreds of square miles of gutted apartments, and flattened factories, would draw the same conclusion.

A LONGER ROAD: THE PACIFIC

The air war in the Pacific was similar in many ways to the fighting in Europe: the USAAF started from an initial disadvantage, suffered shortages of planes and personnel, and finally emerged as an overpowering, war-winning force. Yet

The first American jet fighter, the Bell XP-59 Airacomet. Too large and underpowered to be successful in combat, the P-59 was valuable as a training plane for later jets like the Lockheed P-80.

A restored Messerschmitt Bf 109G coming in to land. While many Spanish-built Messerschmitts still exist, genuine German-built 109s are very rare. Modern test pilots, accustomed to jet engines and tricycle landing gear, find the 109 a handful to land.

there were many differences in climate, living conditions, scale of distances, and perhaps most significant of all, the culture of the enemy. Cold, foggy, or rainy as England or Italy might have been, enduring it was easy compared to the chafing heat of the South Pacific, where temperature, humidity, and rampant insect life made ordinary living miserable. As for distance, while it might be 600 miles from England to Berlin, it was 1,200 from American bomber bases at Saipan to

Tokyo. The Philippine Islands alone were spread across 1,000 miles of sea. The Pacific theater was subdivided into areas, each the responsibility of an air force. The Eleventh Air Force covered Alaska and the Aleutian Islands, colder and foggier than England on its worst day. The Seventh Air Force left its Hawaii haven to fight westward from one island after another. The Thirteenth Air Force fought a tough and vicious air-to-ground campaign. The Tenth served in India, contending with the worst weather and the most difficult terrain in the world. The Fourteenth expanded on the Flying Tiger tradition, defending China by lashing out wherever it could reach to punish the Japanese. Each of the air forces fought with short supplies, too few planes, and too few pilots.

As vast as the distances were, the cultural gap was greater. No matter how monstrous some of the Nazi actions were later found to be, the general concept of Germany as an enemy was conditioned by knowledge that the Germans subscribed to the Geneva Convention in regard to the treatment of prisoners of war. There was also substantial evidence from Red Cross inspections, escaped prisoners, and other sources that while conditions were harsh, they were endurable, and that a prisoner could reasonably expect to live to see the end of the war. It was just the opposite with the Japanese. The Bataan death march, the execution of some of the Doolittle raiders, and the vicious treatment of prisoners of all countries rendered Japan suspect as a hostile, subhuman enemy. The image was borne out by the fact that of all the U.S. prisoners of war held by the Germans, only 5 percent died in captivity. Of those held by the Japanese, 34 percent died.

Fortunately, the tide turned early in the Pacific war, in exactly the way Admiral Yamamoto Isoroku had ruefully predicted it would. After the battles of the Coral Sea and Midway had sapped Japanese strength, the Allied forces under General MacArthur began the island-hopping campaign that systematically pried island after island airbase from Japanese control, so that they could be used for the advance on the next one. The bitter battles were typified by the first, at Guadalcanal. There the "Cactus Air Force," a ragtag combination of Navy, Marine, and USAAF units, won air superiority and permitted the American land forces to win a protracted race with the Japanese for supplies and reinforcements. Victory had been assured as early as November 1942, when a Japanese troop transport with 13,500 reinforcements was destroyed by American ships and aircraft.

And, as in Europe, the USAAF was blessed with strong commanders. The Commanding General of Allied air forces in the South Pacific and of the Fifth Air Force was Lieutenant General George Kenney, who would not only direct an intensifying air war for three years against Japan, but would also be successful in the even more difficult task of getting along with the mercurial General Douglas MacArthur.

Kenney's deputy was one of the great combat leaders of World War II, Major General Ennis Whitehead, known to the Japanese as the "Butcher of

Moresby" because of the ferocity of his aerial assaults. In command of the Thirteenth Air Force was Major General Nathan Twining, the future Chairman of the Joint Chiefs of Staff, and the fourth Chief of Staff of the USAF. Twining, who survived six days drifting in a raft after being shot down in his B-17, was a specialist in interservice cooperation, particularly in close air support with Marine and Navy air units.

Kenney's formula for success was classically simple: destroy enemy air power wherever it could be found. His leadership elicited new tactics and innovative use of old tactics. To destroy Japanese aircraft on the ground, he revived an idea he had conceived in 1928, using parachute bombs for low-level attacks. His A-20s, loaded with twenty-three-pound parachute-retarded fragmentation bombs armed with instantaneous fuses, devastated Japanese airfields.

Of the many heroes who emerged under Kenney's guidance, the most flamboyant was the legendary Major Paul "Pappy" Gunn, who improvised changes in the field that were later adopted on the production lines. One of his first efforts was the installation of heavy armament packs in the A-20s and later the B-25s, the latter ultimately including a ship-killing 75mm cannon. Gunn, whose wife and four children were prisoners of the Japanese at Billibad

Innovation did not always mean success. The Bell P-39 was perhaps the most innovative of the American prewar fighters, with a 37mm engine-mounted cannon, tricycle landing gear, and its engine located midship, behind the pilot. Yet changes in specifications led to deletion of its turbosupercharger and an increase in weight. The result was a fighter unable to engage at medium to high altitudes, and useful primarily in the ground-attack role.

The American long suit in aviation was adaptation and innovation. After experimentation in combat, the armament of the North American B-25H was upgraded to a 75mm cannon and eight forward-firing .50-caliber machine guns for antishipping attacks. The cannon reduced the aircraft's flexibilty for use in other missions, and most later B-25s reverted to a standard glazed nose.

OPPOSITE TOP:

The restored Northrop Flying Wing at the National Air and Space Museum's Garber Facility. The restoration proved to be exceptionally difficult because of the custom construction of the all-wood airframe. The left and right wings were not at all symmetrical, and rebuilding each one took many more man-hours than had been projected.

OPPOSITE BOTTOM:

While the Bell P-39 was not considered successful in American use, it was very popular in the Soviet Union, which received 4,773 of the 9,558 built. The Russians liked the P-39 for its tank-killing ability, but it was also used with great success in air-to-air combat.

in the Philippines, led the skip-bombing attacks conceived of by Kenney and used so effectively against Japanese convoys.

This spirit of innovation characterized the entire American effort and led the way to classic demonstrations of air power, including the Battle of the Bismarck Sea in early March 1943, where American and Australian aircraft sank twelve out of sixteen ships in a Japanese convoy. But the principal effort of the USAAF was dedicated to the destruction of the Japanese homeland, and to this end it entered on two enormous projects, larger than any undertaken before for military purposes. Although conducted on a totally independent basis, they would ultimately work together. The first and most expensive was the Manhattan Project to produce an atomic bomb. The second was a program to produce the B-29, by far the most advanced bomber, and in many ways the most advanced airplane, to emerge from World War II. Both projects were enormously risky, and both would succeed beyond anyone's greatest hopes—and fears, for many recognized immediately the awesome portent for the future.

The B-29 was an example of the farsighted thinking of the little group of Air Corps planners. It began in March 1938, when Boeing provided to the Air Corps a design study for what was essentially a pressurized, tricycle-gear B-17. Pursuing the development of the basic concept over the next year was so costly that Boeing lost $2.5 million, an enormous sum for the prewar years, and the company's very existence was threatened. In January 1940 a specification was issued for a superbomber with a speed of 400 mph, a range of 5,333 miles, and

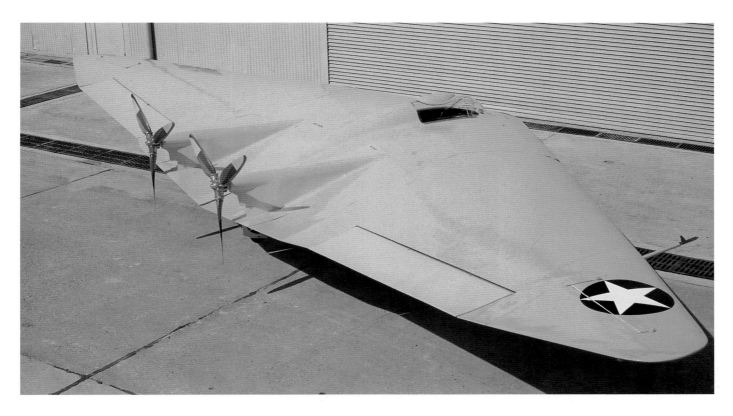

Jack Northrop leans on an early version of his vision of technology, the N-1M flying wing. The pilot, Moye Stephens, has earlier gained fame in a round-the-world flight with explorer Richard Halliburton, recounted in the latter's book, Magic Carpet. Stephens is wearing an early hard hat that looks suspiciously like a polo helmet. The theoretical advantage of the flying wing was a great reduction in both weight and drag. The N-1M led directly to the later Northrop XB-35 and YB-49 bombers, but genuine success was to elude the concept until the advent of the Northrop B-2. The same basic idea was pursued in Germany by the Horten brothers, with equivalent success.

By far the most technologically advanced bomber of the war was the Boeing B-29. Boeing engineers achieved its great leap in performance by assuming some tremendous risks. It was the first pressurized bomber to enter large-scale production, and its gun turrets were remotely controlled. The Wright R-3350 engines were new and temperamental, as were the Curtiss electric propellers. The structure was vastly more modern than that of the B-17, and its heavy weight meant a high wing loading, which in turn required large, effective flaps for takeoff and landing. The contract for the first two aircraft was issued on September 6, 1940; the first combat mission took place on June 5, 1944.

a bombload of 2,000 pounds. Boeing responded with the Model 345, which in the course of time became the XB-29.

There had never been an aircraft like it. It was the world's largest production bomber and the first to be pressurized. Its combination of high gross weight and long, slender wing gave it an extremely high wing loading for the time. A brand-new engine, the 2,200-horsepower Wright R-3350, was designed for it, as were many of its operating features, including a radical remote-controlled gunnery system. Contracts for more than 1,600 aircraft issued before a single one had actually flown. New factories were built for its production, and additional manufacturers were called in to assist. If the B-29 had failed as an airplane, the war against Japan might have been extended for several years.

The first flight was made on September 21, 1942, and combat operations began with a raid on Bangkok on June 5, 1944. It was not until June 15 that the first raid against Japan from Chinese bases was made: forty-seven B-29s bombed Yawata, where much of Japan's steel was made.

The bases in China had been constructed at great cost, and were difficult to supply with fuel and bombs. Not until the island fortress of Truk had been bypassed and the Marianas were captured could B-29 operations begin at an effective level. For many months, the B-29s were operated as designed, at high altitudes above the antiaircraft fire and beyond the capabilities of the Japanese interceptors. The first B-29 to land on Saipan was "Jolting Josie, the Pacific Pioneer," flown by Brigadier General Haywood S. Hansell, the same "Possum" Hansell who had helped create AWPD-1.

The Twentieth Air Force, which operated the B-29s, was unique in that it was not under theater command, but instead reported directly to General Arnold. It was he who set the Japanese aircraft engine and airframe industries as the top target priority.

Unfortunately, the results of a long series of well-planned raids were unsatisfactory. The weather, jetstream winds as high as 180 mph, and the well-dispersed nature of Japanese industry enabled the enemy to endure the raids with little more than moderate distress. It was later determined that in twenty-two missions involving 2,148 sorties, 5,398 tons of bombs had been dropped on Japan. Of this amount, only about one-half had hit primary targets; weather and other factors caused the remainder to be used against secondary targets. The B-29 loss rate was 5.7 percent, meaning more than 100 percent attrition for every 18 raids, far too high to endure.

The Twentieth Air Force Chief of Staff, Brigadier General Lauris Norstad, communicated Arnold's desire that a test raid of 100 aircraft be run against a Japanese city in which incendiary bombs would be the principal weapon. Hansell sent all the available aircraft, 57 B-29s, to drop bombs through a cloud cover on Nagoya in an ineffective attack. As a result, the Japanese defenders formed an exaggerated opinion of their firefighting capabilities that would prove to be terribly costly.

The American capacity to put performance above personal relationships asserted itself again. With personal sorrow, Arnold replaced Hansell with Major General Curtis LeMay, who had distinguished himself with the XX Bomber Command in China. The four men—Arnold, Hansell, Norstad, and LeMay—were all personal friends who had served together in peace and war. The inconclusive results of the B-29 bombing could not be attributed to Hansell personally, but he was the commander, and he had to go. In a nutshell, Hansell the planner was reluctantly replaced by LeMay the operator.

Japan was an entirely different target than Germany had been, and LeMay continued to test both precision bombing and incendiary area-raid tactics to determine the best alternative. He concluded that the Japanese defenses were much less formidable than those of the Germans, particularly at low altitude. After careful consultation with his staff, LeMay decided to gamble by stripping his B-29s of their guns and ammunition to increase the weight of bombs they could carry, and sending them in singly at night, at low altitude. If he succeeded, he would be a hero; if he failed, his career would be over.

The first major test came on the night of March 9–10, 1945. LeMay sent 334 B-29s carrying a total load of 2,000 tons of bombs to attack Tokyo. They found few enemy fighters and only light antiaircraft fire.

The results were devastating to the Japanese. The worst urban fire in history destroyed 267,171 buildings, rendered 1,008,005 persons homeless, wounded 40,918, and killed 83,793. The Americans lost fourteen B-29s.

After the Tokyo raid, every realist in the Japanese military understood that Japan had lost the war. There had been other reverses—the merchant marine was gone and the imperial navy was sunk—but these could be shrugged off and with their selfless spirit of nationalism the Japanese could have continued to resist an invasion, using pikes and swords if the ammunition ran out. But there was no way to deal with the B-29s. The United States had achieved true air power at last, and that is what defeated the Japanese. The formality of surrender would come later, when the atomic bombs dropped on

The glory did not all go to fighter pilots. This scene is long before the development of complete search and rescue service, as wounded soldiers from deep in the jungle in Burma are removed from an amphibious Stinson L-1E of the Tenth Air Force. The unarmed L-1Es were vulnerable to enemy fighters and antiaircraft fire, but nonetheless ranged deep behind enemy lines to pick up casualties.

As in Germany, the pressures of war prevented Japan from achieving the same technical progress as the United States. Thus, in 1945 the Japanese delegation would fly to surrender talks at Ie-Shima in two Mitsubishi G4M1s, painted white with green cross insignia. Called the "Betty" by the Allies and first flown in 1939, the G4M1 was so vulnerable to gunfire that it was informally called the "Flying Lighter" by its crews. Admiral Yamamoto Isoroku was flying in a Betty when he was ambushed and shot down by American P-38s on April 18, 1943.

Hiroshima and Nagasaki lifted true air power to an even more horrible degree of reality.

It is interesting to note that at least three of the top Air Force generals—Arnold, Spaatz, and LeMay—felt that the combination of sea blockade, aerial mining, and strategic bombing was bringing Japan to its knees. They opposed dropping the atomic bomb except as a means of preparing for an invasion. At the Potsdam Conference in late July 1945, General Arnold made these views clear. Yet the Japanese did not acknowledge the Potsdam Declaration, which offered a choice between unconditional surrender and total destruction. The Army Chief of Staff, General Marshall, was certain that a March invasion of the main Japanese islands would be required. Arnold finally concurred in the decision, in part political but primarily military, that the bomb should be dropped.

THE SOCIAL REVOLUTION

Just as air power had revolutionized warfare, so did wartime industrial mobilization revolutionize American society. In a way never before contemplated, women entered the American work force in far greater numbers than ever before, and proved themselves in such jobs as shipbuilding and aircraft manufacture, which had always been regarded as the province of the male. And they did more. The WASPs—Women's Army Service Pilots—showed that women could fly any kind of aircraft as well as men. If the conditions had called for it, they could have flown in combat as well.

There was a similar demonstration, of equal racial capability, in the suc-

After intense political battles and immense persuasion, the USAAF finally availed itself of a tremendous pool of talent when it accepted Nancy H. Love's proposal to recruit well-qualified women as pilots. The first organization was the WAFS (Women's Auxiliary Ferrying Squadron), established in the summer of 1942. Almost simultaneously, Jacqueline Cochran had persuaded General Henry H. Arnold to establish the WASPs, the Women's Airforce Service Pilots. Here Shirley A. Haugan, Tex A. Brown, Betty J. Hanson, Kathryn K. Humprheys, Mary C. Canavan, Gwendolyn E. Cowart, and Virginia Whisonant are seen on the flight line at New Castle Army Air Base, near Wilmington, Delaware.

Women were rare on American aircraft production lines until World War II. They were at first accepted only reluctantly by old line supervisors, but it quickly became apparent that in many ways they were better workers in terms of discipline and attention to detail. Here is a classic "Rosie the Riveter" scene at the Consolidated factory in Fort Worth.

cess of the "Tuskegee experiment." The beginning was the provision, in 1939, for six black colleges and two flying schools to participate in the Civilian Pilot Training Program established by the Civil Aeronautics Authority. Subsequently—and despite opposition by both the Army and the War Department—backing by Eleanor Roosvelt and congressional legislation made it possible to activate the all-black 99th Pursuit Squadron on March 22, 1941. A training field was established at Tuskegee, Alabama, and all black fighter pilots were trained there. Later, as the experiment expanded to include the black

332d Fighter Group and the black 447th Bombardment Group, additional training facilities were established at Chanute Field, Illinois; Selfridge Field, Michigan; and Hondo Field, Texas.

The first five black cadets were commissioned officers and pilots at Tuskegee on March 7, 1942; they were the nucleus of the 99th Pursuit Squadron. The 99th entered the combat zone of North Africa in 1943; the next year it was joined by the 100th, 301st, and 302d Pursuit squadrons to form the 332d Fighter Group. Black units flew combat in North Africa, Sicily, and Italy, escorting the bombers of the Fifteenth Air Force, engaging in aerial combat, and strafing enemy positions. By war's end they had flown 15,000 sor-

Another previously untapped resource became available when a program for black aviators was introduced at Tuskegee Army Air Field, Alabama. Although still a segregated unit, this was the first step toward nondiscrimination in the service. A squadron commander, Captain Andrew W. Turner of Washington, D.C. signals to his crew chief from the cockpit of his North American P-51C. Turner flew sixty-nine combat missions with the 332d Fighter Group and won the Distinguished Flying Cross. He remained with the 332d after the war, and lost his life in a midair collision in 1947.

In the 332d, all duties were performed by blacks, from armament through radio repair. Like their colleagues in every air force, the mechanics changed engines on their P-51s out in the open, regardless of weather.

Sergeants J. C. Whitman and J. R. Brewster engaged in the art of Arctic survival in an igloo improvised beneath the wing of their crashed bomber. Similar efforts at postcrash survival—most not recorded, many not successful—occurred in every theater of the war, in every climate.

Not all the flights were in cloudless skies or ended smoothly. This P-47D collided with an Italian aircraft on landing at Foggia, Italy, on December 29, 1943. The ruggedness of the aircraft is apparent— despite a collision, it is relatively intact. The open window and extended shoulder straps are testimony to the pilot's quick exit after the plane came to a stop.

ties and destroyed 261 enemy aircraft. Commanded by the brilliant black leader Brigadier General (later Lieutenant General) Benjamin O. Davis, Jr., the men from Tuskegee were proudest of the fact that they never lost a bomber to enemy fighters. Less well known, but perhaps an even greater achievement, was the influence they had on the events that led ultimately to the postwar Executive Order 9981, issued by President Truman, calling for equality of treatment and opportunity for all members of the military.

There was another quiet social revolution as well: the impact of young Americans—healthy, well-paid, well-equipped, and endlessly generous—on the people throughout the world with whom they were suddenly based. The pattern was recorded a hundred times. The Americans would land at some forsaken outpost—in Alaska, in the South Pacific, in China—and the same events would repeat themselves. First there would be tents and construction equipment, then a runway and some rough maintenance hangars. As time progressed, the buildings became more luxurious and the natives began to be welcomed. Eventually there were almost ritual scenes of vaccinations, medical treatment, and children being fed in the mess halls. Even after the war, in the newly occupied territories, the prohibitions against fraternization were ignored from the start, and the instinctive American goodwill took over.

THE COST OF AIR POWER

The great victories in Europe and the Pacific had been won at a terrible cost of more than 120,000 Army Air Forces casualties, one-third of them suffered in combat, for the air crews were, in the old military phrase, at the "sharp end of the stick." The AWPD-1 planners had estimated losses of 2,133 planes a month. Actual losses averaged 1,449 a month, for a total of 65,200.

Yet the costs had to be weighed in terms of lives saved. Some doubt that the invasion of Europe would have been possible without overwhelming air power—the German army was the finest in the world, even more brilliant in defense than it had been on offense. And air power made the invasion of Japan unnecessary. In the hard economics of war, the investment of lives in air power paid off manyfold in the savings of lives in every other service.

CHAPTER FIVE
The Paradox of Nuclear Air Power 1946–1964

Even skeptics as hardened as the Navy battleship admirals realized that the mating of the B-29 and the atomic bomb had established air power as *the* dominant military-political force, one that exceeded even the most visionary predictions of its prophets. The Soviet Union immediately began making copies of B-29s that had been interned during World War II, while flogging their own and captured German scientists to create nuclear weapons. Great Britain and France were determined to be nuclear powers, and set about fashioning both the science and the weapons to do so. In the United States, the Navy saw an immediate need for aircraft carriers large enough for the huge bombers necessary to carry nuclear weapons.

But the combination of air power and nuclear weapons created a paradox. It lay in the fact that the drastic hazards and moral implications of employing the nuclear option would stymie first the United States and subsequently every

OPPOSITE:
A crew chief on the wing of a shining silver Cessna T-37 watches the Thunderbirds perform in a scene from Sam Lyon's film Visions.

A C-130B makes a hot-rod takeoff from the desert in a painting by Mike Machat.

177

emerging nuclear power. A decade after the end of World War II, at the beginning of the most threatening arms race in history, when both the weapons and the delivery systems had been vastly improved, the nuclear option remained too terrible to use. Yet the mad concept of mutually assured destruction grew out of this like a weed in a midden heap, an insanity that caused each superpower to arm itself with 10,000 times the power necessary to destroy the planet. (Smaller nuclear powers like France and England had to be content with the capability to ruin only a continent or two.)

Yet what were the perceived options? For the United States and Western Europe, it was obviously impossible to match the conventional military might of the Soviet Union and its allies, postured as they were for an offensive strike that could turn the Cold War hot overnight. Therefore, a Western nuclear capability was essential. To the Soviet Union, it was obvious that having used atomic weapons once, the United States would use them again—therefore, it felt a Soviet nuclear capability was essential. The Cold War became a stalemate, one that first stimulated, then voraciously devoured the economies of the participants.

The nuclear paradox resulted in the creation of a second definition of air power that no visionary had ever prophesied—saving the land battle by interdicting an attacking enemy. When in 1950 North Korean forces swept down the peninsula, penning the motley collection of U.S. and South Korean troops in the perimeter at Pusan, it was the Air Force that hammered the attackers, stiffening resistance until help could come. That it was an antiquated Air Force, flying World War II crocks dragged out of storage, was all the more to its credit. That it had become an antiquated Air Force was to the shame of the American Congress.

DEMOBILIZATION DÉJÀ VU

When World War II ended, on September 2, 1945, the USAAF had a strength of 2,253,000 personnel, and approximately 70,000 aircraft, of which 54 percent were in commission. By December 1946, only fifteen months later, strength had fallen to about 24,000 aircraft, of which only 18 percent were combat-ready. (This wastage is horrifying to present-day warplane buffs who spend hundreds of thousands of dollars to resuscitate old fighters from rusting hulks. Immediately after the war, thousands of aircraft, many brand new, straight from the factory, were pushed into landfills, dumped off cliffs, jettisoned into the ocean, or, more commonly, cut up for scrap.)

The drawdown in personnel was even greater; by May 1947 the USAAF had only 303,000 on duty. The war was over and the civilians who had gladly served when it was necessary wanted to go home—and their congressmen wanted them there.

The threat of another war seemed remote. The victory had been complete, and the only potential threat, the Soviet Union, was exhausted by the war. Yet the men who had led the USAAF to victory had not planned on such a precipitous drop in strength. Studies directed by General Arnold in 1944, and confirmed by his successor, General Carl Spaatz, indicated that the minimum strength required to maintain both a military and industrial base capable of expanding for a new conflict was 105 groups, a little less than half the size of the wartime USAAF. After the war this was seen as far too expensive, as was an alternate plan for 78 groups. Lieutenant General Ira Eaker, now Deputy Commander to Spaatz, finally came up with a recommendation for 70 groups as the rock-bottom minimum for the postwar Air Force. This would be backed up by 27 Air National Guard and 34 Air Reserve groups. It was not to be. By December 1946 the USAAF had dwindled to 55 groups, and of these only 2 were combat-ready.

Fortunately, this runaway diminution of strength was offset in part by the vision that had characterized Hap Arnold. Not a scientist himself, not really able to describe precisely the supersonic aircraft and intercontinental missiles he envisaged, he nonetheless placed tremendous importance on research and development. In November 1944 he named Dr. Theodore von Karman to head an AAF Scientific Advisory Group. It would release its findings in the book *Where We Stand*, followed by publication of a mammoth thirty-three-volume report called *Towards New Horizons*. This was the beginning of an effort that would expand at an ever greater rate, each new scientific breakthrough calling for more experimentation and study. An often overlooked feature of von

The late 1940s were a transitional time for the bomber force, with hundreds of B-29s still available and the new Consolidated B-36 Peacekeeper just coming into service. Design work on the B-36 had begun in 1941, when there was concern that Germany would overrun all of Europe, and would have to be bombed from bases in the United States. Development of the 230-foot-wingspan plane took time, and it did not make its first flight until August 8, 1946. By then a new enemy, Russia, had emerged, and despite strong opposition from the U.S. Navy, almost 400 of the aircraft were procured. The long-range B-36 was 1940s technology, but it did its part in keeping the peace until the last one was withdrawn from SAC on February 12, 1959.

Derived from the XP-80, the Lockheed T-33 became the free world's standard jet trainer.

One method of loading research aircraft planes was this hydraulic lift. The EB-50A mother plane was lifted, and the Bell X-2 research plane was rolled underneath.

Karman's work was his recommendation that the Air Force adopt the German system of providing a single-manager type of organization with adequate resources and funds. This philosophy evolved into the Weapon Systems Project Office method that managed the explosion of advanced developments. Arnold appointed the veteran combat leader Curtis LeMay to be Deputy Chief of Air Staff for Research and Development, a key post that would lay the groundwork for the weapons LeMay would later have at his disposal in the Strategic Air Command.

The USAAF had fought World War II largely with weapons designed before Pearl Harbor, but the pressures that had so vastly expanded production had caused funds to be lavished on research, and a new generation of aircraft was on the drawing boards. This was enriched by the wealth of information captured from the Germans on jet and rocket engines, swept wings, and a thousand other subjects. The natural urge to experiment was accelerated by the nuclear incubus, the knowledge that the Soviet Union would develop an atom bomb of its own, perhaps in ten or fifteen years. In fact, it would be less than five.

Even though consciously trying to reduce spending, Congress continued to think in terms of huge appropriations. Much procurement was still tied to wartime budgets—1944 money was used to purchase 100 B-36s and 498 Lockheed P-80 jet fighters, while 1945 money would buy another 417 P-80s and 100 Republic F-84s. And because home-district factories had to be considered, even the immediate postwar budgets had funds for research and development and for limited production. Yet the collapse in production was terrifying. The country that had been building planes at the rate of 100,000 a year in 1944 ordered only 662 airplanes in 1946 and 769 in 1947.

Ironically, although the USAAF was literally disintegrating in terms of personnel, combat strength, and production capability, a host of new aircraft were emerging, strange shapes and sounds in the sky that would revolutionize air power and carry it beyond anything Douhet, Mitchell, or anyone else had imagined. With their jet engines, swept or delta wings, exotic electronics, and nuclear capability, they were expressions of what Carl Spaatz described as "technical air superiority," an important concept that prevails to this day.

The pace of development was frenetic. In the past engine development had always governed—and limited—improvements in aircraft performance. It took longer to develop reciprocating engines than airframes, and the increment of increase in power was always relatively small. Piston-engine development reached a practical peak during the war with the advent of the huge Pratt and Whitney R-4360, a twenty-eight-cylinder "corn-cob" radial that ultimately produced 3,500 horsepower. The R-4360 and its rival, the Wright R-3350, were complex, and in their early years, trouble-prone. More importantly, it was

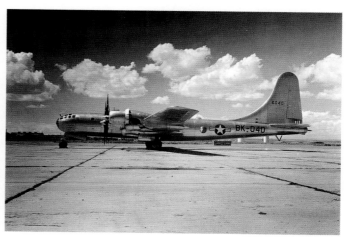

The first operational jet fighter for the USAAF was Lockheed's sleek P-80. The prototype XP-80 flew 143 days after the contract was signed on January 8, 1944; its direct descendant, the T-33, is still flying in several air forces around the world. The P-80 won the first jet-versus-jet combat, shooting down a MiG-15 in Korea. Easy to fly and effective in the ground-support role, the P-80 is yet another example of Kelly Johnson's engineering genius.

The F-84 had a tremendous load-carrying capacity; here it is shown armed with HVARs (High Velocity Aerial Rockets). As with all aircraft, the more weight, the longer the takeoff, and it was jokingly said of the F-84 that if a runway were built around the equator, Republic would build an aircraft that couldn't take off on it.

Loading a tiny research aircraft such as the Bell X-2 into a mother plane was not easy. It had to be rolled into a special pit, and the mother plane, here a B-29, positioned over it. Large nuclear weapons were loaded into B-50 bombers in a similar manner.

evident that further increases in piston-engine power could come only at tremendous expense in power plants that would be prohibitively heavy and extraordinarily complex. As an additional inhibiting factor, propellers were reaching the upper limits of efficiency as their blade tips reached the speed of sound, and no solution was in sight.

The jet engine arrived to save the situation. Jet engines were light, small, and had the great advantage of having only rotary motions to contend with, rather than the pounding oscillations of a reciprocating engine. The development cycle was relatively short, and the power output went up rapidly. Before Frank Whittle in Great Britain and Hans von Ohain in Germany demonstrated their practicability at the end of the 1930s, jet engines were discounted on the basis of high fuel consumption. This disadvantage was partially offset by the fact that jet fuel was both inexpensive and easy to refine compared to aviation gasoline, but few realized how much the relative fuel economy improved at the high altitudes and airspeeds where the jet engine performed best—and piston engines could not match.

To optimize the jet's performance, totally new airframes with pressurized cabins and swept wings had to be designed. These were features of two of the most signficant aircraft in history, the North American F-86 Sabre and the Boeing B-47 Stratojet. Both would have a profound influence on later aircraft design, and both would be of immense political and military importance. They were joined by a host of prototypes of almost every configuration. A few, like the North American B-45 and Northrop F-89, would enter production and serve well; others, like the Convair XP-81 and the Martin XB-51, would make brief appearances only to fail to gain production contracts and quickly slide into oblivion.

One of the unsung heroes of the supersonic flight test program, Chalmers "Slick" Goodlin lowers himself into the hatch of the Bell XS-1, suspended in the bomb bay of a B-29 mother ship. Goodlin made the first powered flight in the second XS-1 produced, No. 6063, on December 9, 1946, experiencing a small engine fire. He also made the first powered flight in the first XS-1, No. 6062, on April 11, 1947.

Piston-engine transport design reached a peak of refinement with the Republic XR-12. Designed by the master, Alexander Kartveli, the gorgeous Rainbow first flew on July 2, 1946. The Air Force decided that the Boeing RB-50 could do the reconnaissance task, and lost interest. In the meantime, Pan American had decided that the forty-passenger Rainbow was too small for its use. The second prototype crashed, while the first was used for artillery practice at the Aberdeen Proving Grounds. It was a sad end for one of the most beautiful airplanes in history.

Surprisingly, some of the foremost proponents of strategic bombing now saw aircraft going the way of coast artillery and the battleship, to be replaced by the ballistic missile. Even the always-outspoken bomber veteran Major General Hugh Knerr, a logistic genius who had survived a career-long quarrel with Hap Arnold, said, "The aerial missile, by whatever means it is delivered [i.e., even if not by an airplane] is the weapon of the Air Force."

And while this strange mixture of a drawdown in strength and a buildup in potential was occurring, another battle was being fought for the long-sought goal of an independent air force.

THE BIRTH OF THE UNITED STATES AIR FORCE

The first legislation for an independent air force had been introduced in March 1916 by Congressman Charles Lieb of Indiana. Over the next twenty-one years there would be more than fifty similar attempts, but it was not until President Harry Truman threw the weight of his office behind the request in 1945 that an independent air force became a certainty. It was still not an easy task. The Navy was adamantly opposed to the idea, out of fear that it would be placed at a political disadvantage in the competition for funds.

The services labored over the next two years to reach an agreement that became the National Security Act of 1947, which provided in part that an independent United States Air Force be established. The official birthday of the Air Force was September 18, 1947, when the first Secretary of the Air Force, W. Stuart Symington, was sworn in. Just eight days later, General Carl Spaatz reached the top of his profession when he became the first USAF Chief of Staff. Spaatz was a three-victory ace in the First World War, and in the Second a combat leader said never to have made a mistake. This tough warrior was also that rarest of commodities, a commander truly beloved by both his subordinates and his English allies—a tribute to his intelligence, fairness, and good common sense.

In his previous capacity as Commanding General of the Army Air Forces, Spaatz had assessed the many detailed studies that had been made and, anticipating eventual independence, had established three functional combat commands: Strategic Air, Tactical Air, and Air Defense. These would remain the Air Force's basic structure until 1979, when the Tactical Air Command absorbed the Air Defense Command. Later, in 1992, in the wake of the monumental reduction of the services following the breakup of the Soviet Union, there would be a further streamlining of the structure.

THE COLD WAR BEGINS

In August 1945, when Japan surrendered, U.S. forces were operating in almost every military theater; two years later, only minor forces remained in Germany,

Japan, and a few strategic outposts. Exhausted as the Soviet Union was, it still had the will to resume both its traditional expansion and its political infiltration into the countries that neighbored it. The most successful American response was economic. The Marshall Plan was created to shore up Europe from Communist aggression, repairing its ravaged economy. Ultimately, more than $20 billion would be sent to revitalize Europe, and additional funds were sent to speed Japan's recovery. In 1947, no one could have predicted that American aid would succeed so well in strengthening Europe to resist the Soviet Union's tendency to expand. And certainly no one could have predicted that forty-five years later another $20 billion in aid would be required, this time for the preservation of the remnants of the dissolved Soviet Union.

Earlier, on March 5, 1946, Winston Churchill had proclaimed that an Iron Curtain had descended across the continent, "from Stettin in the Baltic to Trieste in the Adriatic." The curtain was soon extended to Romania and Czechoslovakia, and by April 1948 the Soviet Union prepared to test the will of the United States by blockading Berlin.

Hitler's proud capital had been reduced to rubble by Allied bombing and Russian artillery shells. Now it was completely surrounded by the Russian zone of occupation and divided into an East Berlin dominated by the Soviet Union, and a West Berlin occupied by France, Great Britain, and the United States. The Soviet Union wanted the Western Allies to leave the city, and progressively restricted road and rail traffic until June 22, 1948 (the seventh anniversary of the Nazi invasion of Russia), when all barge, rail, and highway traffic was halted. The Russians had thirty full-strength army divisions in their zone, the Allies only a few weak divisions. There could be no question of a ground battle.

But the U.S. Military Governor, General Lucius D. Clay, and his British and French counterparts, dared to stay and to supply the 2 million German citizens with the necessities of life by an airlift through the three air corridors that led from Allied areas into Berlin. Clay telephoned Major General LeMay, now Commanding General of the U.S. Air Forces in Europe and asked, "Curt, can you transport coal by air?"

Nonplussed, LeMay asked him to repeat the question, and replied, "Sir, the Air Force can deliver anything." LeMay then threw together a scratch unit of the ubiquitous C-47s flown by behind-the-lines pilots, and on June 26, airlifted 80 tons of supplies into the city. It was soon determined that Berlin required 4,500 tons of essential supplies daily, and a major undertaking code-named Operation Vittles got underway.

The new Air Force Chief of Staff, tall, lean, athletic Hoyt Vandenberg—the youngest full general since Ulysses S. Grant—threw the weight of his service's resources behind the effort, culling planes and crews from all over the world, including two groups of B-29s. These were sent to England without atomic weapons—the USAF's "equalizers" as Vandenberg called them—but the Soviet Union understood the message. Vandenberg also saw to it that

TOP LEFT:
German children understood from the start that where the Americans had once used four-engine aircraft to destroy Berlin, they were now using them to save it. Some pilots would drop candy via parachutes.

TOP RIGHT:
German crews worked eagerly and willingly to unload the C-54s. The principal cargo was coal; food was second most important.

seventy-two Military Air Transport System C-54s were brought into the operation, along with the necessary support staff. By July 31, 2,000 tons a day were being transported, less than half the requirement, but still enough to make the Russians increase their harassment tactics—jamming radios and buzzing with fighters.

LeMay was a brilliant combat commander, but there was an airlift specialist waiting in the wings, Major General William C. Tunner, who had done a masterful job flying over the Himalayas during World War II. Using thirteen bases in India and six in China, Tunner had delivered up to 72,000 tons a month to China in the biggest, most successful airlift operation in history.

Tunner came in five weeks after the start of the Berlin airlift and regularized it, laying down an operational system that functioned as much like a conveyor belt as an airline. As soon as possible, he selected the Douglas C-54 as the airplane of choice (he would eventually have 319 of them at work), and he prescribed the routes, altitudes, and airspeeds that the planes would fly.

Flying from bases at Wiesbaden, Rhein-Main, Fassberg, and Celle, the airplanes cruised at 170 mph, with 500-foot altitude separation and a three-minute interval between aircraft to land, at Gatow, Tempelhof, and later, Tegel. The three-minute interval allowed 480 landings every twenty-four hours at Tempelhof and Gatow; day and night, a plane landed or took off every ninety seconds, until the airlift began to wind down.

Tunner sought to reduce ground time with new procedures and by forbidding the air crews to leave their planes when they landed; instead, refreshments, flight clearances, and weather information were brought directly to them, as German civilians competed to off-load the supplies. One twelve-man German crew unloaded 12,500 pounds of coal in five minutes, forty-five seconds, a record that won a precious pack of cigarettes per man. Refueling time was cut from thirty-three to eight minutes, and ground time was reduced to thirty minutes. If either weather or mechanical malfunction interfered with their landings,

the C-54 pilots were instructed to pull up and return to their start point. Nothing was allowed to interfere with the seamless landing, off-loading, take-off sequence.

Tunner insisted on standardization in everything from preflight briefings to piloting. He issued an edict that he would reduce to copilot any pilot who failed to land with a ceiling and visibility *greater* than 400 feet and one mile, and would court-martial any who landed with a ceiling and visibility *less* than 400 feet and one mile. All traffic was strictly controlled, with an increasingly expert Ground Controlled Approach (GCA) system available for landings in bad weather.

The routine was hard on both planes and pilots. The C-54s had their origin in the 1940 Douglas DC-4 passenger airliner, designed to take off at high gross weights, cruise for several hours burning off fuel, and then land. In Berlin, hauling everything from fuel to macaroni, they were landing almost 20,000 pounds over the landing weight of the original design. Engines, brakes, and tires were worn terribly in the process. Coal was the major cargo, and its abrasive dust seeped into the aircraft and engines, causing major problems. A huge maintenance facility was established at Burtonwood, England, while Erding in Germany provided routine supply and maintenance. Every 1,000 flying hours, the C-54s were returned to the United States for complete overhaul.

The system worked, and on April 15, 1,398 aircraft brought in 12,940.9 tons of goods, a performance that impressed the stoic Russians; the blockade was lifted at one minute after midnight on May 12. The airlift continued, phasing down in the process, and finally terminated on September 30, 1949, one month ahead of the scheduled closing date. It had delivered a total of 2,325,000 tons of food, fuel, and supplies to Berlin. U.S. aircraft had flown 189,963 flights, in 586,827 hours, for 92,061,863 miles.

Amazingly enough, the operation had been fairly safe, with the accident rate only half that of the entire Air Force. There had been twelve crashes, in which thirty-one Americans lost their lives. In monetary terms, the entire operation cost the United States just under $200 million. In political terms, the Cold War's first crisis had been overcome by American resolve, and without the use of weapons.

THE GROWTH OF THE STRATEGIC AIR COMMAND

Reinforced by the assessment of the United States Strategic Bombing Survey, as well as the comments of leaders of both Germany and Japan, the United States Air Force was convinced that strategic bombardment was more than the essential key to victory; with a nuclear capability, it was the key to world peace.

When the Strategic Air Command was established in 1946, it was but a shadow of the USAAF at its peak. General George C. Kenney, the victor of the Pacific air war, was named head of the command, and he found that he had only nine bombardment groups and two fighter groups at his disposal. His B-29s did not have intercontinental range, nor did they have more than a token nuclear capability.

However, Kenney became occupied with advocating the independent air force, rather than with whipping what came to be known as SAC into shape. It stumbled along, ill-equipped, poorly manned, and virtually untrained for two years, until the Soviet seizure of Czechoslovakia in April 1948. Then, President Truman clearly defined the nature of the Cold War emergency by citing Russia as the potential enemy. The blockade of Berlin had dispelled all doubts about Stalin's intentions, and there was never any possibility of fielding an army that could match the Soviet bloc's in size. The answer was air power, and the answer to air power was LeMay.

Probably no leader in modern history had the personal impact on his command that Curtis LeMay did on the Strategic Air Command. By intellect, force of will, and unrelenting energy, he imprinted the command with his personal style, changing it from what had become essentially an expensive flying club into the single greatest instrument of war that the world had ever known. It is not an understatement to say that LeMay personally was the architect of the instruments of what has been called the *Pax Americana*, and he built his command at the time of greatest possible peril. Yet it speaks to the growing sophistication and complexity of the Air Force management systems that when LeMay became Chief of Staff in 1961, he was unable to imprint himself upon the entire service as he had done so indelibly with SAC. It was not that LeMay was in any way diminished; rather, it was that within the Pentagon, the bureaucracy could stifle any man, even one of LeMay's titanic force. An era had ended, and neither LeMay nor any of his able successors was able to impart a personal style on the entire Air Force as had the early leaders like Mitchell, Arnold, and Spaatz.

LeMay was utterly dismayed with his new command in 1948, and immediately set about conforming it to his own vision of a striking force, one that would defend against any potential atomic attack by being so powerful that it would be capable of delivering an annihilating blow to any enemy. This was essentially the same philosophy by which England had ruled the seas for two centuries, and LeMay was convinced it was now the only defense possible for the United States. To make his task easier, he brought in as his deputy a man whose name described him perfectly, the autocratic Major General Thomas Power.

The two men set about their work with skill and passion, determined to create a force that would be ready to go to war on an instant's notice. LeMay instituted a program of intensified training and evaluation that has been continuously refined to this day, but flight crews were far from his only concern. He established the same high criteria for every aspect of SAC life, including maintenance, logistics, weather reporting—everything. In some areas legislative and budgetary considerations impeded his progress. Family housing was unsatisfactory at many bases, and was reflected in the number of officers and men who chose to leave the service rather than subject their families to the strain of the substandard living conditions of SAC.

The September 23, 1949, disclosure of the Russian explosion of an atomic bomb lent increased urgency to LeMay's efforts. By 1950 the results began to be evident. SAC now had 962 tactical aircraft, with jet bombers about to enter the inventory. It had just demonstrated its reach with the flight of the Boeing B-50 "Lucky Lady II" nonstop around the world using in-flight refueling. LeMay's confidence in his people increased to the point that he initiated on-the-spot promotions for exceptional crew members. For the first time since he took command of SAC, LeMay felt that he had forged a weapon that could preserve the peace through nuclear deterrence.

And then he was ordered to send his units to war in Korea, to fight with conventional bombs.

THE FORGOTTEN WAR

The UN-mandated "police action" in Korea has often and correctly been called the "forgotten war" for a variety of reasons. Foremost, it was the first war that the United States did not pursue to victory, electing instead to enter protracted armistice negotiations. Not before, during, or after the war did we have a strong interest in Korea, other than its proximity to Japan, and we had no desire to either enter a land campaign against Red China or start an atomic conflict with the Soviet Union. There were other considerations as well. World War II had ended, and people were eager to get on with their lives in an economy showing the first signs of a boom.

An odd side aspect of aviation history is that although America clearly won the air war in Korea, that fact has also been forgotten. Few now remember

Development of the P-80 into a two-place interceptor, the F-94, began in 1949. An afterburning Pratt & Whitney J48 engine was installed in the F-94C, and the nose was modified to hold twenty-four 2.75-inch rockets. A pod with twelve additional rockets could be carried on each wing. The F-94 enjoyed a ten-year career in Air Force and Air National Guard units, not being retired until 1959.

Having learned how essential escort fighters were in World War II, the USAF tried desperately to find a way to provide protection for bombers in the jet age. As no jet fighter had the range required, a number of experiments were tried with "parasite" fighters especially designed to be carried by the bomber and released for defense purposes over enemy territory. This is the McDonnell XF-85 Goblin, a tiny aircraft that mercifully never entered production.

the utterly valiant work done by the crews flying World War II equipment under some of the worst weather and operating conditions in history to save the UN forces from both tactical and strategic defeat. Night after night the aging Douglas B-26s would skim through the black, narrow valleys destroying North Korean traffic. War-weary B-29s bombed endlessly, by day when they could, by night when jet fighter opposition made it necessary, but missing operations on only a score of days throughout the entire war. Even less well known are the critically important efforts of the Combat Cargo Command, which used a motley collection of Curtiss C-46s and Douglas C-47s before more modern—and more demanding—Fairchild C-119s were available. They hauled troops in and evacuees out and carried ton after ton of cargo where no roads reached. Ancient F-51s, some literally pulled from cosmoline storage, *saved* the war at Pusan after their twin-brother F-82s had scored initial victories. The ground troops were grateful to the L-19 and T-6 Mosquitos, the Forward Air Control aircraft whose pilots would get down in the weeds with the infantry to offset the enemy's numerical superiority. Innovation was the order of the day. When the B-26s couldn't get adequate flares for their night-bombing work, C-47 "Lightning Bugs" were loaded with Navy Mark VIII pyrotechnics that worked like a charm, giving four to five minutes of near-daylight illumination in which the B-26s could strafe and bomb.

All this has been overlooked, but the jet war is remembered, particularly the duels between swept-wing North American F-86s and MiG-15s in that triangular corner south of the Yalu River called MiG Alley. The scale was smaller than in World War II, but its importance was just as crucial: the preservation of air superiority. Yet in still another inversion of common practice, it was the sustained killing power of obsolete ground attack airplanes

The speed of jet fighters made jet bomber development vital. The North American B-45 was the first American production jet bomber, and as an essential interim step, used piston-engine design philosophy. Equipped with four General Electric J47 engines, the straight-wing B-45 had a maximum speed of 579 mph. The B-45 did not have ejection seats, and was a difficult aircraft from which to bail out; consequently members of the four-man crews were not entirely comfortable with it. A reconnaissance version, the RB-45C, saw service in Korea.

The first aircraft to gain a U.S. victory in the Korean War was a North American F-82 Twin Mustang, shooting down a North Korean Yak-9 fighter. Essentially two lengthened P-51H fuselages joined by a new center wing section and tailplane, the F-82 served as a long-range escort fighter and a night-fighter. On February 28, 1947, Lieutenant Colonel Bob Thacker (now a master radio-control model builder) and Lieutenant John Ard flew Betty Joe nonstop from Honolulu to New York, taking 14 hours, 31 minutes, 50 seconds to cover the 4,968-mile distance.

After World War II, 2,068 AT-6 aircraft were modified to become AT-6Gs for use in the pilot-training program, which began to expand rapidly after the start of the Korean War. If you could fly the T-6, you could fly anything. Some T-6s saw service in Korea as Mosquitos, flying as forward air controllers.

and bombers that permitted the reestablishment of bases for the F-86s. Of this, more later.

A DIVIDED KOREA

At the end of World War II, Korea, ruled ruthlessly by Japan for more than forty years, was divided at the 38th parallel as a convenient way to accept the surrender of Japanese forces. The Soviet Union created the People's Democratic Republic of Korea, under Chinese control, north of the parallel. South of the parallel, free elections were held to establish the Republic of Korea. Two separate political trends were established, each reflected in their military postures.

In South Korea, all of the occupying U.S. troops except for a small advisory force had left by July 1949. In contrast, China had provided North Korea not only with training but with many regular army units hardened in the long Chinese civil war just ended. The Soviet Union equipped the North Korean army and navy with first-rate weapons. The North Korean air force, however, was ill equipped with about 160 aircraft, including 62 IL-10 Sturmovik and 70 Yak-3 and Yak-7B piston-engine fighters.

On June 25, 1950, the North Korean army swarmed over the 38th parallel in a march to the sea, intending to conquer and annex South Korea. The USAF's first task was to cover the evacuation of American dependents by surface vessel from the port of Inchon. North American F-82s from the 8th Fighter-Bomber Wing at Itazuke, Japan, were assigned the job. On a similar mission two days later, the F-82s were covering the aerial evacuation of 851 civilians from airfields near Seoul airfield when five North Korean Yak fighters attacked. Three of the Yaks were quickly shot down, First Lieutenant William G. Hudson getting the first, to open one of the most difficult campaigns in U.S. history.

The South Korean army, outnumbered, poorly trained, and ill equipped, collapsed. Even as he solicited United Nations approval, President Truman ordered the old war-horse General Douglas MacArthur to take the necessary military action to defend Korea. Keenly aware of how long it would take to get American ground forces into action, MacArthur called on the Far Eastern Air Force (FEAF) to hit the North Koreans with everything they had for the next thirty-six hours.

The Douglas B-26 served again in Vietnam, doing night interdiction work, just as it had in Korea. This restored example was originally an A-26B.

It wasn't much. Eight combat squadrons were sent into action, two of Douglas B-26 light bombers, two of twin-Mustang F-82, and four of F-80s. Their targets were anything of military value from Seoul north to the 38th parallel. B-29s from Okinawa soon joined in, and for the next six days these minimal forces prevented a Dunkirk for American forces. The sheer momentum of the North Korean attack had compressed the remnants of the Republic of Korea's army and the slowly building U.S. contingent in the perimeter around Pusan. Against 150,000 North Korean troops, organized into thirteen rifle divisions, a tank brigade, a mechanized division, and a tank division, were pitted four American divisions, five badly mauled and demoralized Republic of Korea divisions, and a Marine brigade.

Because jet fighters were unable to operate from the unimproved South Korean airfields, six squadrons of the venerable North American F-51s were introduced, refugees from storage depots. Squadrons that had just converted to F-80 jets found themselves going into combat with Mustangs on a day's notice. Working with Forward Air Controllers flying North American L-17s (Navions), the F-51s were launched time and again to keep the North Korean forces in check. F-80s continued to operate from Japan, flying at the very limits of their range, and returning to Japan with absolutely minimum fuel.

The pace of the air war increased steadily. The Fifth Air Force, led by Major General Earle C. Partridge, demonstrated the flexibility of air power by its quick reaction to target changes, sometimes diverting a mission en route in response to an Army request. The Eighth Army Commander, Lieutenant General Walton H. Walker, later stated for the record that he could not have stayed in Korea without the Fifth Air Force's support.

The tide turned rapidly. On July 24, General MacArthur had assumed the duties of Commander in Chief, United Nations Command, and on September 15 he launched his daring Inchon invasion, which began the rout of North Korean forces.

Inchon was in many ways reminiscent of June 6, 1944, D-day in France. Lieutenant General George E. Stratemeyer, a genial collegiate type despite his

The marvelous Grumman SA-16 Albatross entered service with the USAF in 1948, and served in a variety of search and rescue roles. Tough, and able to land and take off in seas that would swamp another amphibian, the Albatross saved many lives in peace and war. Its superb characteristics came not so much from technical advances, although it was thoroughly modern, but instead from the high standards of quality that were a Grumman Aircraft Engineering Corporation tradition.

The Douglas C-124 was a development of the earlier C-74, in turn a development of the C-54. This, the C-74 prototype, was distinguished by an unusual "bug-eye" cockpit canopy that Douglas had used (without success) on its XB-43 jet bomber. Only fourteen were built, and they had a conventional canopy. Curiously, the more massive C-124, with basically the same power, cruised at 230 mph, some 35 mph faster than the smaller C-74.

years of tough combat command experience, first directed his Far Eastern Air Force to fly aerial reconnaissance (in part to determine the high- and low-tide heights of the sea walls that would have to be scaled), then to begin an interdiction campaign to take out enemy rail lines, bridges, and tunnels to isolate the area. U.S. fighters roamed over North Korean airfields to suppress the enemy fighters and then launched a massive resupply effort as the UN troops moved inland. The Navy and Marines provided the close air support for the invasion.

Meanwhile, in a coordinated effort in the south, B-29s laid down a carpet bombing attack that helped the Eighth Army break out of the bridgehead at Pusan and sweep north. The weather began to clear and the Fifth Air Force mounted more and more close support sorties, using rockets and napalm to break Communist resistance. Mosquitos, T-6 trainers used as Forward Air Control aircraft, worked directly with U.S. ground forces to counter the heavy enemy tank attacks.

An almost unheralded parallel effort was the successful strategic bombing campaign, in which the Far Eastern Air Force Bomber Command in a single month used its B-29s to destroy North Korea's capacity to support its troops in the field. It was a tribute to the methods LeMay had instilled in his crews. (When Chinese aerial opposition stiffened, the B-29s turned to night bombing, and carried on for the remainder of the war, ultimately dropping 167,100 tons of bombs in 21,328 combat sorties, a major effort by a force that never exceeded 100 aircraft.)

One of the most successful parachute operations in history helped bottle

up the retreating Communist forces. On October 20, 1950, seventy-one C-119s and forty C-47s of General William Tunner's new Combat Cargo Command dropped 2,860 paratroopers and 300 tons of equipment to straddle the main roads north of Pyonyang. General MacArthur was airborne in his own aircraft to watch the operation. Backed by savage air support, the paratroopers startled the North Korean troops so badly that they fled their strongly fortified positions. The paratroopers of the 187th Regimental Combat team killed an estimated 2,700 of the 6,000 troops they engaged, and took another 3,000 prisoners.

The North Korean forces were routed, pursued by elements of the Eighth Army that were being supplied almost totally by airlift. United Nations ground forces followed them beyond the 38th parallel, despite warnings from the Chinese that they would intervene. In a series of events of which Desert Storm would be reminiscent forty-one years later, the United States interpreted its UN mandate to repel the North Korean invasion and restore peace to the area as authority to pursue military operations above the 38th parallel. General MacArthur assured President Truman that the Chinese would not intervene, basing his assumptions in part on the fact that the "Chinese had no air force."

It was a fateful, near-fatal conclusion.

MIG ALLEY

The Chinese did exactly what they said they were going to do, but on a far greater scale than anyone had envisaged. The initial Chinese intervention was

ABOVE LEFT:

The venerable Douglas B-26 was a main-stay of interdiction in Korea. Bombers from the 452d Light Bomb Wing used the "Y" intersection in these railroad tracks as an aiming point for their napalm bombs. Developed late in World War II, napalm proved devastating in Korea.

ABOVE TOP:

Helicopters came of age during the 1950s, gaining engine power that gave them sufficient range and altitude capability to work anywhere in the world. The Piasecki H-21 Workhorse lived up to its name. Shown here at Goose Air Base, Labrador, it was used for resupply of remote radar warning stations. Later it was armed with machine guns for combat in Vietnam.

ABOVE BOTTOM:

The H-21 was used in even greater numbers as a rescue aircraft.

The North American F-86 in a painting by William Phillips. The F-86 was one of the best-loved fighters in the history of the Air Force—technically advanced, but still small enough to be a delight to fly.

by air, as first piston-engine fighters, then swept-wing jets—MiG-15s—attacked American aircraft. The first all-jet battle in history took place on November 8, 1950, when F-80s of the 51st Fighter Interceptor Wing were jumped by MiG-15s. The F-80s were clearly outclassed by the MiGs, a brilliant design that combined Russian and German technology with a derivative of the Rolls Royce Nene jet engine the British had sold to Russia a few years previously. Even so, first blood went to the Americans, when Lieutenant Russell J. Brown downed a MiG-15.

The MiGs represented a real threat to air superiority. If employed in sufficient numbers, they would unquestionably drive the UN aircraft from the air at the time of greatest need, for more and more Chinese troops had crossed the border, and the UN forces were being roughly thrown back.

Orders began to come from MacArthur's headquarters that would be echoed one war later in Vietnam. To slow the oncoming Chinese reinforcements, the General wanted the bridges across the Yalu destroyed, but only the portions on Korean territory. There was to be no violation of Manchurian territory or airspace. As a result, the bombers had to make their runs parallel to the river, exposed for the greatest length of time not only to antiaircraft fire but also to Russian-built—and probably Russian-flown—fighters that would circle at altitude, then make a diving attack across the Yalu through the bomber formations before streaking back to safety.

Fortunately, the MiGs were not aggressive, and there was time to bring in

the 4th Fighter Interceptor wing of F-86 Sabres from the United States. On December 17, Lieutenant Colonel Bruce Hinton of the 336th Squadron scored the first of his unit's four victories over MiGs that day.

Less well known, but perhaps even more important, was the arrival of the 27th Fighter Escort Wing of straight-wing Republic F-84 Thunderjets. As the Eighth Army fought its desperate retreat, sometimes the only thing that changed destruction to escape was the timely appearance of the Thunderjets, laden with rockets, napalm, and bombs. The F-80s of the 49th Group made the waters of the Chongchon River literally run red with the blood of Chinese infantry. Air attacks accounted for more than 33,000 Chinese dead by the end of December.

So overwhelming was the Chinese strength—estimated at over 500,000 men—that they pushed on past Seoul, overrunning the F-86 bases and forcing the Sabres' return to Japan. With their short, 490-mile range, the early-model Sabres were thus temporarily out of the war. The Chinese had inverted doctrine, gaining air superiority through controlling the airfields. At once, they began stockpiling huge quantities of MiGs in the Manchurian sanctuary, so that they could be brought down into Korea for the final push.

However, the continual attrition by air attack and stubborn ground defenses had bled the Red army and by January, General Lin Pao, commander of the enemy Fourth Field Army, realized that his attack had failed. As vast as his numbers were, he was unable to progress against the UN forces, and he

Three pilots of the 49th Fighter Bomber Wing who have just completed an F-84 mission deep behind enemy lines. Going to war no longer meant just donning a white scarf and goggles; F-84 pilots were encumbered with hard hats, parachutes, G-suits, survival kits, side arms, first-aid supplies, navigation kits—the list went on and on—all this for a mission that rarely exceeded two hours.

The mark of a good basic design is the amount of "stretch" in it—its potential for variation. The straight-wing Republic F-84 was developed into the highly successful F-84F and RF-84F, which used about 60 percent of the original aircraft's parts and tooling. Called the Thunderstreak by public affairs types and Lead Sled by pilots, the F models had larger engines, swept wings, and upgraded equipment.

A formation flight of P-80s, speed brakes deployed to slow them down.

200

informed a visiting delegation that the failure of the Chinese offensive was due to a lack of Chinese air support.

The UN forces' counterattack drove the Red army forces back far enough that air bases could be reestablished for F-86s, and the air war in MiG Alley resumed, still with almost every condition advantageous to the Communists. Flying from bases in the Manchurian sanctuary, the MiGs could choose the time and place of attacks. The F-86s were operating at the limit of their range, and had only a few minutes to spend on station. There were about 300 MiGs available against 90 to 127 F-86s, although these were nominal strengths, with probably no more than half available operationally on either side at a given moment. The F-86 was considered superior to the MiGs in most respects. The MiGs had a higher ceiling and a better rate of climb, but the Sabres had better armament and were better gun platforms.

At the start of the conflict, the Sabre F-86 pilots were generally more experienced, but as time went on, new pilots right out of flying school joined the F-86 units, some firing their guns for the first time in combat. On the whole, however, the USAF training and spirit were superior to that of the Communists, who were only occasionally aggressive. In the end, the figures told the story: 792 MiGs were shot down, at the cost of 78 F-86s, a ten-to-one ratio that was to breed a costly degree of overconfidence in the next war.

Perhaps the most important use of air power in Korea was diplomatic. As the peace negotiations at Panmunjom dragged on, apparently unending and unendable, Air Force Chief of Staff Hoyt Vandenberg began pressing for more extensive action. At the same time, John Foster Dulles let the Chinese know through Indian Prime Minister Jawaharlal Nehru that America was frustrated enough to use atomic weapons in Manchuria. Vandenberg authorized the transferral of nuclear weapons to Okinawa, in preparation for the time when they might be used. The Chinese got the message, and peace negotiations accelerated.

The effects of the bitter "police action" in Korea lingered on in the Air Force. For the first time in American history, it was recognized by both the Congress and the public that a permanent professional military establishment of huge proportions was going to have to be maintained. Korea was the training ground for the USAF, endowing a professional force with the degree of discipline that had existed during World War II and was being reestablished in the Strategic Air Command. In the next decade the Air Force would triple in size, and as it did so would add an entirely new dimension to its capability—the intercontinental ballistic missile. That would be air power's first tentative step toward becoming space power.

THE COLD WAR INTENSIFIES

The Strategic Air Command built up its strength at an incredible rate. For many years, its mainstay was the ten-engine Convair B-36, huge and ponderous but with the range and altitude capability to reach any target in Russia. These were first supplemented with almost 2,000 B-47s, which were then superseded by a mixture of the long-lived B-52 and the shorter-lived but beautiful supersonic Convair B-58.

The Boeing B-47, first flown in 1947, took four years of development before it entered operational service. There were only 12 in the fleet in 1951, but the numbers grew rapidly, from 329 in 1953 to 1,533 in 1958. The B-47, with its in-flight refueling capability, gave SAC an intercontinental weapon of overpowering might. In its early years it was virtually invulnerable to interception. I well recall flying it in an orbital pattern, trying to let contemporary Air Force interceptors climb high and fast enough to catch us. In the event of a Communist invasion of Europe, the USAF war plan called for a concerted attack on the Soviet Union, described by former Secretary of the Air Force Thomas K. Finletter as the "front-to-rear concept," in which the fleet of B-47s would roll up all targets from the borders back to the sources of production and governmental direction. A six-day attack would have left the Russian armies to wither in the field, their homeland demolished. United States losses would have been relatively low.

There was no invasion of Europe because the Soviet Union was well aware of the B-47's capabilities. Yet the B-47 was a curious mixture of old and new technologies. Its swept wings and jet engines would point the way to future bombers and to the entire fleet of jet transports that now unite the world, but its structure was based on older technology that did not lend itself to the stresses of high-speed, high-altitude flight. Metal fatigue was an early and con-

Convair expanded on its delta-wing theme to create the world's first supersonic bomber, the B-58 Hustler. It was an utterly original design, with a bomb load carried in an external pod rather than internally, and with panels of bonded honeycomb sandwich skin to resist heat. The B-58 had no peer anywhere in the world from the time of its first flight on March 1, 1956, to its final retirement in January 1970. Its career was cut short by a combination of factors, including high operating costs and a very high accident rate—out of 104 aircraft built, 25 were lost.

The competition for a jet bomber to fulfill the B-29's role was intense. Convair submitted the aesthetically beautiful XB-46; it was elegantly styled but conservative, and was discounted early in the competition.

The tradition of Martin bombers reached back to the GMB of World War I, and the firm was anxious to reestablish itself in the jet age. Its offering, the six-jet XB-48, was less conservative than the XB-46, but handicapped by a high-drag engine installation. Martin had developed the bicycle-type landing gear, which was also being used on the Boeing XB-47.

The most radical of the competing bombers was Northrop's YB-49, an eight-jet development of the YB-35. Its low-drag design also had an extremely low radar signature, a fact not fully appreciated until many years later when the Northrop B-2 appeared.

The furor over the Northrop bombers was academic, for the Boeing XB-47 was clearly the most outstanding bomber in the competition by a very large margin. It had everything—speed, range (with in-flight refueling), altitude capability, and perhaps most important of all, Boeing's long history of success with heavy bombers. The XB-47 was the most important jet bomber in history because of its own primacy with SAC, its fostering of the follow-on B-52, and its siring of the 707/KC-135 series. Among its advanced features were swept-wing (first on a production bomber), suspended-pod engine installation, bicycle gear, drag and brake parachutes, and a small crew—only three men.

The Northrop firm was elated when a production contract for thirty-six jet YB-49s was awarded in 1948. The protracted difficulties in the B-35 and B-49 flight test program resulted in the cancellation of the contract in 1949, and only one YRB-49A was completed. The two jet engines in pods under the wings degraded the flying wing's streamlining.

Built before the days of computer-enhanced stability augmentation systems, the Northrop wings lacked stability, and were not a good bombing platform. Vertical surfaces were added, departing somewhat from Jack Northrop's vision of a pure flying wing.

One of the saddest events in aviation history. Eleven of the fifteen large flying wings manufactured are shown here in an open-air production line. These are YB-35s being converted to YB-49 configuration. All of these aircraft were cut up and disposed of, destroyed on the direct orders of the Secretary of the Air Force, Stuart Symington. The order led to years of controversy, in which Jack Northrop and his adherents charged that a political conspiracy had forced cancellation of the flying wing.

Part of the Boeing brain trust that developed the B-47 bomber. From the left: George Schairer, Edward C. Wells, George Martin, and Robert Jewett. They were proud of the design, without knowing that it would pay the way for Boeing's domination of the commercial jetliner market for decades to come.

205

Painted black for its night-fighter role, the F-82 assumes an almost sinister look.

A B-47B flown by the author with the 4925th Test Group (Atomic) at Kirtland Air Force Base, New Mexico. This was one of the few remaining B models that had long bomb-bay doors.

Originally designed as a high-altitude bomber, the B-52 was versatile enough to undertake the low-level roll.

tinuing problem with the B-47s, and they were soon phased out in favor of a larger aircraft, the Boeing B-52, the "long rifle" of SAC. Like the B-47, it was intended to be a high-altitude nuclear bomber, one that would streak in alone to take out a city. Fortunately, the only wartime use of the B-52 was in a non-nuclear capacity, when it carried "iron bombs" in both the Vietnam and the Persian Gulf wars.

The biggest change in the mission, capability, and psychology of the Air Force came about as a result of a directive from President Eisenhower in September 1955 to give the intercontinental ballistic missile top priority. With development, the size of the hydrogen bomb had been reduced so that it was now feasible to build a missile with a 5,000-mile range. The reduction in size also meant that a new family of tactical weapons could be developed to be carried by fighter bombers. Suddenly, the Tactical Air Command—and the carrier-borne aircraft of the Navy—saw a whole new world of missions open up.

Since 1946, the USAF had been developing nuclear-capable, long-range pilotless aircraft, the Northrop SM-62 Snark and the North American SM-64 Navaho. In 1946 work had also begun on an ICBM when Convair created the MX-774, an innovative extrapolation of German V-2 technology. The MX-774 fell to the postwar budget cuts, and the development of pilotless aircraft was dropped, for they were as subject to the improved Russian defenses as manned aircraft. (Snark advocates had maintained its development until it became operational in February 1961, only to be withdrawn from service in June of the same year.)

BOTTOM LEFT:
The Northrop SM-62A Snark program was more ambitious than successful. The world's first intercontinental missile program, it ran from 1946 to 1957, and may better exxemplify the results of advocacy than missile performance. Technically the Snark was highly advanced, using a stellar-inertial guidance system, swept wings, and J57 turbojet engine. Two solid-rocket boost motors, each of 130,000 pounds thrust, hurled the Snark from zero-length launchers. Completely air transportable, it is here being disgorged from a Douglas C-124. In the background is the unusual French Breguet 763 Provence double-decker transport.

BOTTOM RIGHT:
The Air Force pursued the pilotless guided missile, but never as strongly as the development of bombers or ICBMs. About 1,000 supersonic Martin B-61 Matadors came into inventory between 1951 and their retirement in 1966. Able to carry 3,000 pounds of conventional or nuclear explosives, the Matador had a range of about 500 miles.

207

At the same time the USAF was building up an air force both to fight the Korean War and to maintain a strategic deterrence, it was also developing an incredible intercontinental ballistic missile force. In the process of doing so, it fielded an armada of liquid-fueled Atlas missiles as an interim step even as it was preparing a second generation of more reliable, more accurate Minuteman missiles. It was a triumph of management as well as engineering.

The offensive strategy of the Soviet Union was always based on the concept of a first strike by their intercontinental missiles. The new U.S. missiles, solid-fueled and launched from silos, presented the Soviet Union with an unsolvable problem, for the fleet of Minutemen could almost instantly be launched upon notice of a Soviet attack. The situation was called MAD—mutually assured destruction—and it deterred nuclear war.

Even as the Boeing B-47 fleet was building into a tremendous force, the Strategic Air Command called for a replacement. General Curtis LeMay wanted an aircraft much larger and more capable than the B-47, one that would have the capacity to grow over the years. Boeing responded with the B-52 prototype. While the aerodynamics were similar, the B-52 had vastly more sophisticated structure and equipment. The B-17, regarded as a sky giant when it was rolled out, is here dwarfed by the YB-52, which made its first flight on April 15, 1952.

Once again a handful of individual leaders came together, this time to create a viable ICBM program. The new group included politicians, civil servants, military leaders, and members of industry. A young man described by colleagues as both a "sparkplug who did a tremendous job in expediting the development of the missile" and an irascible, cold, unpleasant bastard, was Trevor Gardner, a Special Assistant for Research and Development to Secretary of the Air Force Harold Talbot. In 1953 Gardner recruited an illustrious ten-man committee to study the problem of nuclear missiles, including among others Chairman John von Neumann, Clark B. Millikan, Simon Ramo, and a lean young colonel, Bernard A. Schriever. All were distinguished and hard-working.

Radar listening posts in Turkey had established that the Soviet Union had a lead in the missile program, and Gardner pushed the acceleration of the Convair Atlas. A systems engineering concept was essential, one in which all of the elements of a weapon system, including design, testing, production, training, logistics, deployment, and maintenance, were considered simultaneously and analyzed continuously. Because of the urgency of what in the later election contest between John F. Kennedy and Richard M. Nixon became known as the "missile gap," there was a tremendous amount of concurrence in the development of the Atlas, and concomitantly, a tremendous amount of risk. The project was blessed by a series of advances in key areas—structure, control, reentry—and the result was an operational Atlas missile capability by 1959.

As with the B-47 and B-52, SAC's buildup in missile strength proceeded rapidly. By 1961 there were twenty missile squadrons, including Atlas, Titan, and Minuteman units, although the latter two did not yet have missiles in place. But the liquid-fueled Atlas and Titan ICBMs, first-generation missiles, had reliability problems, and the quick introduction of the Minuteman solid-fuel ICBM placed the entire arsenal on a new, higher plane. The first Minuteman unit of ten missiles became operational on October 24, 1962, at the time of the Cuban missile crisis.

The missile force was to the Air Force what the Air Service had been to the Army—a newfangled branch of service that both required and elicited a different type of individual for service. Despite the importance of their demanding jobs, missile crews did not feel that they had the respect flight crews commanded, and they knew they did not have the flight pay. It took years of conscious effort to overcome the second-class-citizen syndrome of the missile force, a feeling heightened by the remote locations of most missile stations.

THE SERIES OF CRISES

The Cold War began to flash hot with terrifying frequency. Among the dozen aircraft that were attacked and destroyed by Soviet MiGs were SAC "snoopers," ferret aircraft that probed the enemy electronic capability, including a B-29 in 1952, an RB-47E in 1960, and B-66A in 1964. We now know that many crew members survived these attacks, only to be imprisoned in Soviet gulags or psychiatric hospitals. The reconnaissance mission was a deadly game of cat-and-mouse, each side learning from the other, and it would lead to surveillance from U-2s, SR-71s, and satellites.

Even more serious were the political games of other countries, games that occasionally erupted into war. In 1956 SAC had gone on alert when the English, French, and Israelis had invaded Egypt after the nationalization of the Suez Canal. It did the same in July 1958 when Lebanon faced intervention by

Lockheed produced the XF-90 long-range penetration fighter powered by two Westinghouse J34 engines, but the aircraft was seriously overweight and was not placed in production.

209

the Russians. Within a few hours, 1,100 aircraft were ready for takeoff, and the Soviet Union backed down. Later that year a similar provocation by China against Taiwan was tempered by SAC's quick reaction. By May 1960 SAC had achieved its self-imposed goal of having one-third of its 3,000 bombers and tankers on a fifteen-minute-alert status. President Kennedy increased this to 50 percent of the force in the following year, in response to heightened world tension.

The effect of the alert system on families and crew members was devastating, for it was compounded by additional training for war readiness. Crew members routinely worked 80 to 100 hours a week, effectively creating single-parent families long before the term became current. The impact was reflected directly in increased numbers of separations and divorces.

The crews on alert lived in a special facility near the flight line, away from families and initially devoid of creature comforts. In many ways, the alert-crew status was similar to that of the missile crews. Later, the alert facilities were made more livable, and provision was made for families to visit at intervals. It was nonetheless one of the most demanding regimes ever placed on peacetime crew members.

All of the cost, sacrifice, and effort paid off suddenly in the October 1962 Cuban missile crisis. A SAC U-2 reconnaissance plane had overflown Cuba on October 14 and obtained photographs of Soviet intermediate-range ballistic missiles being installed. The B-52 airborne alert program was intensified, and the 200 operational ICBMs were brought to an alert status. In the famous catch-phrase of the time, the United States and the Soviet Union went eyeball to eyeball—and the Soviets blinked.

THE DRIFT TO DISASTER

The rapid growth of the Air Force in size and power was more than matched by the increased demands placed upon it. The policy of nuclear deterrence

The McDonnell Douglas F-101 represents the peak of late-1950 technology, with its high-mounted elevator, twin J57 engines, and the Falcon air-to-air missiles nestled in its belly.

The Convair F-106 Delta Dart was an extensively modified version of the earlier F-102 Delta Dagger interceptor. The delta-wing F-106 was equipped with the very sophisticated Hughes MA-1 electronic guidance and fire-control system, which work with the SAGE (Semiautomatic Ground Environment) national air-defense system. The F-106, with a top speed of 1,500 mph, was the best interceptor in the world when it appeared in squadron service in 1958. None of the pilots who flew it so proudly would have believed that it would serve as an interceptor for three decades before its retirement in 1988.

One of the most important elements of the electronic revolution is the airborne command post, introduced as the Boeing EC-135C. The Strategic Air Command maintained an EC-135C in the air continuously for decades until the end of the Cold War. The command post carried a crew of five, a general officer, and a ten-man staff for the radar and communication equipment.

Although strongly resembling the Navy's carrier-based Douglas Skywarrior, the Douglas B-66 was virtually a new design, tailored to Air Force needs and intended to fulfill the Douglas B-26's role. Only 206 were procured, but the B-66 was a versatile jack-of-all-trades for the Air Force, serving initially as a bomber and then in night, radar, and weather reconnaissance missions. Serving with the 41st and 42d TEWS of the 355 Tactical Fighter Wing at Takhli, Thailand, the EB-66Cs fought for seven years in the electronic countermeasures role, going north to blank out enemy radars for penetrating bombers and fighters.

had succeeded. There had been no nuclear exchange; instead, there was a nuclear equilibrium.

As early as 1955, a Composite Air Strike Force had been established to deal with what came to be known as "brush-fire wars." Unfortunately, the maintenance of an Army–Navy–Air Force team capable of meeting all possible situations was simply too expensive, and the country remained committed to the use of atomic weapons as a deterrent to all wars, large or small.

The concept of fighting a limited war was put to test by proxy in Indochina, where minor assistance had been given to the French since 1950 in their bitter eight-year "war without fronts." Now, the French were beleaguered as the Communist Vietnamese forces squeezed them out of one position after another. Trapped in a self-inflicted Verdun-like battle at Dien Bien Phu in March 1954, the French appealed for direct U.S. intervention. For a brief period, the use of U.S. atomic weapons was contemplated. This was swiftly dropped in favor of the possibility of a strike by B-29s. In the end, nothing was done. Dien Bien Phu fell to General Giap. Eleven thousand French soldiers were captured, half of whom never returned; the French were forced to leave Indochina.

Under the terms of the 1954 Geneva Protocols, the states of Laos and Cambodia were established. Vietnam was divided at the 17th parallel with the Democratic Republic of Vietnam to the North, supported by China and Russia. To the south was the Republic of Vietnam, supported by the United States. It was as if the Korean problem had been transplanted twenty-one degrees south.

President Eisenhower recognized the elected regime in the Republic of Vietnam and promised support, having accepted the "domino theory" that all of Southeast Asia would fall one by one to the North Vietnamese if they were not checked. To this end, the United States sponsored the Southeast Asia Treaty Organization (SEATO), to correspond to NATO in Europe. As the French, in their agony, relinquished authority and responsibility for training the

The Lockheed F-94C in flight. This was a classic blend of second-generation jet aircraft technology with second-generation airborne electronics. Its capability was far greater than the World War II night-fighters, but far less than would be achieved in just a few years with the F-89 and F-102 interceptors.

Not even the great Douglas Aircraft Company could create a winner every time. The C-133 Cargomaster was plagued by development troubles early in its career, and then beset with fatigue problems as the earlier difficulties were ironed out. The four-turbo-prop cargo plane was fast, with a maximum speed of 359 mph, and it could carry almost every vehicle in the Army inventory.

Not really suited to refueling jet aircraft, the Boeing KC-97 soldiered on for years until replaced by the Boeing KC-135. Refueling the B-47 was difficult, especially as fuel was transferred and the B-47 had to increase its speed to avoid stalling. The KC-97 had to begin a descent at full power just to be able to stay ahead of the B-47. Later model KC-97Ls were fitted with a single J47 jet-engine pod under each wing, which greatly improved their performance.

The rapid expansion of the Soviet bomber force caused the USAF to develop several interceptors. The Northrop F-89 Scorpion was one of the best, although it had a long, troubled development. Some F-89 pilots jokingly claimed that the difference between an F-89C and an F-89D was that the wings fell off the C, while the engines blew up on the D. The vintage cars parked in front of this Scorpion include a Jaguar XK-120, an MG-TD, and a Porsche Type 356. The airplane and all three cars are collector's items today.

A brand new Lockheed F-94B. Aircraft wear rapidly in the field, and after just a few hundred hours will bear lots of scars from wind and weather.

Open wide—a C-124 discharges an Army field piece.

215

Successor to the F-86, and the first of
the "century" series fighters, the North
American F-100 Super Sabre signaled a
new era in fighter planes when it first flew
on May 25, 1953. Affectionately called
the "Hun" by its pilots, the F-100 was the
world's first operational supersonic fighter.
Heavy, fast, and rugged, the F-100 could
carry almost twice the bomb load of a
Flying Fortress. It was the Air Force's
mainstay in Vietnam for years, and was
the first Wild Weasel aircraft. Four Air
National Guard squadrons, from Colorado,
Iowa, New Mexico, and New York, flew
the F-100 in Vietnam. After its retirement from first-line service, the airplane
went on to a second career as the QF-100
target drone.

Cleanliness is important for more than
appearance. Oil, dirt, and the residue of
bugs can seriously detract from an aircraft's
speed, even one as powerful as this North
American F-100.

The Douglas plant at Tulsa, Oklahoma,
with Douglas B-66s being built in the
foreground and Boeing B-47s being modified in the background. This is a good shop;
you can tell from the neat parts room, clean
floors, and general air of orderly progress.

South Vietnamese, the United States reluctantly began to assume those duties.

The term "Viet Cong" came into the American vocabulary as a result of terrorism against South Vietnamese forces, and inevitably, their American advisers. In 1961, the American policy of the global containment of Communism had been badly shaken by the Bay of Pigs fiasco in Cuba and by the erection of the Berlin Wall. President Kennedy began to lean heavily on the advice of former Army Chief of Staff General Maxwell Taylor, who wished to see his service restored to a position of predominance in American military strategy. Taylor, in turn, was influenced by his deputy, Walter Rostow, an intellectual with untried theories on counterinsurgency. On their advice, Kennedy established a strategy of flexible response to aggression at any level, from nuclear attack to a local guerrilla operation. A direct result was the buildup of the American military presence in the Republic of Vietnam from a total of 875 in 1960 to a peak of 536,134 in 1968. The thin edge of the aerial wedge was inserted in 1960, when twenty-five U.S. Navy AD-6 aircraft, the venerable Spad from Korea, were sent to the Vietnamese air force.

Official U.S. involvement began in October 1960 as a result of conversations by then–Vice President Lyndon B. Johnson and the President of the Republic of Vietnam, Ngo Dinh Diem. It would build steadily over the years, costing ever more money and ever more lives. In the end it would be the first war that the United States lost, and it would divide the country almost as bitterly as had the Civil War a century before.

TOP LEFT:

Clinging like a bat to a limb, the Ryan X-13 Vertijet perches on its mobile launch platform, which was raised and lowered hydraulically. Almost as much thought had to go into the launch platform as into the aircraft itself.

TOP RIGHT:

The desirability of VTO, vertical takeoff, was always obvious; the technique to obtain the capability was not. The Vertijet was far more successful than most of its competitors, for it took off and landed vertically many times. The problem that would continue to handicap the concept was the limited fuel load that could be carried in VTO aircraft.

CHAPTER SIX
The Numbers Game
1965–1972

The military leadership of the Air Force and its predecessor organizations was always strong, even if it varied widely in its approach and emphasis. Leaders like Mason Patrick and Benjamin Foulois had been able to survive when times were tough, enduring minuscule budgets and facing opposition from a War Department opposed to either an expanded or an independent air force. H. H. Arnold was a facilitator like General Dwight Eisenhower, gaining the support of such key figures as the Assistant Secretary for Air, Robert Lovett, and the Chief of Staff, George Marshall. Arnold thus enabled the service to prosper and become ready for independence.

The immediate post–World War II period was filled with change and confusion until the dismantling of the military services was brought to a halt by the escalating Cold War. Then, in the decade after Korea, three independent developments occurred that had a vital, interrelated effect upon the military.

OPPOSITE:
A painting by Nixon Galloway captures the beginning of an attack as McDonnell Douglas F-4Es roll in over the Mekong River.

Only two XB-70 Valkyries were built; the first was flown on September 21, 1964, the second on July 17, 1965. Designed as a B-52 replacement, to cruise at 70,000 feet at Mach 3, the B-70 mission was eliminated by the advent of the surface-to-air missile. The two craft did valuable test work that had application to later aircraft, but the $2 billion program ended on a sad note when the second one was destroyed in a midair collision with an F-104 chase plane while on a public affairs photo mission.

One of the most controversial warplanes of all time, the General Dynamics F-111 suffered difficulties on an initial deployment to Vietnam in 1966. The story was entirely different in 1972, when F-111s of the 474th Tactical Fighter Wing flew long missions over some of the most difficult territory in the world. Flying just 500 feet off the ground, depending totally upon their instruments, the F-111s would sneak beneath the hostile radar to drop bombs upon a totally surprised enemy. The F-111's versatility stems from its swing-wing design.

These precipitated the U.S. involvement in Vietnam and, at the same time, made it inevitable that we would lose that war.

The first development was in communications. By 1964, events all over the world could be monitored in real time in Washington, D.C. It became possible for the Commander in Chief to issue orders directly to the field on a day-to-day basis, a tempting prospect to most leaders and irresistible to Lyndon Johnson and Richard Nixon.

The second development was the whiz-kid managerial style of micromanagement that had been thrust upon the Pentagon by Secretary of Defense Robert McNamara, a man with an incredible mastery of quantitative analysis—the king of the number crunchers. McNamara had an intimidating ability to recall statistics and to recognize any inconsistency with previous data. Adding up columns of numbers as soon as they were flashed on the screen, he could destroy any briefer whose data were wrong. This became the outward and visible sign that military equipment could be procured on the basis of in-depth statistical analysis, using the same techniques as at the Ford Motor Company, where McNamara had been president. At Ford, these methods produced the Edsel; in the Pentagon they produced, among other things, the ill-fated all-purpose, joint-service, swing-wing TFX fighter that was jokingly called the switchblade Edsel.

It was but a step from procurement to using the same mathematically elegant but practically imperfect techniques to conduct military operations. The result was a decision to wage "capital intensive" warfare against guerrillas: to create a billion-dollar electronic battlefield, using sensors to detect the footsteps of rice-laden peasants, and employing computers to send $5 million jets against $2,000 trucks. Aircraft sorties became valuable for their *numbers* rather than for their results, just as in the ground war body counts became the grisly substitute for elusive victory. The United States had all the data—and no strategy.

McNamara's irretrievable error was his failure to understand that the corporate concept of a bottom line cannot be translated into the life-or-death considerations of military requirements. Although Chapter Eleven bankruptcy may be a viable business strategy, defeat is not an appropriate military one.

And it was here that some say that some members of the top Air Force leadership also failed, for instead of stopping the gradual but relentless inanity, they stayed on to "contain" it. But containing it led to giving the Department of Defense what it demanded. Thus, four fighters, each carrying half its load of armament, would be launched against a target in order to generate more sorties for DOD's voracious numbers maw. That four half-armed fighters were twice as costly to use and exposed to twice the danger of two fighters with full armament loads was not considered—except by the crews. And this is but one small example of the sort of interference in operational matters that was fostered by the worship of numbers and the long-distance conduct of the war.

Ironically, in the light of his later protestations, it was McNamara who, in March 1964, made the first recommendation that bombing operations should be conducted against North Vietnam.

The third critical development was the emergence of an inordinate sensitivity of politicians, particularly those in the White House, to public reaction to television news coverage of military events. The effect was to order military operations conducted in a telegenic manner or to conceal those that were not. Both options were fatal to credibility, to public esteem, and to fighting a war. They cost Lyndon Johnson the presidency. After having seen what appeared to be convincing progress toward winning the war, the American public was unprepared for the violence of the twin events of January 1968, the siege of Khe Sanh and the Tet offensive. Even though both of these campaigns were major defeats for the North Vietnamese and Viet Cong (45,000 casualties) they were not perceived as such by the American viewing audience, who were dismayed at the level and strength of the enemy effort.

For U.S. military leaders in all services, these three developments came to be a vise from which there was no escape. In contrast to World War II and Korea, when the government had set policies for the military to fulfill in the conduct of military operations, the government now daily directed military operations in terms of location and level of intensity, sometimes not only prescribing targets and times of attack, but even selecting the ordnance to be used. As rapid as communications were, inevitably there was sufficient lag time as orders passed from the White House through the various headquarters—the

The first Air Force ace in the Vietnam War was Captain Steve Ritchie (second from right, standing). He has just shot down his fifth MiG-21. This group includes, from the left, Captain Gary Shoulders; Captain John Madden, who would later lose his life; Captain Charles DeBellevue, who would be the leading ace with six victories; Captain Ritchie; Captain Larry Petit. Below, from the left: Captain Mike Francisco, Captain Billy Graham, and First Lieutenant Don Binkley.

Pentagon, Thirteenth Air Force in Hawaii, Seventh Air Force in Saigon—for the real situation to be completely altered, often because of leaks to the Viet Cong. The result was wasted sorties and vicious ambushes.

The Department of Defense and the White House established an intricate and variable set of "rules of engagement" that subordinated military action to short-term political considerations. And, with some interruptions, it followed almost to the end the incredible policy of graduated response—warfare by measured escalation, designed to correspond nicely to "provocations." Each enemy slap was to be met with one only slightly harder, a concept deriving more from a Laurel and Hardy two-reeler than from Clausewitz. This parody of warfare did not deter the enemy; instead it was a training program, military aerobics for an exceedingly apt pupil. In the comfort of Washington offices, it was determined that air operations were to deliver a political message instead of devastating damage in a war that would be played by "signals." Thus, we signaled the North Vietnamese of our desire to negotiate in good faith by halting the bombing, hoping that they would then cease their relentless assault on the villages of the South. The problem was that they understood our signals as signs of weakness, not of strength, and redoubled their assaults.

It is easy to understand the enemy reaction. American policy alternated between retaliation and graduated response as mindlessly as a lawn sprinkler. After American bombing halted in 1968, North Vietnam brought in Soviet equipment and Soviet advisers to completely rejuvenate the air defense system, building forty surface-to-air missile sites around Hanoi alone, a defense capacity unequaled since World War II.

In our vacillation we alienated the South Vietnamese population by using techniques of defoliation and bombing that destroyed their means of livelihood. The insane decision to use high-altitude precision bombers to battle clever, mobile, well-informed guerrillas resulted in some 10 million craters from B-52 bombing alone ruining our *ally's* countryside! In 1968 and 1969, a megaton (1 million tons) of ordnance was dropped on South Vietnam to fight North Vietnamese forces, five times the amount employed against the invader's territory in North Vietnam. It took 502,000 tons of bombs to win the war against Japan, and 6.2 million tons to lose it in Vietnam.

Throughout the early 1960s, the military services, rarely in accord on most subjects, had been in total agreement on one, that the United States

An F-4D of the 25th Tactical Fighter Squadron demonstrates the wide variety of armament with which a Phantom could be fitted. The weapons include two AIM 7E Sparrows, six CBU 39 Gravelmine pods in SUU-41 dispensers, and a KB-18 strike camera. This aircraft was shot down in April 1969 by flak over Laos while executing a dive-bombing attack. The crew, Major Dennis Winkels and Captain Bob Anderson, glided back across the Mekong River, then ejected successfully near Nakhon Phanom when both engines flamed out.

The grim side of the air war. Lieutenant Colonel J. L. Hughes, his wounds bandaged, is forced to walk barefoot between two guards who were quick to beat him.

should not become engaged in a land war in Asia, most especially a guerrilla war. There was also general governmental agreement that the United States had no vital interests in Vietnam, and that, in any event, the supplies for Vietnamese opposition would be from unassailable sources. Just as in Korea, there would be sanctuaries, this time in China, Laos, and Cambodia. Under General John McConnell, Curtis LeMay's successor as Chief of Staff, the Air Force recommended that if we were *forced* into a contest with North Vietnam, the quickest solution would be a decisive bombing attack against ninety-four important industrial targets in that country, to vitiate North Vietnam's war-making capability. It was admittedly a Neanderthal approach, the leveling of a country with massive bombing, but in retrospect it certainly had these virtues: (1) It would have worked, for it did in 1972. (2) It could have been done with minimum losses, for North Vietnam had not yet built its sophisticated defense network of surface-to-air missiles (SAMs), antiaircraft batteries and MiG interceptors. (3) At least it would have been our enemy's country being bombed rather than that of our ally. This advice was rejected.

Captain M. N. Jones is forced to stand upright in a truck, under heavy guard in a parade of American prisoners in North Vietnam.

The Boeing Bomarc IM-99B interceptor missile was an important element of the U.S. continental air defenses for almost a decade after it was placed in service in the early 1960s. Located in a protected shelter, the Bomarc could be fired within thirty seconds of receiving an alert signal. In tests, targets were intercepted at altitudes as high as 80,000 feet, and as far away as 400 miles. Air defense control centers guided the Bomarc's attack by radio.

For twelve agonizing years, from John Kennedy's first commitment to Lyndon Johnson's total engagement to Richard Nixon's "bomb them to the negotiating table" withdrawal, the new-style Department of Defense leadership would force the military leadership to act while simultaneously limiting its capabilities.

The only possible way for the United States to have lost in Vietnam was to commit huge land forces; the only way it could have won was with an overwhelming air strike. Until the very end of the war, whiz-kid management elected to do the opposite in both cases, fielding half a million soldiers before selecting "Vietnamization" in 1969 as a euphemism for bugging out of a losing war and a destroyed country.

In the process, it would fall to the men and women of all services to take up the slack of the abject failure of civil and military leadership, to do the best possible job under the worst conditions, and for the first time in history to find themselves reviled by the public for doing so.

SLIPPING INTO THE QUAGMIRE

Although usually called the Vietnam War, the fighting in Southeast Asia actually embraced three countries, all involved in civil wars of ancient history and savage character. A three-way civil war raged in Laos; Communist guerrillas, the Khmer Rouge, were on the ascent in Cambodia; and South Vietnam was being eased ever closer to submission by the Viet Cong. The United States made a decision to prevent the dominoes from toppling by shoring up the South Vietnamese with military equipment and training. With free and anti-Communist Thailand as one bookend and a viable South Vietnam as the

TOP LEFT:
The original Atlas ICBM was phased out, replaced by the solid-fuel Minuteman missile system in 1962. Within three years after production began, 800 Minuteman I missiles were on alert in midwestern defense complexes. An upgrade program began in 1964, with Minuteman II and Minuteman III missiles being introduced. By 1967, 1,000 Minuteman missiles were on site. The nuclear armed missiles have a range of 6,000 miles and a speed of 15,000 mph.

TOP RIGHT:
Boeing was successful in bringing in the Minuteman fleet on budget, and on schedule. When operational, life in a silo tended to be both stressful and monotonous; only by convincing the crews and their families of the importance of the mission was the Air Force able to provide job satisfaction. One problem was that the visual excitement of a launch was confined to the rare test missions, like this one at Vandenberg Air Force Base, California.

other, stability might be maintained in the corner of the world that had been known as French Indochina.

The initial USAF involvement was picaresque. On October 11, 1961, President Kennedy authorized the deployment of an element of the Jungle Jim 4400th Combat Crew Training Squadron to South Vietnam, under the code name Farm Gate. In the modest Farm Gate force were 151 officers and men, equipped with four Douglas RB-26s, four Douglas SC-47s— both relics of World War II and Korea—and eight North American T-28 trainers. All aircraft bore Vietnamese Air Force markings. Stationed at Bien Hoa Air Base, north of Saigon, the personnel were enthusiastic and believed in their role.

Then, like coins falling from a torn pocket, the stream of aircraft began to build. Four McDonnell RF-101s were brought in for reconnaissance. They were followed by forty Sikorsky H-21 helicopters, thirty T-28s, and sixteen Fairchild C-123 transports. On November 30, six more C-123s were sent for Operation Ranch Hand, which spread the infamous Agent Orange, a dioxin compound used to defoliate the jungle and expose enemy troop movements and concentrations. Each bit of help rendered was so valuable that more was immediately needed.

The nominal task was to train and equip the Vietnamese Air Force. The VNAF did grow in the process, from 6 squadrons and 97 ill-maintained planes in 1962 to an effective force of 14 squadrons and 285 planes in 1965. But it was not enough, and never would be enough. The Americans were also tasked to conduct combat-training operations against guerrillas quartered in civilian areas, but "to avoid killing or injuring noncombatants." In essence, the troops were told to perform combat operations, but not let any blame flow back to the U.S. government. As a nod to legality, it was required that a Vietnamese pilot be on board for all fighter and armed helicopter missions. In most cases they were; in emergencies they often were not.

The first USAF plane was lost in Vietnam on February 2, 1962, when a C-123 crashed on a training mission. (The first lost anywhere in Southeast Asia was an SC-47 shot down in Laos on March 23, 1961.) As the "advisory phase" of USAF involvement mutated into direct involvement, another 2,256 would be lost.

THE ANTE IS RAISED

In the spring of 1965, Viet Cong forces increased their activity. A mortar attack on Bien Hoa Air Base that destroyed five Martin B-57s was matched by an attack on an American barracks in Saigon. Further, the black-pajama-clad Viet Cong were now fighting regular set-piece battles with the South Vietnamese forces. The result was a decision to use USAF tactical air power directly, including bombing infiltration trails in Laos (Operation Barrel Roll) and targets in North Vietnam.

One of the most overlooked and underrated weapons of the Vietnam War was the unmanned reconnaissance vehicle or drone. Lockheed DC-130 launch and control planes could carry up to four Ryan Firebee drones. The photographic information the drones brought back was remarkable for its coverage and its clarity. In Vietnam they flew dozens of different kinds of missions, from simple photographic reconnaissance to dispensing leaflets, taking electronic counter-measures, and assessing bomb damage.

Although not a signatory to the 1954 Geneva Protocols, the United States had abided by the protocol injunction not to introduce jets as bombers or fighters. (Jets had been used for reconnaissance since 1961.) On August 5, 1964, North Vietnamese torpedo boats attacked U.S. ships in the Gulf of Tonkin; two days later the Congress passed the Tonkin Gulf resolution, grant-ing the President greater authority to strike back at North Vietnam. The first result was the introduction of thirty-six Martin B-57 bombers and several squadrons of North American F-100 attack planes, as well as a squadron of Convair F-102 interceptors. Shortly thereafter, thirty B-52s arrived at Andersen Air Force Base, Guam, while thirty-two KC-135 tankers were deployed to Okinawa. The B-52s were temporarily kept in reserve as the bombing opera-tion called Rolling Thunder began in the North.

The operation was flown primarily by Republic F-105 Thunderchiefs, supersonic fighter-bombers with a great load-carrying capability, and fondly called the "Thud" in wry reference to their huge size and weight. For attacks in the South, the Martin B-57 and the F-100 were used, the latter recalled from Air National Guard units. The Rolling Thunder targets were reminiscent of Operation Strangle in Italy and the interdiction in North Korea, with some inhibiting refinements. Traffic along roads, bridges, rail lines, and radar sites were eligible targets, but it was forbidden to hit surface-to-air missile sites or the MiGs visible on North Vietnamese airfields. North Vietnamese dikes damming the water for rice paddies were also off-limits; they consequently became a favored site for antiaircraft batteries.

Washington's thinking became incredibly convoluted. It wanted the war to be contained without killing any Russian and Chinese advisers at the air-fields and missile sites. SAM sites were ruled off-limits while they were being built and equipped. They were off-limits while training went on. They were even off-limits when they were operating in a search mode, looking for a target. They became "on-limits" only when their radar locked on an American aircraft preparatory to firing missiles. Thus, for months the pilots were forced to ignore sites that could have been taken out with little risk, only to have to attack them when they became lethal. In a similar way, MiGs were not to be attacked unless they showed "hostile intent," by turning in to make an attack of their own.

The telephone-pole-sized SAMs were dangerous, but could be outmaneuvered by a twisting dive beneath them. Unfortunately, this took the fighters down into the range of automatic antiaircraft fire, and losses began to rise.

Over the next two years, the USAF and the Navy accelerated their efforts under Rolling Thunder, flying nearly 170,000 sorties, dropping hundreds of thousand of tons of bombs, and killing almost 30,000 civilians. In response, the hardy North Vietnamese dispersed their facilities, increased their imports of arms, petroleum, and food from Russia and China, and steadily increased the strength of their defenses. They soon built the most effective air defense system in the world, and brought into operation MiG-21 fighters equipped with Atoll missiles, which corresponded to the American Sidewinders.

In the meantime, the United States public was growing weary of the war, as the government demonstrated its inability to reach the Vietnamese leaders with either bombing or bombing pauses. There was an urgent need to keep Russia and China from formally entering the war, even though both nations were already heavily involved with men, advice, armaments, food, petroleum, and every other commodity. As a result the United States fell into the same fatal dance with the North Vietnamese that had forced France from the country, a mesmerized willingness to fight the war on enemy terms.

THE SIREN SONG OF TECHNOLOGY

Having ruled out a massive air strike against North Vietnam, the leaders in Washington seemed to have two possible solutions to the war. The first was to win it with technology that would make it too costly for the North Vietnamese to continue, to create an economic Verdun in which capital-intensive means would overcome labor-intensive means. The second was to find a face-saving way to abandon South Vietnam, to declare victory and go home.

The North Vietnamese were sustaining the Viet Cong (and their own regular units) in South Vietnam with supplies brought down a route known colloquially as the Ho Chi Minh Trail, an intricate set of roads, rivers, and paths shielded by a triple canopy of jungle. The trail had been used for centuries by guerrillas and was as familiar to them as Route 66 was to U.S. vaca-

tioners. The straight-line distance from Saigon to Hanoi was roughly 600 miles; the trail was many times longer than that as it twisted through Laos and Cambodia, crossing into South Vietnam at intervals. There were actually three different arteries. One truck route carried cargo and personnel through the Nape and Mugia passes through Laos. Another corridor was primarily for personnel who infiltrated on foot from Laos to South Vietnam. A third came from Cambodia, carrying material unloaded from foreign ships. Thousands of Russian-built ZIL-157 trucks carried up to five tons of supplies each. Interspersed with the truck convoys were bicycles with racks of rifles and humans with sacks of rice. When attacks temporarily took out bridges or roadways, human labor portaged the material to the next point, indefatigable as a trail of ants scurrying with their burdens.

The versatile C-130 cargo plane was also used in the special operations role as the AC-130 Spectre, using a side-firing cannon.

The United States had made a command decision not to attack the supplies at their source in Hanoi and Haiphong Harbor. Instead of destroying the reservoir of supplies, it elected instead to attempt to dam the many rivulets flowing from it. As a consequence of this clouded reasoning, the comparatively easy target of a ship in Haiphong Harbor carrying 500 SAMs was off-limits. Instead, the Air Force was required to take the missiles out one by one, after they were installed, ready to fire back.

Not surprisingly, much of the technology developed was too sophisticated to be useful in an engagement against the primitive supply lines. Defense Secretary McNamara authorized $2.5 billion to be invested in Igloo White, the Air Force element of a larger system known as the McNamara Line, which consisted in part of air-dropped sensors that detected troops or trucks by acoustic or seismic means and relayed this information to an orbiting aircraft, usually an RC-121 Constellation. The data were relayed to Task Force Alpha at Nakhon Phanom where they were analyzed and an appropriate strike force called up.

Igloo White naturally had defects and limitations, chief among them the intelligent Vietnamese response. When they spotted an acoustic sensor parachuting down, they would locate it, then run a single truck back and forth near it for hours, sending back the signal that an army was going by. Alternatively, they would cover it with a wicker basket so that it couldn't pick up any sound at all.

The reaction to Igloo White difficulties was to pour more funds and more facilities into the campaign, including the development of specialized equipment and ordnance to complement the system. Ultimately, billions more would be spent. Although millions of dollars of enemy supplies were destroyed, the net total arriving in the hands of the Viet Cong steadily increased. It was not unlike the current war on drugs.

There were other technical developments, but more importantly, Air Force personnel were able to expand upon the equipment and develop tactics that amplified their value. In every arena—rescue, gunship, remote-piloted vehicles, cargo, in-flight refueling, reconnaissance, forward air controllers, bombing, and especially air combat—the new technology was vastly amplified by the skills of the users. From a hard, dirty war there flowed two positive elements. The first was the level of expertise gained using high-technology equipment, skills that were to mold the future. The second was the camaraderie engendered by prevailing against adverse circumstances. Both of these are best illustrated by looking at some of the major air missions. These include air-to-air combat, bombing raids in the North, the role of the B-52, aerial refueling, reconnaissance and forward air control, strategic and tactical airlift, gunships, and search and rescue. In considering each of these, it must be remembered that every aircraft sortie was backed up by thousands of individuals in a wide variety of jobs ranging from armament to aircraft repair to logistics, mess, and medicine, in a supply train that reached halfway around the world. There is no way to descibe

each of the contributory efforts, but they are implicit in the success of the air missions.

AIR-TO-AIR COMBAT: FIGHTING THE MIGS

Just as in Korea, public interest in the air war centered around the air-to-air combat with Russian- and Chinese-built MiG fighters. Unlike Korea, in Vietnam there was no longer a U.S. 10-to-1 victory ratio. The ratio between 1965 and 1967 was about 3.5 to 1; from late 1967 to 1968 it fell to 2 to 1. The truth was that the U.S. prewar combat training had not been vigorous enough, with too much concern about flying safety and not enough about simulating the rigor of battle. As a result of tougher training after 1968, the USAF victory ratio climbed to 3 to 1, still nowhere near the Korean War, nor equivalent to the startling 13-to-1 ratio established in 1972 by the Navy as a result of the training encountered in what became known as the Top Gun program. As we will see, the Air Force learned from this, too.

A number of factors led to the decrease in the victory-to-loss ratio. One of the most important was that the North Vietnamese Peoples Air Force (VPAF) was strictly controlled from the ground, refusing combat under all but the most favorable circumstances. Like the Imperial German Air Force of World War I, the Communists believed in letting the customers come to the shop.

The Americans had a disadvantage in position. Because of political agreements limiting the number of U.S. forces in Vietnam, many of the U.S. bases were located in Thailand, roughly 500 miles from Hanoi. It was necessary to

ABOVE:
A McDonnell Douglas F-4D from the "Triple Nickle" squadron, the 555th Tactical Fighter Squadron, stationed at Udorn, Thailand.

RIGHT:
The "smart bombs" that figured so brilliantly in the Persian Gulf War were first introduced in combat in Vietnam. This is an F-4E equipped with two laser-guided bombs and two Sparrow missiles.

OPPOSITE TOP:
An F-4 of the 8th Tactical Fighter Wing, the Wolfpack, taxies out at Ubon, Thailand. The Wolfpack was commanded by Colonel Robin Olds.

OPPOSITE BOTTOM:
An Air Defense Command Convair F-102 interceptor patiently rides herd on a Tupelov Tu-95 Bear. The Bear entered service in 1956, and is still flown.

The Convair F-102 was the first delta-wing aircraft capable of exceeding Mach 1. Like the early F-4s, it was armed only with missiles—a first for an American fighter. It also introduced the "Coke bottle" fuselage, because it required area-ruling to be able to go supersonic. Called the "Deuce," the F-102 served in Southeast Asia for seven years at Tan Son Nhut AB in Saigon, and at Udorn in Thailand.

refuel aircraft close to the border, giving the enemy radar systems full warning that an attack was coming.

Further, a paradox was found in the principal fighter the USAF deployed. The McDonnell Douglas F-4 Phantom was undoubtedly the best fighter in the world during the 1960s, and was in many ways ideally suited for the Vietnam War. It had a long range, could refuel in flight, was fast, could carry a heavy load, and had a twin engine capability that saved many a pilot when flak damaged one power plant. What it could *not* do was dogfight effectively with the MiG-17s, 19s, and 21s it encountered, because the lighter MiGs elected to fight with horizontal hit-and-run tactics, sometimes popping up from behind to fire a missile from the six-o'clock (tail chase) position, then diving away. The principal MiG mission was to interfere with bombing attacks, seeking to force the incoming F-4s and F-105s to jettison their bombs before getting on target, a strategy that took full advantage of the encumbrance of U.S. rules of engagement and prevented the F-4s from mixing it up with the MiGs.

Dogfighting was further hampered because the first F-4s to reach Vietnam were armed only with missiles that had originally been intended for use against enemy bombers. In the split seconds that were available between the time the MiG was identified as hostile and it had evaded, there wasn't time to aim, arm, and fire the missiles. A gun was needed in this sort of combat. As a quick fix, rapid-firing gun pods were mounted on the centerline attachment point, but pilots were not satisfied until the introduction of the F-4E, with its internal six-barrel 20mm rotary gun. In the meantime, both the Air Force F-105 and the Navy Vought F-8 pilots were using their guns with success against the MiGs. Identification was later improved by the introduction of

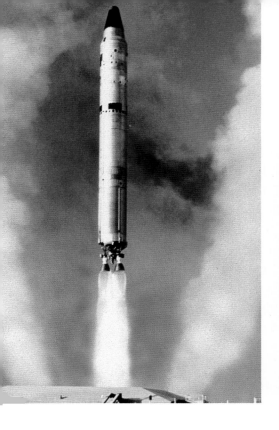

electro-optical equipment, but the smaller MiGs were usually able to spot the larger F-4s first.

Frustrated by the prohibition to take the MiGs out on their airfields—a basic tactic in all previous air wars—the USAF occasionally resorted to subterfuge to lure the MiGs into attack. One of the principal attempts was Operation Bolo, led by Colonel Robin Olds, commander of the 8th Tactical Fighter Wing. Olds, a former West Point football player and a twenty-victory ace in Europe in World War II, crafted a formation that would appear on the Communist radar screens as a standard strike force comprised of F-4s and F-105s. Instead, the entire formation was made up of F-4s. Another group of F-4s was stationed to take on any MiGs that would come in at high altitude, while still another was positioned to intercept any that tried the more typical low-altitude tactics. Weather interfered somewhat, but the Communists took the bait and seven MiGs were shot down.

Between 1968 and 1972 there was virtually no air-to-air combat; instead of fighting MiGs, the F-4s were turned into bombers and escort fighters. In 1972 air fighting flared briefly, this time with more successes.

BOMBING THE NORTH: "GOING DOWNTOWN"

Few aircraft have had so inauspicious a beginning as the Republic F-105 Thunderchief. A long series of accidents early in its service life made it notorious, but in Vietnam it became, like the Republic P-47 and F-84 of two earlier wars, the supreme fighter-bomber. It was the fastest aircraft in the theater, able to streak through the tough North Vietnamese defenses, drop its bombs, then,

TOP LEFT:
Titan II was the largest ICBM ever deployed by the United States, with a launch weight of 330,000 pounds and a range of up to 9,000 miles. After almost thirty years of service, the Titan II was retired from its nuclear-deterrent task and put into service as a boost vehicle for satellites.

TOP RIGHT:
Swift and powerful, and the ultimate refinement of a concept that began with the P-47, the Republic F-105 Thud epitomized American air power over Vietnam. The F-105 had the range, speed, and bomb capacity to take on the toughest missions, from bombing Hanoi and Haiphong to taking out the hotly defended bridges. It also assumed the Wild Weasel role.

if necessary, dogfight its way out, using its internal gun to kill MiGs. One bitter measure of its value are its losses; of the 833 F-105s built, 382 were lost from 1965 to 1972.

The Thud, as it was called, became the workhorse of the war. It was enormous for a fighter, with an internal bomb bay capable of carrying up to 8,000 pounds of bombs, at a speed close to 1,400 mph. It was armed with a wide variety of missiles, and a six-barrel 20mm cannon that was effective in both air-to-air and air-to-ground work.

Operating out of Korat and Takhli Royal Thai Air Force bases, the Thuds performed 75 percent of the missions against North Vietnam during Operation Rolling Thunder. When "going downtown" (bombing Hanoi) was authorized, the Thuds would lead the way both in bombing and in casualties. The Thud crews came to realize that they had only a 50 percent chance of surviving a 100-mission tour.

As arduous and dangerous as the Thud's regular duties were, it was given the even more hazardous "Wild Weasel" task of suppressing SAMs. (The term "Wild Weasel" refers to the mission, and is applied to whatever type of aircraft is conducting it.) Countermeasures against enemy radar go back to World War II, and in Vietnam, the F-100 Super Sabre had been used effectively in the Wild Weasel radar-killing role. But in the North, where speed was vital, the F-105s had to slow down to stay with the older F-100s. There soon evolved paired hunter-killer teams composed either of all F-105s or a mix of F-105s and F-4Cs. One team was two Wild Weasel planes carrying air-to-ground missiles; the other team was two planes with conventional bombs. The Wild Weasels would go in harm's way to seek out SAM sites by offering them-

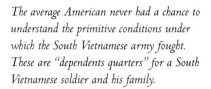

The average American never had a chance to understand the primitive conditions under which the South Vietnamese army fought. These are "dependents quarters" for a South Vietnamese soldier and his family.

The F-111 appears somewhat ungainly at ground level, with its gear and flaps extended and its wing swept forward. Once airborne, with the gear up and wings swept to the rear, it gains an arrowlike sleekness.

North American F-100s refueling from a KC-135 tanker. The venerable F-100 Hun was a little long in the tooth when the Vietnam War came, but it distinguished itself in the ground-attack role.

selves as targets. When the SAM radars illuminated them, they would launch radar-homing Shrike (or later, Standard Arm) missiles to destroy them. As soon as the radar-homing missiles were launched, the other team would roll in with conventional bombs.

It was an incredibly hazardous, nerve-racking job, in which split-second timing meant the difference between life or death, for once the SAM battery had locked on and launched, the radar-guided SAM would home on the Wild Weasel. It required the Wild Weasel teams to have a complete understanding of both the American attackers' and the North Vietnamese defenders' tactics. The Wild Weasels would go in about five minutes ahead of the bombers, lure the SAMs into revealing themselves, then work them over all during the attack. They would remain on station as the attackers left the target area, earning their motto, "First in—Last out."

The SAM site operators were clever, experienced soldiers who worked closely with their antiaircraft and fighters. There was a constant evolution of tactics on both sides that made the fight tougher every day of the war, but it was a battle that the Wild Weasels won. In the final days of the great raids on Hanoi and Haiphong, the SAMs were simply salvoed without radar guidance, because the SAM site crews could not turn their radars on without a Wild Weasel attack destroying them.

FROM ARC LIGHT TO LINEBACKER II:
THE ROLE OF THE B-52

The XB-52 made its first flight on April 14, 1952. It was intended as a high-altitude nuclear bomber, capable of single-plane missions to the heart of the Soviet Union. No one in the Air Force or at Boeing would have predicted that twenty years later it would still be in use in Vietnam in the totally different role of an aerial artillery platform, dropping iron bombs in formation from relatively low levels. It is still more unlikely that they would have predicted its use still another twenty years later in the same role in the Persian Gulf War.

The Vietnam debut of the B-52s—the BUFF (Big Ugly Fat Fellow)—was not auspicious. Twenty-seven B-52s took off on the long eighteen-hour round-trip from Andersen Air Force Base on Guam to drop conventional bombs against an unseen Viet Cong target. Results were unsatisfactory, and two aircraft were lost in a midair collision. Despite this, within a very few weeks the B-52s were accepted as an innovation—artillery support delivered by air. Flying at 30,000 feet, the B-52s were unseen and unheard by the enemy, which was forced to break up its ground elements, spreading them out so that they would not be caught in a carpet of bombs. Less than a year after beginning operations, B-52s were dropping an average of 8,000 tons of bombs a month in what were known as Arc Light operations. At Khe Sanh, General Giap's troops were decimated by unbroken waves of six B-52s attacking every three hours, dropping bombs as close as 900 feet to friendly lines.

Although most of the early missions involved elaborate mission planning, the Combat Skyspot bombing system was soon introduced for operational flexibility. The B-52s would arrive at a specific point and be picked up by the MSQ-77 radar system. They could then be directed exactly to where they were to release their bombs. The system allowed B-52 flights to be diverted to targets of opportunity, but it gave a sense of remoteness to their actions that eroded crew morale, already strained by tension, fatigue, and boredom.

Assigned for administrative reasons for 179 days at a time to "temporary" duty at Andersen Air Force Base or at U-Tapao in Thailand, air crew life was a monotonous round of briefing, flying, and sleeping. Crew members mockingly called themselves "coconut knockers" for the hours they spent bombing the jungle, but the B-52s were reputedly the weapon most feared by the Viet Cong. The hard-working ground crews, including the armament people who endlessly assembled the 500- and 750-pound bombs, worked as many as eighty-four hours a week during surge periods.

Eventually, the B-52 came into its own in an hour of desperation, when U.S. diplomatic activity seemed bankrupt. By 1968 the United States was

General Curtis LeMay must be given credit for the B-52's versatility. The original B-52 bomber mission could have been performed more cheaply by a reengined B-47. LeMay would have none of it, saying that he wanted an aircraft large enough to be able to adapt to change. The B-52 fulfilled his requirement perfectly.

The B-52, not an aesthetic triumph from any angle, appeared to its greatest disadvantage on the ground. Here it groans to a halt after landing, its brake chute streaming, spoilers fully deployed, and cross-wind landing gear engaged to keep it straight down the runway.

aware that it had to disengage from the Vietnam War. Henry Kissinger, then Assistant for National Security to President Nixon, engaged in some historic secret negotiations with the North Vietnamese leader, Le Duc Tho. The discussions were intended to provide a framework by which the United States could leave North and South Vietnam nominally at peace, with a reasonable military parity, and withdraw its forces. The basic concept was that the war would be "Vietnamized": the South Vietnamese forces would be so trained and strengthened that they would not require U.S. support, which could then be withdrawn with face saved.

On October 23, 1972, Kissinger announced, "Peace is at hand," and all bombing was halted north of the 20th parallel. The North Vietnamese used the period of cessation to do intensive repairs to the railroads and bridges, gearing up for a major assault. On December 13, the United States finally recognized that the North Vietnamese were drawing the negotiations out deliberately, taking advantage of the rising tide of opposition to the war in the United States and preparing a military victory rather than a diplomatic one. The peace talks were broken off, and the recently reelected President Nixon made the decision to attack the enemy so vigorously that it would prefer to negotiate

rather than continue the endless guerrilla warfare. The attack was to be called Linebacker II.

For the first time, the artificial rules of engagement were lifted in an operation that originally called for three days of maximum effort over Hanoi and Haiphong. The B-52s were to do radar night bombing of military targets.

Linebacker II started on December 18, 1972, with an attack by seventy-five B-52s. They were joined by other Air Force and Navy elements to suppress both SAMs and fighters. The enemy defenses were heavy; over 200 SAMs were fired, and three B-52s were lost. In the Hanoi Hilton, the American prisoners of war cheered the sound of the falling bombs, and were gratified by the increasingly frightened response of their brutal captors.

The second day was worse. Ninety-three B-52s were launched, and six were shot down, almost a 7 percent loss rate, intolerable over an extended period. Ninety-nine bombers attacked on the third day. Despite the loss rate, the decision was made to continue beyond the original three days planned. On December 26, new tactics were introduced, with all of the B-52s attacking their targets simultaneously, four waves over Hanoi, three over Haiphong. Despite an increased level of SAM firings, only two B-52s were lost. Then the B-52s and

The last of the line, the B-52H, will probably soldier on in a variety of roles for at least the next decade. Intended as a high-level nuclear bomber, the B-52 became a low-level attacker, then just flying artillery, dropping iron bombs. It has been given new tasks as a maritime reconnaissance and antishipping aircraft, and no one can say that it will not have new missions in the future.

*Four Vought A-7Ds from the 355 Tactical
Fighter Squadron queue up to refuel from a
KC-135 tanker. The ability to refuel gives
a flexibility to attack aircraft, which can
take off with a maximum bomb load, then
take on a full fuel load in the air before
departing on a mission. The A-7s did
excellent work both in the Vietnam and the
Persian Gulf wars.*

the fighters turned to the destruction of the SAM sites. The following raids,
the tenth and eleventh, were almost unopposed, and the North Vietnamese
returned to the negotiating table—forced there by Linebacker II.

The Strategic Air Command had flown 729 sorties against one of the
most heavily defended targets in history, dropping 15,000 tons of bombs and
sustaining only a 2 percent loss rate—fifteen airplanes. Another 1,000 sorties
were flown by other Air Force and Navy aircraft. By the eleventh day, North
Vietnamese opposition had been hammered into the ground; there were no
more SAMs to be fired and no more SAM sites to fire them from. Had the
Linebacker II been allowed to continue, it is virtually certain that North
Vietnam would have been forced to surrender. From a desperation weapon,
thrown in to relieve beleaguered defenders, the B-52 had become the ultimate
weapon in the war.

YOUNG TIGERS: AERIAL REFUELINGS

Among the many unsung heroes of the war were the crews of the Boeing
KC-135 tankers that refueled the attack aircraft in flight. Although they did

not themselves employ arms against the enemy, they were in effect a force multiplier; by having the tankers on station, the value of the fighters and the B-52s was doubled and redoubled.

Aerial refueling has come to seem so routine that the extraordinary skill it requires and the extreme danger implicit in the operation are often overlooked. The tanker is 300,000 pounds of fuel and metal moving at 500 mph, making first a rendezvous and then the gentlest of midair collisions with an equally swift mass of metal and fuel, the receiver aircraft. Conditions in Vietnam added to the equation the hazards of performing this a dozen times on a single mission, perhaps in turbulent thunderstorms at night, operating in radio silence and with a minimum of lights.

Prior to 1965, the KC-135s had been overworked just providing refueling to B-52s and tactical aircraft on their routine training missions. When the combat requirement of the Vietnam War to refuel fighters, bombers, and reconnaissance aircraft was added, the tanker work load became overwhelming.

Tankers permitted the fighters to take off with much greater armament loads, and then top off with fuel when airborne. During the strike, the tankers would orbit, waiting for the fighters to come streaming back, often damaged and dangerously low on fuel, to refuel again before the flight home. Some tankers acted as aerial tow trucks, letting damaged fighters latch on to their refueling booms and then towing them to within gliding distance of their bases. Others prowled into North Vietnamese airspace to rescue fighters too short of fuel to make it to the refueling area.

The demand for tankers increased steadily. As early as 1965 there were 55 stationed in Southeast Asia; by Linebacker II, 195 were required. The KC-135s made 813,378 refuelings during 194,687 sorties, and off-loaded almost 9 billion pounds of fuel, the numbers conveying nothing of the danger and anxiety involved. It was hard, hazardous work, and the pressures of war forced the vulnerable tankers to fly day and night in every sort of weather, sometimes passing into the combat zone itself, although the KC-135s were as vulnerable to gunfire as prewar hydrogen-filled airships like the *Hindenberg* were to lightning. Operating in radio silence in their oval pattern orbits, the tankers would service thirsty aircraft as rapidly as possible, always at risk of collision. Their rewards were mainly psychological—a fighter pilot saying, "Thanks, you can count that as a save," as he broke away. But for the tanker, he would have had to abandon his aircraft. A tanker crewman rarely had to buy his own drinks on a fighter base.

RECONNAISSANCE, FACS, AND FAST FACS

There were many kinds of reconnaissance in Vietnam, including electronic, photographic, and direct visual observation by Forward Air Controllers. Each was demanding, and each had its own rewards.

One of the personnel revolutions in the Air Force was the systematic rotation of pilots from desk jobs through combat assignments in the Vietnam War. Pilots were taken from routine duty and placed behind the stick of advanced aircraft like the McDonnell F-101B, photographed here from the cockpit of another 101. The transition programs were carefully designed, and most pilots were successful in it. Some were not able to handle the more advanced aircraft, and to their chagrin were relegated to other duties.

The bureaucratic difficulties that constrained the photographic reconnaissance efforts are a capsule picture of the hazards of joint commands. The bravery of the crews and the hard work of the photo processors as well as of the photo interpreters simply could not overcome the impediments created by the command structure. The Military Assistance Command, Vietnam (MACV), which controlled reconnaissance, set up its Target Research and Analysis Center in Saigon to determine the location, timing, and manner of reconnaissance missions. It was an impossible situation that denied the Air Force the capability to select its own targets from reconnaissance photos. These crucial command, doctrinal, and operational issues were never fully resolved, and the Air Force had to continue to obtain its target information from MACV.

The photo reconnaissance effort began as early as 1961. There were two Air Force photo-processing units in Southeast Asia, one at Ton Son Nhut Air Base in Saigon, and the other at Don Muang Airport, near Bangkok. Reconnaissance was undertaken by McDonnell RF-101 Voodoos, fast, long-range jets; later Martin RB-57s came in to assist them, and these were soon supplemented by McDonnell Douglas RF-4s and Douglas RB-66s.

Photo reconnaissance was difficult in the area because of the triple layer of jungle foliage. To compound the problem, the weather was often bad, and the enemy tended to operate at night. Innovation was called for, yet the task of reconnaissance continued to be impeded by a growing civil and military bureaucracy. Infrared photography, which detected heat from enemy vehicles or camps, was new at the time and not yet up to the demands of the Southeast Asian environment. The very volume of photographic and infrared information

Reconnaissance versions of the McDonnell Douglas F-101 continued to do invaluable work in Vietnam, providing most of the long-range reconnaissance in the North until superseded by RF-4Cs.

obtained placed almost impossible demands on the processing equipment, which was difficult to keep operating in the temperature and humidity found in Southeast Asia. Ice wrapped in plastic had to be placed in the chemical solutions to keep them within proper operating temperatures.

Despite the command difficulties, the reconnaissance crews carried on, plunging unarmed into hotly defended zones to bring back essential photographs. In Vietnam, visual reconnaissance assumed the importance it had gained in World War I. The intimate nature of warfare in Vietnam—brothers fighting against brothers in their own villages—made visual reconnaissance absolutely critical.

The very speed and power of the jets, combined with the elusive nature of the targets, made the Forward Air Controller (FAC) even more valuable in Vietnam than he had been in any previous war. The FAC had the responsibility for assuring that a target was an enemy and that no damage was inflicted on friendly personnel or installations. The only way to combine the tasks of targeting the enemy and shielding the friendly was to fly low and slow in the combat area, vulnerable to everything from a thrown rock to antiaircraft fire.

The FAC's job was first of all to find the target, then call for fighter-bombers, either via an airborne command post or from a direct air support center on the ground. When the attack aircraft arrived, the FAC assumed total control of the attack, beginning the proceedings by firing "Willy Petes," white phosphorous rockets, to mark the targets. He would alert the fighter-bombers to flak concentrations (having ferreted them out as a target), suggest lines of run-in for the best attack, and then assess results. If the attackers missed, the FAC would provide corrections, using the traditional "clock" method (giving directions to the target as it would relate to numbers on a superimposed clock face) or a prominent landmark. A special talent was necessary to marshal fighter-bomber aircraft of vastly different performance—F-100s and Douglas A-1E Skyraiders, for example—and maneuver them in and out of the target area to get maximum utilization from them and give maximum damage to the enemy.

After the fighter-bombers departed, the FAC would do bomb-damage assessment, calling in another wave if required. During the whole engagement, the FAC was a sitting duck, who had to be as worried about accidentally damaging the civilian population as he was about hitting the enemy. Combat had to be cleared with local civilian officials, and the FAC had to be familiar with the attack methods the U.S. and RVN armies used.

The FAC became a radio central, maintaining contact with the airborne command post, controlling the attacking fighters, and talking to the units on the ground, as well as to other FACs in the area. In addition, there might be four or five flights of fighter-bombers awaiting his instructions. While he did this, he had to fly his airplane, avoid the flak, watch his fuel supply and do the hundred other things required to survive in combat over hostile territory.

In the beginning, the FACs flew Cessna O-1s, basically the same airplane as the L-19 of the Korean War, and very little different from civilian puddle-jumpers. With neither armor nor self-sealing fuel tanks, it had a maximum speed of 115 mph when light and clean. Speed fell off by 30 percent when carrying the usual load of marking rockets.

In 1967, specially modified versions of the tandem twin-engine Cessna Model 337 Skymaster were put in service. With larger windows, additional hard points to which weapons could be attached, some armor, and the capability to carry a gun pad, the O-2A was an improvement but still did not have sufficient armament, armor, speed, or escape gear. The FACs got an even more modern aircraft in 1968, when the twin-turboprop North American OV-10A Bronco began operations. Equipped with four forward-firing machine guns, and strong points for mounting both rockets and bombs, the FACs at last had an aircraft that not only offered them a better chance for survival, but let them carry offensive weapons with some punch to defend themselves.

Even the OV-10A was too limited in range and speed to operate deep in enemy territory, and by 1967 the North Vietnamese were able to bring intense antiaircraft fire to bear even in the South. When the faster two-seat F-100s were introduced they were called Fast FACs, code-named Misty. They were superseded by F-4s, which would conduct high-speed visual reconnaissance in high-threat areas in Laos, Cambodia, and North Vietnam. Only the most experienced veterans, in first-class physical condition, were qualified to fly the demanding Fast FAC mission, which involved four to five hours of low-level flight pulling constant high-G turns. When a Fast FAC found a target, it would request a strike from the airborne battlefield command and control aircraft

Forward Air Controllers fought a very personal war, for they flew their Cessna O-2s low and slow directly over the enemy, exposed not only to antiaircraft fire, but also to rifles and machine guns. The enemy hated the FACs, for they knew their mission: assigning targets for U.S. fighter-bombers. The job called for far more than courage; it also demanded a deep knowledge of enemy and U.S. tactics to make the most of the available air power.

Despite the growing antiwar sentiment in the United States, it was still necessary to recruit new members for the Air Force, and the Thunderbird aerobatic team was one of the best means to do this. Thousands of young men and women made up their mind to join the service after watching the Thunderbirds perform. Here they fly Northrop T-38s.

Another workhorse, the Lockheed C-141 Starlifter, photographed at U-Tapao Royal Thai Air Base in Thailand. The C-141 was well liked by its crews because it was not only reliable, it was comfortable.

The Lockheed C-130E fulfilled its role as an intratheater transport, operating out of small fields and, when necessary, air-dropping cargo at places where it could not land. The C-130 was a strong aircraft as the C-47 was: able to carry bigger loads and to take more punishment than its designers had ever intended.

The crew of a Lockheed C-5A Galaxy faced a bewildering array of instruments. A diplay like this is now sadly obsolete in the day of the "glass cockpit" equipped with cathode-ray-tube instruments.

(usually a C-130), then, like its lower-speed cousins, mark the target with Willy Pete and assess the results.

All FAC work called for bravery and devotion to duty. It also involved long hours of study, noting every element of the terrain below so that any change—a new shrub, leaves bent down by tires, freshly turned earth, anything—would be noticed, for the Viet Cong were masters of camouflage. One of the most demanding missions was Night Owl FAC: handpicked crews with specially equipped F-4s that conducted night dive-bombing attacks in the light of their own flares.

The pilots who became FACs were usually volunteers, but not always; they could be assigned from any mission—transport, fighter, reconnaissance— and expected to learn their trade. It was work at the sharp end of the stick, as valuable for saving innocent lives as for hitting the target.

CARRYING THE LOAD: STRATEGIC AIRLIFT

Strategic airlift was more important in Vietnam than it was in either World War II or Korea, for neither the harbors nor the roads of South Vietnam permitted timely unloading of ships. Thirty-four squadrons of the Military Airlift Command were dedicated to it. There were twenty-one squadrons of the faithful "Old Shaky" Douglas C-124, three of the trouble-plagued Douglas C-133, seven of the Lockheed C-130, and three of the Boeing C-135. Only the C-124 and C-133 were truly cargo aircraft, and both were obsolete. The C-124 took almost two weeks to make the round-trip between California and Vietnam, flying ninety-five hours in the process. The C-133 was slightly faster, but had a checkered history of safety problems that restricted its operation. The Air Force Reserve and Air National Guard provided invaluable help with their even older equipment, including double-deck Boeing C-97s and twin-boom Fairchild C-119s.

The first major boost to cargo capability came with the introduction of the Lockheed C-141 in 1965, which could carry twice the C-124's cargo twice as fast and twice as far. The second boost came in 1969, when the controversial Lockheed C-5A became operational; ultimately seventy-three of these giant Galaxies saw service.

But the efficiency of transport depended upon far more than aircraft and crews. A science of air transport grew up, centered upon efficient aerial ports using new materials-handling systems, and a new concept of the mission. During February 1968, at a time when airlift resources were strained to meet the buildup of forces in Korea caused by the North Korean seizure of the USS *Pueblo*, an emergency airlift was made of 6,000 troops and equipment from the 82d Airborne Division and the 5th Marine Division. These troops, flown from the United States to Saigon, were vital in stemming the Communist Tet offensive.

The gigantic military airlift operation performed two other functions, less critical to winning the war, but perhaps even more important in human terms. The first was to bring weary soldiers back from Vietnam for R&R—rest and recuperation. The second was the poignant repatriation of the prisoners of war in February 1973.

CARRYING THE CARGO: TACTICAL AIRLIFT

Tactical airlift began in Vietnam with four obsolete Douglas C-47 Gooney Birds. It grew over time, supplemented with more C-47s, de Havilland C-7A Caribous, and Fairchild C-123 Providers. It came into its own with the arrival of the Lockheed C-130 Hercules, an immensely strong four-engine turboprop that could carry all but the largest pieces of Army equipment.

As invaluable as tactical airlift had been in previous wars, it was far more so in Vietnam. It was also far more vulnerable, because the transports operated routinely in the combat zone. Some analysts have written that tactical airlift was more important in Vietnam than the interdiction provided by tactical fighters.

In the Vietnam "war without fronts," Air Force transports were vital in important search-and-destroy operations conducted in remote regions. Besides carrying men and cargo to the scene of battle, the transports were used in major parachute assaults. The war's only battalion-size drop occurred during Operation Junction City in early 1967. The transports lifted multibattalion task forces to the battle area, and then resupplied them with fuel, food, and ammunition. The C-130s and C-123s would land amid mortar fire and artillery shelling, off-load cargo and take on wounded, then fly out through the hail of enemy shells. It was backbreaking, knuckle-biting work, and it went on routinely, day after day. At Dak To, in November 1967, a stream of C-130s delivered 5,000 tons of supplies, flying in and out of a shell-damaged 4,200-foot asphalt strip runway.

At Khe Sanh, four months of aerial resupply kept 6,000 defenders able to resist heavy pressure from General Giap's troops. When heavy shellfire prevented the C-130s and C-123s from landing, they were guided by radar to precise drop points over the Khe Sanh runway, using the LAPES (Low-Altitude Parachute Extraction System) delivery.

From 1962 to 1973, tactical airlift carried more than 7 million tons of passengers and cargo within South Vietnam, almost ten times that carried during the Korean War. In the process, it lost 126 aircraft in operations, with 269 crewmen killed or missing.

GUNSHIPS

In early 1963, the Viet Cong began to increase the extent and ferocity of their attacks on hamlets and outposts in the so-called safe areas of South Vietnam, and were threatening to disrupt the pacification program. There was simply not enough artillery or attack aircraft to provide fire support to the hundreds of trouble spots, and jet fighters were not an effective weapon to use against the guerrillas at night.

The problem was solved in part by the development of one of the most potent weapons of the Vietnam War, the side-firing gunship. Equipped with cannon and gun ports reminiscent of a ship of the line, the aerial gunship was the joint product of inspiration and desperation, a brilliant example of the way innovative airmen teamed up to overcome operational difficulties.

The idea of cannon side-firing from an aircraft was first suggested by Gilmour MacDonald in 1942, for attacking submarines. MacDonald resubmitted his idea to the Air Force in 1945 and again in 1961. In the meantime Ralph Flexman, a Bell Aerosystems engineer, became aware of a flying technique developed in the mid-1950s by an American missionary named Nate Saint. Saint would lower mail, food, and medical supplies to natives on the ground via a very long rope, while making pylon turns in his aircraft, a maneuver in which the pilot sights his wingtip on a point on the ground and circles around it. The bucket at the end of the rope could be guided very accurately.

Flexman saw that Saint's technique could be used to sight MacDonald's side-firing gun. The concept was approved and under the direction of Lieutenant Colonel John C. Simons, was given years of testing in everything from a T-28 to a C-131. Captain Ronald W. Terry became project leader, managing the installation, the tactics, and the somewhat tougher job of selling the idea within the Air Force. Eventually, the cargo bay of a venerable Douglas C-47 was fitted with a battery of SUU-11a Gatling guns for trial at Eglin Air Force Base, Florida.

The program had a great deal to recommend it, including the fact that there were were plenty of C-47s around to be converted (becoming FC-47s) and no shortage of crews to man them. There were some who questioned whether the ancient C-47 could survive in a battlefield environment, but all doubts were removed after the combat debut of the FC-47 in a day mission on December 15, 1964, and an even more impressive night mission on December 23, when the test aircraft broke up a Viet Cong attack on an outpost in the Mekong River Delta area.

Once proven, the go-ahead was given to put a battery of three GAU-2B/A 7.62mm miniguns into twenty-six aircraft, now designated AC-47s. The seven-man AC-47 crew consisted of two pilots, a navigator, two gunners, a loadmaster, and a flight engineer. The miniguns were in short supply, however, and the first AC-47s operated with only one or two per aircraft, none getting a full battery until 1965. Twenty of the AC-47s were assigned to the 4th Air Commando Squadron and deployed to the Republic of Vietnam, where in late 1965 it seemed that a general Communist takeover was inevitable.

The 4th Air Commandos. using the radio call sign Spooky, went right to work, flying 277 combat missions in the remainder of 1965, most of them at night. They were extraordinarily effective in shoring up South Vietnamese defenses. The AC-47s gunships came to be called Spooky, Dragonship, or Puff— the latter two names, inspired by the song "Puff the Magic Dragon," referred to the incredible outpouring of flame and smoke when the guns were fired. On one mission, a record 43,500 rounds of ammunition and 96 flares were expended by a single Spooky to save a besieged outpost.

As the gunship unit developed experience, its mission was expanded to include reconnaissance, convoy escort, and forward air control, and its geographical coverage was expanded into Laos.

The demand for gunships went up in terms of both numbers and capabilities. As more ancient C-47s were converted into gun-toting Gunship I AC-47s, larger, faster, more modern aircraft were selected for conversion. Gunship II was the AC-130 (call sign Spectre), a four-engine Lockheed turboprop transport conversion designed for interdiction of roads and armed reconnaissance at long range. There were two kinds of Gunship III, Fairchild AC-119Gs, call sign Shadow, and AC-119Ks, call sign Stinger. The USAF gunships became more and more sophisticated as the war progressed, with improved capabilities in target acquisition and fire control and far better illumination systems, which had come to include huge 1.5 million candlepower variable-beam searchlights.

The gunships were extremely cost effective in terms of the numbers of trucks destroyed, but more importantly in the number of lives saved in defending villages and forts, thanks to the tremendous volume of accurately aimed firepower. Flying gunship missions was lonely, dangerous work, but the rewards for saving forces on the ground or destroying enemy supplies were immediate and apparent.

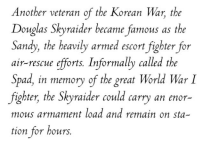

Another veteran of the Korean War, the Douglas Skyraider became famous as the Sandy, the heavily armed escort fighter for air-rescue efforts. Informally called the Spad, in memory of the great World War I fighter, the Skyraider could carry an enormous armament load and remain on station for hours.

SEARCH AND RESCUE

The perception of the United States' participation in Vietnam has changed in recent years. The veterans, once the object of contempt in the eyes of a small but vocal part of the community, are now seen as the heroes they were, men and women who were trying to do their duty. Of all the missions in Vietnam, the one that best captures this spirit of good intent is that of the search and rescue teams, who risked their lives day in and day out for their motto, "So That Others May Live."

By 1968, every air crew member flying in Southeast Asia knew that if he went down, every effort would be made to rescue him, regardless of the location, the cost, or the impact on other missions. The knowledge was a boost to the morale that made it a bit easier to fly into the heart of the enemy defenses.

Search and rescue operations started in a small way, and for political reasons did not increase at the same rate as the military buildup. The very first rescue capability in Southeast Asia came about in 1961, when sixteen Sikorsky H-34 Choctaw helicopters were provided to Air America, an ostensibly civilian company conducting air operations in the area. Air America made several rescues, even though it was not trained in the technique. The enemy was quick to react, and saw almost from the very first that a downed pilot provided an opportunity to set up an ambush, a "flak trap" to shoot down the rescuers.

As the American presence grew, the customary official Sea-Air Rescue (SAR) capability was not provided because USAF pilots were not supposed to be flying combat missions. The provision of an adequate SAR force would have been an admission that this was not true.

The Wright Cyclone engine of the Spad always leaked oil, but it could take punishment and keep on turning. Revetments were necessary at all airfields to protect against Viet Cong mortar and rocket attacks.

Bureaucracy and politics continued to delay the establishment of a true SAR capability through 1964, despite the rapid rise in capability of the enemy antiaircraft, especially over the Plain of Jars in Laos. It was not until November 1964, after more than twenty aircraft had crashed or been shot down, that the first official, trained search and rescue capability became available in a theater where the hazards grew daily.

The first helicopters supplied to the rescue units were Kaman HH-43Bs, small, unarmored, and with inadequate range. The Kamans had been designed primarily for local rescue work around an airport, so in 1965 Air America continued to do most of the air crew recovery work. The very inadequacy of the Kaman brought about some new concepts, and the idea of a rescue task force came into being. Originally, it consisted of Grumman HU-16 Albatross amphibians as control ships, HH-43 helicopters as rescue craft, and A-IE

Unsung, but never forgotten by the pilots who trained or fought in it, the Cessna T-37B "Tweetybird" has had a thirty-year career as a trainer and an attack plane, and it may yet have another decade of use.

Sandies—as the rugged Spads were now designated—as armed escorts. The airborne control plane stayed at altitude, above the range of small-arms fire; the escort fighter-bombers put down suppressing fire to keep the enemy away from the downed air crew; and the helicopters went in to make the rescue.

By the end of 1965, trained crews and significantly improved helicopters became available. The new aircraft included the Sikorsky HH-3E, which was much faster, and carried a comforting 1,000 pounds of armor to protect the crew and passengers. The Sikorskies soon became famous as "Jolly Green Giants" because of their green-and-brown camouflage scheme. In addition, Douglas HC-54s replaced the Albatross amphibians as airborne mission controllers.

The conduct of rescue operations was extremely risky. The rescue helicopters endured everything from attacks by MiGs to running the gauntlet of

FOLLOWING PAGE:
The Northrop T-38 trainer was first flown on April 10, 1958. After more than thirty years of service, the supersonic T-38 is slated for well-deserved retirement. However, the replacement cost of a new trainer aircraft is so high that it is possible that the T-38 will be put through a modernization program and used for another thirty years.

Six Northrop F-5Es, each with different markings. The F-5E was used by many air forces around the world, and finally found acceptance in the USAF as an Aggressor Force airplane in Red Flag exercises. The small size and high performance of the Northrop fighter made it a suitable substitute for the MiG-21 in simulated combat.

antiaircraft fire in a flak trap. The escorts suffered too: the A-IE Sandy had the highest overall loss rate of any plane in Southeast Asia, ranging up to 6.2 per 1,000 sorties.

By January 1, 1967, the rescue effort had been given a new title, the Aerospace Rescue and Recovery Service, and it employed fifty helicopters in Southeast Asia. A hard analysis had been made of rescue attempts in the previous years, and it was determined that 47 percent of all unsuccessful rescue attempts were caused by the helicopter's lack of speed in getting on site. If a helicopter could reach a downed air crew member in fifteen minutes, the chances for rescue were excellent; if it took thirty minutes or more, the probability of a successful rescue went down sharply. Helicopters were staged out of advanced air bases in Laos, and would go on station while raids against the North were being conducted. After aerial refueling became possible in 1967, the Jolly Greens were able to spend much more time in the air, ready for action. Performance capability was increased further with the arrival of the Super Jolly Greens, HH-53Cs, which were twice as heavy as the HH-3Es and carried three 7.62mm miniguns with which to suppress enemy flak.

By 1969, rescue missions usually consisted of a Jolly Green or a Super Jolly Green, escorted by two flights of two A-IE Sandies, and controlled by an HC-130P control plane. A FAC was usually at the rescue site, and was on-scene commander until the Sandies arrived. The A-IEs would survey the crash scene and direct fire against any enemy opposition. If the enemy was there in force, additional fighters could be called in, even diverting those on a mission to the North. Finally, when the Sandy on-scene commander decided it was safe, the helicopter would go in to make the rescue, sometimes dropping a "jungle penetrator" line to pick up the downed crewman, or sending a pararescue crewman down to assist him.

The last SAR operation took place as a part of Operation Freewind, the final massive evacuation of Saigon, when Air Force and Marine Corps helicopters flew mission after mission to ferry out the South Vietnamese patriots who dared not face the Communist occupiers. The American withdrawal from Vietnam ended with the desperate last lift-off from the roof of the American embassy.

In the administration of the Vietnam War, quantitative analysis—number crunching—came to be dominant. In time, numbers and statistics became more real to the far-off commanders in Washington than combat itself. Yet of all the numbers generated, the following are the most meaningful. From 1965 through 1972, the USAF lost 2,254 aircraft, with 6,200 crew members killed, captured, or missing. During the same period, the Aerospace Rescue and Recovery Service saved 3,883 lives, in an effort unparalleled in history. It is fair to say that of all of the missions in the war, none was more daring or more satisfying than that of rescue and recovery. Certainly no numbers were more important.

LESSONS TO BE LEARNED

The United States Air Force entered the war in Southeast Asia when it was ordered to do so, and it withdrew the same way. As senseless as the entire intervention had been, there were still lessons to be learned from it, for there were certain to be other wars in other times. And the war had one positive legacy: a new group of leaders would emerge who were well grounded in the advanced technologies and tactics of the times.

Major James R. Compton, a pilot with the 13th Tactical Fighter Squadron and his Weapon System Operator, Captain Ronald E. Fitzgerald, were both injured when shot down in their F-4 Phantom over Southeast Asia. Here, Compton is being evacuated from his home base at Udorn, Thailand, for medical treatment in the United States.

CHAPTER SEVEN
Drawing Conclusions from Vietnam 1973–1979

The profound social effects of the Vietnam War disconcerted military personnel and their families. Men and women who had always been proud of their uniforms were now gratuitously insulted on the street by those who had protested the war. In films and in the media generally, the military became the butt of jokes, stereotyped as warmongers who lacked the exquisite sensitivity of the war protesters and the draft evaders. It was a difficult time, and the military, especially the Air Force, turned within itself to compensate, coiling like a giant spring to prepare for the next leap forward.

An important element of this inward look was the changing nature of the military as a whole and of the Air Force in particular. The concept of life in a garrison atmosphere, isolated in a special community, had continued even

OPPOSITE:
One important result of the Vietnam War was the recognition that air combat training had to be made more realistic and rigorous. In his painting Guns at Cedar Pass, *Bill Phillips captures the instant in a Red Flag exercise when the F-15 brings an aggressor aircraft into its sights.*

The Boeing AGM-86B, an air-launched cruise missile, won the long, well-publicized competition over its General Dynamics counterpart, the Tomahawk. Both missiles were used with devastating effects in the opening moments of the Persian Gulf War. Here an ALCM is launched during the competition, which not only selected a missile but effectively extended the useful life of the B-52G carrier plane.

after World War II. This was in part due to tradition, but in greater measure to the acute housing shortage that made any available base quarters desirable. One of the greatest economic changes in Air Force life was that many families now routinely purchased homes when transferred to a new station, something that had been unheard of a generation before. This in turn led to far more community involvement, which indeed became an informal element in performance evaluation.

As with the rest of the population, more wives began to work, and the need for day-care centers rose. Among enlisted men it was not uncommon for a husband and wife to have four jobs between them, two regular and two part-time, just to make ends meet.

The Air Force, like the other military services, had grown almost indistinguishable from the civilian community in terms of both problems and achievements. If the civilian community prospered, so did the military; if drugs became a problem in the civilian community, they plagued the military as well. Instead of skewing the service's bell curve away from the civilian norm, the vol-

A unique situation, rarely commented on, is that there has never been a complete test of a U.S. intercontinental ballistic missile weapon system: the launch of an ICBM from an operational unit ending with the detonation of the nuclear warhead on a target. All the elements have been tested exhaustively, but the complete scenario has never been run, and with the end of the Cold War may never be run. This Minuteman, like most ICBMs that were test-fired, was launched from a special test facility.

unteer force had the effect of making the military the mirror image of the community from which it came.

There was a danger implicit in this. The concept of "duty, honor, country" was being replaced by monetary incentives determined by marketplace standards, even though it was obvious that there was no way that the services could ever be economically competitive in the long run. Curiously, even as the Air Force sought to adopt the standards of the business community in terms of pay and working conditions, it became more necessary than ever for the service to take care of its own.

One signficant measure of this was a vastly increased emphasis on education, both within the technical specialities of the service and for personal improvement. Another significant change was the genuine acceptance of racial integration; minorities were fully integrated into the Air Force both officially and in a practical sense, although there were still some individuals who were bigoted. In a similar way, women were beginning at least to have truly equal service opportunities, with more and more positions opening to them.

As great as these social changes were, there were even more dramatic changes in the military workplace. During the long agony of the Vietnam War,

The Convair F-102 Delta Dagger remained in service with the Air Force until 1973, and the Air National Guard flew it through 1976. The portly delta-wing fighter was also used by Turkey and Greece. Almost 400 F-102As were placed in storage at Davis-Monthan Air Force Base, Arizona, and more than half of these were converted to drone aircraft for target and research use. Even as a drone, the Delta Dagger broke new ground as the first full-scale drone without provision for a pilot. Designated PQM-102A, it was flown under radar control to test advanced new missile systems.

The Soviet Union continued to deploy new weapons, aircraft, and missiles. The growth in throw weight and accuracy of their new ICBMs induced the United States to field a new fleet of missiles. This is the first flight of the MX, an ICBM long delayed by congressional debate, but ultimately deployed as the LGM-118 Peacekeeper. Since the dissolution of the Soviet Union, attempts are being made to reduce the number of ICBMs on both sides.

the USAF had to maintain the nuclear deterrent of its bomber and missile forces. More importantly—and in the long run, far more intelligently—it had to continue spending a significant portion of its budget on research and development, to offset the skyrocketing expenditures in that field by the Soviet Union, which achieved one spectacular goal after another. We tend to think of Russia's Sputnik, the first satellite, as the catalyst of American efforts, forgetting that over the years the Soviet Union continually improved its intercontinental ballistic missiles even as it expanded its space exploration and continued to set new aviation records. There was no apparent evidence that there was trouble within the Communist system. On the contrary, Soviet influence was extended to every corner of the globe in a spirit of adventurism that hearkened back past 1917 to the era of Peter the Great, manifesting itself in Afghanistan, Africa, and Central America.

In today's strange mixture of euphoria and uncertainty following the end of the Cold War and the almost simultaneous dissolution of Communism in most countries, it is difficult to remember the magnitude of the threat of the Soviet Union and its allies at the end of the Vietnam War. In 1973 the USSR, with 3,425,000 men and women under arms, had 1,527 intercontinental ballistic missiles, 628 submarine-launched missiles, and 600 intermediate-range missiles. Its long-range air force, the equivalent of the Strategic Air Command, had 700 medium-range and 140 long-range bombers. Its ground forces were backed up by 4,500 tactical aircraft, almost 3,000 interceptors in its air defense forces, and 6,000 more aircraft in the Soviet navy. Sixty-four antiballistic-missile missile launchers ringed Moscow, where the careful preparation of an elaborate civil defense system indicated a willingness to take losses. Elsewhere, the country was defended by more than 10,000 surface-to-air missiles, backed up by the most extensive antiaircraft and radar systems in history. The Warsaw Pact nations greatly outnumbered the NATO forces in manpower and equipment, particularly tanks.

There was nothing to indicate that these vast forces were anything but well trained, well equipped, and well motivated. The Soviet armed forces were immunized by privilege, training, and discipline from the then-secret ills racking the Communist economy. The memories of Khrushchev's warnings still echoed in American ears, from brandishing the Soviet ICBM capability to his shoe-pounding escapade at the United Nations to his boast, "We will bury you!" We thought the threats were real, and so did Mr. Khrushchev and his immediate successors, for as George F. Kennan related about the Russian in his memoirs, "The better things go for him, the more arrogant he is."

The concern was reinforced by a steady succession of new Soviet weapons. Fighters poured off the assembly lines in bewildering variety and number—the MiG-23, 25, 27, 29, and 31; the Sukhoi-17, 20, 22, 24, 25, and 27. Bomber production increased with the modernized Tupelov "Backfire" and "Blackjack" bombers, the latter a B-1B equivalent. Even more frightening was

The success of the Aardvark, General Dynamic's long-nosed, swing-wing F-111, in the Vietnam War vindicated a design that had been the subject of controversy for years. The F-111 served TAC as the F-111F, while the FB-111A provided SAC with a pinpoint delivery system in the most adverse weather. The FB-111A uses the Short Range Attack Missile (SRAM) as its principal weapon. The EF-111A Raven version was developed later for electronic countermeasures.

the deployment of the Soviet SS-17, SS-18, and SS-19 missiles, which had unprecedented accuracy and power to execute the USSR's acknowledged first-strike strategy. The ten-ton SS-18 in particular cast doubt on the survivability of USAF ICBMs. There were substantial improvements in support equipment, with the development of tankers, AWACS-type aircraft and, more significantly, an intensification of pilot training that moved away from dependence upon ground control.

    The Air Force realized that it would have to work harder, train harder, and be far more flexible to meet the changes of the post–Vietnam War world.

Engine and airframe technology had leapfrogged electronic development during the 1960s and 1970s. Aircraft like the Convair F-106 Delta Dart were able to remain in service for many years, their electronic systems being periodically updated. Such longevity made it possible for Air National Guard and Reserve units to fly first-line equipment, fully equivalent to that being flown in the regular Air Force.

In figurative terms, the Air Force spat on its hands and tugged up its pants to prepare to do more with fewer resources.

A new style of leader emerged. the military man well versed in politics. able to defend the budget as well as the coastline. A succession of Chiefs of Staff—Generals John D. Ryan, George S. Brown, David C. Jones, and Lewis Allen, Jr.—lent a management emphasis to the use of resources so that the maximum amount of fighting capability would be achieved, while still matching research and development and training to the next generation of weapon systems. The slogan "You're in the Air Force to Fly and Fight—and Don't You Forget It" took on new meaning for everyone.

General Allen managed the key transitional period between the Carter reductions and the Reagan expansion; he was one of a rare breed of scientist-pilots in the mold of Jimmy Doolittle. It was on Allen's watch that the USAF Space Command (discussed in the next chapter) was created, pointing the way to the apotheosis of air power—space power.

The diminished resources that the various Air Force chiefs so skillfully managed stemmed not so much from an approximately one-third reduction in Congressional appropriations as from three elements shared with the civilian sector. The first was the greatest economic slowdown since the Great Depression of the 1930s. Four recessions between 1971 and 1982 almost brought the nation to its knees and prompted President Jimmy Carter to make devastating comments on the nation's malaise. The Air Force's budget problems were beset by the same double-digit inflation that choked the nation's economy. The budget was further taxed by the changeover to a professional volunteer force, which made pay comparability with civilian employment a necessity. The pay raises ultimately forced personnel costs up to about 40 percent of the total Air Force budget.

At the same time the Air Force had to address a host of challenges, some old, some new. Many of these derived from the peacekeeping process of détente started by President Nixon as a step away from mutual assured destruction (MAD), perhaps the most appropriate acronym in history. The transition between the two concepts, MAD and détente, began with the interminable Strategic Arms Limitation Talks (SALT), which codified a rough nuclear balance with the Soviet Union.

Maintaining this balance for the future required that a great deal of the USAF research and development expenditure would be in far more esoteric areas than in the past, areas that were a closed book to all but the most prescient. The most demanding was in Command, Control and Communication (C^3) but there were also advanced new radars, lasers, missiles, munitions, exotic metals, and other new materials. These elements were difficult to defend in a budget, for many were top secret, and their benefits would not be visible to Congress or the public for decades. In most instances, the public only became aware of the remarkable effects of this long-term R&D at the time of the

Persian Gulf War, when they were manifested in AWACS, J-STARS, satellite systems, Stealth fighters, and smart bombs. These of course were only the most visible results of the R&D; the bulk of research had resulted in projects and programs that did their jobs silently but indispensably in the background.

After Vietnam the basic principle of Air Force existence had changed from making war to a concept of combat-readiness, in which the Air Force would maintain its deterrent power and still be able to react to smaller wars that might occur anywhere in the world. At the same time, the Air Force embarked upon an ambitious reequipment and modernization program to counter deficiencies made evident in Vietnam. In the process, the leadership created doctrine and policies to ensure that while the new equipment was being procured, there would be sufficient training and spare parts provided to use it. This sounds neither particularly brilliant nor especially difficult. In fact it was both, because in the competition for funds it was far easier to defer the procurement of spare parts or the implementation of training than to defer the purchase of aircraft or equipment. The reasons are simple. New aircraft possess implicit propaganda and public relations value, and have many natural advocates. Units in the field want them, the commanders see a need for them, the manufacturers want to sell them, and congressmen want the business to go to their districts. Spare parts have far fewer advocates, and training even less.

The results of skimping on those things often do not appear until later (indeed, they may never appear, if the interval between wars is long enough), but when they do appear, they are inevitably disastrous.

Despite the many pressures, the USAF managed to maintain a balanced posture, keeping the minimum numbers of spares on hand by means of new accounting and inventory techniques (it was called increasing the "teeth-to-tail" ratio at the time), and expanding training at every level from the mechanic on the line, to the Air Force Academy, to the professional military schools.

EDUCATION AND TRAINING

The very nature of flying, with its requirement to understand aerodynamic principles, engineering, meteorology, navigation, ballistics, and much, much more, meant that personnel had to be both well educated and continuously trained. From the early days of the Air Service, regular officers were most often graduates of West Point, while reserve officers might come from civilian colleges, ROTC, or aviation cadet programs.

The need for continual technical training was recognized early on with the establishment of the Air Service Engineering School at McCook Field in 1919. From the first small class of November of that year there grew the Air

The role of the Boeing B-52H has expanded steadily over the years; it now includes sea surveillance, minelaying, anti-surface warfare, maritime interdiction, defense suppression, and precision strikes with air-launched cruise missiles. It has been modified almost annually, and the process goes on: B-52Hs will receive the AGM-129A advanced cruise missile, and will carry twelve on underwing pylons.

Force Institute of Technology (AFIT), which has trained thousands of officers both in-house and at civilian universities over the years. In the years that followed, the Air Corps Tactical School, which concentrated on tactics and doctrine, was established. It was the precursor of the Air University, which has a wide range of professional schools for officers and airmen.

The Air Force Academy, established in 1954, has made a profound impression upon Air Force educational standards, and has graduated more than 24,000 officers. As West Point is for the Army, it will become the primary source for general officers in the future. It was from the Academy's ranks that many of the Vietnam veterans came who called for the establishment of more rigorous combat training in the form of Red Flag.

RED FLAG

In studies of fighter pilots in four wars, a significant statistic stands out: a pilot's chances of survival go up dramatically after his fifth mission. A profound corollary emerged during the Vietnam War: the chances of both surviving those first five missions and of inflicting damage on the enemy will go up dramatically if training is made very realistic.

The kill ratio—the number of enemy planes downed compared to the number of U.S. planes downed—in the Vietnam War was significantly lower than the kill ratio achieved in the Korean War. The Navy addressed the problem in 1968, and achieved significant success with what is today popularly called the Top Gun program, imprinted indelibly upon the public's memory by the film of the same name. Top Gun is primarily designed for fighter-against-fighter combat, teaching the hard lessons of dogfighting.

The general assessment of USAF training after the Vietnam War was that it was excellent for peacetime, but lacked the rigor required for combat operations. After graduating from flying school, and then being checked out in a first-line fighter, young pilots did not have a chance to simulate anything like real combat. A number of factors interfered: environmental considerations, the expense of munitions and fuel, and more often than not, flying safety. To offset this, three programs were created, the most famous of which is Red Flag, the combat-simulation program conducted in the United States. A corresponding program for Air Force units in the Far East is called Cope Thunder. In Europe, there is an Aggressor unit—U.S. personnel acting the roles of enemy forces— against which Air Force units train.

Unlike Top Gun, Red Flag is a miniwar game using composite forces, not just a dogfighting exercise. The war—carefully mimicking possible scenarios in Europe and the Middle East for the most part—lasts six weeks. A first-line fighter squadron is the core unit, and it may have representatives from as many as nineteen other squadrons, each of which participates for two weeks. A typical mission might include RF-4Cs, F-16s, F-15s, F-111Fs, KC-135s, and

B-52s encountering aggressor squadron aircraft simulating the planes and tactics of the putative enemy. Units of Allied nations, most often France and England but also many other pro-Western countries, frequently participate. The value of these joint programs was proved in the Persian Gulf War.

In addition to airborne exercises, Red Flag simulates the entire electronic spectrum of enemy radars, SAMs, and radar-controlled antiaircraft. For firing practice, there are ground targets of tanks, aircraft, and gun emplacements, some of them real, some simulated.

The flying in Red Flag is very close to combat; the only things lacking are actual bullets and missiles being fired. Aircraft and crew members are pushed to the very limits of their capabilities, with no quarter asked or given. The value of the Red Flag exercise is reinforced in the electronic wizardry that tracks it and preserves it for further review. Each aircraft carries an electronic pod, looking much like a blunted missile, that transmits the flight data—position, air speed, altitude—to the ground for both real-time display and to be recorded for playback. Arguments between pilots as to who won or lost a dogfight are settled by close analysis of the Air Combat Manuevering Instrumentation electronic presentations—four-color video screens that

For the aircraft enthusiast, one of the sadder developments in the history of modern warfare is the increasing tendency toward low-visibility paint schemes in which even the national insignias are barely visible. These veteran B-52s are from Fairchild Air Force Base's famous 92d Bomb Wing.

The USAF Thunderbirds against a sunlit sky. There was considerable congressional opposition to the idea of the Thunderbirds acquiring the new and expensive F-16s that were just equipping first-line units. A compromise was reached—the Thunderbirds' F-16s retained a full combat capability, and in an emergency, could go immediately to war.

portray what happened in the air. There are no excuses or assumptions in Red Flag.

The air crew members who come to Red Flag are already well trained, proficient, and well motivated. Red Flag is the polishing process that takes them beyond routine combat situational awareness into a world in which the war plan is seen as a whole. The hard, and risky, engagements are carefully analyzed, and the combatants have a chance to talk about them afterward. Unfortunately, budget cuts have forced the cancellation of Red Flag, in what will probably prove to be false economy.

Just as the professionalism and expertise of the Strategic Air Command influenced the character of the entire Air Force in the 1960s, so have the realism and rigor of Red Flag exercises influenced other training in the service. The attention to detail, the meticulous analysis, the enthusiasm, have become the standard throughout the Air Force.

THE ELECTRONIC REVOLUTION

Nowhere was training more necessary than in the handling of the massive electronic revolution, which was changing the Air Force as not even jet or rocket

The Lockheed C-5B Galaxy has been transformed from an intertheater troop carrier to a mercy aircraft, carrying tons of supplies to former enemies. Shown here in three-tone camouflage, the Galaxy has outlived the controversy that surrounded its inception to become a reliable workhorse. Just visible is the twenty-eight-wheel undercarriage originally intended for operation out of unimproved fields.

The Lockheed C-130 Hercules is probably one of the most welcome warplanes in the world, for it is invariably chosen for humanitarian missions to countries that either have suffered a natural disaster or are recovering from the aftermath of war. Conceived as military transport to combat the Communist menace, C-130s are now flying supplies to trouble spots within the former Soviet Union. C-130s have been in production for more than thirty years, and the 2,000th example recently came off the line.

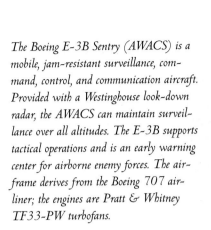

The Boeing E-3B Sentry (AWACS) is a mobile, jam-resistant surveillance, command, control, and communication aircraft. Provided with a Westinghouse look-down radar, the AWACS can maintain surveillance over all altitudes. The E-3B supports tactical operations and is an early warning center for airborne enemy forces. The airframe derives from the Boeing 707 airliner; the engines are Pratt & Whitney TF33-PW turbofans.

engines had. Beginning in the late 1950s, the Cold War spurred electronic technology far faster than hot wars had in the past, with dramatic effect upon future developments.

The expense and the degree of risk in the electronic revolution were comparable to that of the World War II Manhattan Project. The revolution was spread out among several hundred programs that included the general development of computers and software, as well as systems for electronic countermeasures, radars, command and control, satellites, navigation, and landing. Electronics was to become both the sword and the shield of the American military, as the Gulf War made evident.

Electronic warfare has tracks back through nine decades of history, first occurring during the Russo-Japanese War of 1904, when Russian operators heard the Japanese using radios to direct the bombardment on Port Arthur and sent out signals to jam them. Development was slow but steady thereafter, passing through the rather primitive radios used in World War I to the very advanced radar systems of World War II. Electronic countermeasure development similarly ranged from simple to sophisticated, from Window, the aluminum-foil chaff used to deceive German radars in the raid on Hamburg, to devices that alerted a pilot to radar surveillance (from which came the "fuzz-busters" of today's speeding motorists), to shells and missiles that home in on the radars tracking them.

The development of modern electronics systems was extraordinarily expensive. At times as much as 26 percent of the entire defense budget was being invested in electronic hardware. It was also time-consuming. It was not uncommon for half a career to be dedicated to the pursuit of a single element of a new system. One of the most important differences was the need for an entirely new class of personnel able to work in the abstract on the great ideas of the future. A special organization, the Electronics Systems Division (ESD), was established to recruit, train, and exploit the ideas of such individuals. Head-quartered at Hanscom Air Force Base, Massachusetts, ESD was the equivalent of the famed Aeronautical Systems Division (ASD) of long history at Wright-Patterson Air Force Base. Like ASD, ESD, in concert with the most advanced companies in the industry, set nearly impossible requirements, then worked miracles to achieve them.

Unlike conventional hardware, such as aircraft or engines, there was no quick way to procure a single electronic system, which by its very nature had relationships both broad and deep with other systems. The entire architecture of electronic warfare had to be developed simultaneously, and the rapid changes and advances in the field had to be integrated across the board. This placed intellectual demands on the planners even greater than the demands they placed on the budget.

The process was more difficult because it was so agonizingly long term, some projects requiring five or ten years to come to fruition, consuming dollar and manpower assets for the entire period. Not all were successful. In some cases the threat changed or disappeared. In others it was simply not possible to achieve all that was desired, as when the Air Force attempted to develop a generic, all-purpose electronic warfare capability, going beyond combating specific enemy equipment to address as yet unknown threats. It was too much to achieve, and the effort failed, even though it yielded many spin-offs. Yet the USAF electronics revolution was a success in general, and proved itself both in the hot-war victory in the Persian Gulf and the Cold War triumph over a bankrupt Communist system.

THE GREAT SPY PLANES

The electronics revolution was matched aerodynamically over the years by a number of aircraft, including the Lockheed F-117 Stealth fighter and the Northrop B-2 Stealth bomber. But the best evidence of aerodynamic refinement, created a generation before, were two of the most remarkable aircraft of all time, the U-2 and the SR-71. Both were Lockheeds and both were the products of the famous "Skunk Works" where Kelly Johnson and later Ben Rich led the most innovative team in aviation history.

While the two aircraft originated long before the Vietnam War, and operated through it, the true story of their development and use did not become public knowledge until the mid-1970s. The sailplanelike U-2 made its first flight on August 1, 1955; it continues in active service in modified form as the TR-1 and ER-2. The U-2 gained its greatest fame—or notoriety—on May 1, 1960, when one of the planes, piloted by Gary Powers, was shot down

The breadth of Kelly Johnson's design genius at Lockheed was amazing. It ranged from the utter simplicity of the original U-2 at right (really just a powered glider) to the rocketship sophistication of the SR-71. Yet even the U-2 was suitable for updating, so that it reentered production and took on a new life as the TR-1.

Few aircraft have captured the imagination of the world like the Lockheed SR-71 Blackbird. Capable of Mach 3 speeds at altitudes in excess of 80,000 feet, its unparalleled performance was never even approached by the aircraft of any other nation. The SR-71 was ultimately retired from USAF service, only to begin work with NASA as a research aircraft.

by a fusillade of surface-to-air missiles over the Soviet Union. This gave Premier Nikita Khrushchev the opportunity to savage President Eisenhower, causing the Paris summit meeting to collapse and signaling the end of the era of high-altitude intrusion by bombers. The U-2 served for many years thereafter, however, flying missions over virtually every square inch of the earth's surface. It was a U-2 that uncovered the missile sites being built in Cuba in 1962.

The U-2 was created from the mating of a basic Lockheed F-104 fuse-lage to a slender wing of great span. The resulting high-aspect ratio, the rela-tionship of wing length to width, helped the U-2 fly at great altitudes and for long distances. Despite its relatively small size, it was continually improved over the years with new cameras and highly classified new electronic gear, ultimately including the J-STARS system.

Unlike the U-2, a gentle, almost ladylike airplane, the Lockheed SR-71 was a raging bull. It represented a tremendous leap forward in perfor-mance, combining the altitude and range capability of the U-2 with a blister-ing sustained cruise speed more than three times the speed of sound. The first official flight of the A-12 version took place on April 26, 1959. Later recon-naissance versions were to be called RS-71, but in announcing the existence of the program, President Lyndon Johnson referred to it as the SR-71, which remained the permanent designation.

Affectionately called Blackbird, in tribute to its ebony color, the SR-71's lines gave it some stealth attributes, while its 2,100 mph speed and 80,000-foot altitude capability gave it immunity to interception. The USAF used it for global reconnaissance, dispatching it instantly to any potential

On its last official mission, en route to storage at the Smithsonian Institution's National Air and Space Museum, the Lockheed Blackbird set a new transconti-nental speed record at 2,124.41 mph. The Blackbird's greatest asset was the ability of its special reconnaissance equipment to cover as much as 100,000 square miles of ter-ritory per hour, day or night, rain or shine.

Even though the U-2 was a relatively simple aircraft, it was extremely demanding to fly because its light structure was vulnerable to excessive G forces. This is one of two trainers built, the Lockheed U-2CT. A raised instructor's seat was installed in place of the main equipment bay.

trouble spot in the world on missions that might last from two to twelve hours. Although the airplane was easy to fly, the missions were arduous because of the astronautlike pressure suits the two-man crews wore. Unlike satellites, which follow a predictable orbit and map the terrain below in precise sequence, the SR-71 fleet was extraordinarily flexible, able to go anywhere from Antarctica to the heart of Africa, until annual operating costs of $300 million forced the Air Force to retire them. Three were transferred to NASA for research work.

As with the U-2, the aerodynamics of the SR-71 were but a platform for the cameras and the electronic surveillance gear—mostly classified and all products of the electronic revolution, a revolution that still goes on in aircraft of more fantastic capability whose existence is not acknowledged.

Even more sophisticated electronics are included in the satellite systems that have taken over the reconnaissance role, and which monitor events in every country of the world. These latter-day successors to Sputnik also point the way to exotic future antiballistic missile defense systems.

NEW PROCUREMENT

Despite the reduction in available funds, the years immediately after the Vietnam War saw a surge in the development of totally new designs, and the modernization of older ones. These efforts were driven both by the deficiencies in USAF aircraft and missiles revealed during the war, and by the impressive series of new planes being produced by the Soviet Union. There was another factor. Even before the war in Vietnam had ended, the Air Force was anxious to create its own designs, for it was embarrassed that two of its most recent procurements, the McDonnell Douglas F-4 and the Vought A-7, had originally been designed and built for the Navy.

In the previous decade, the procurement climate had changed drastically because of the increase in costs and the intensive scrutiny of the process by Congress, the media, and the public. Instead of having several companies producing fighter and bomber prototypes for evaluation, Secretary of Defense McNamara had inaugurated Total Package Procurement (TPP), elaborate paper competitions in which as many as three freight-car loads of documentation were submitted for analysis. The fatal flaw of TPP was that there was no

Many developments were successful, but did not go into production because of budget limitations. One of these was the Boeing YC-14, designed to replace the Lockheed C-130. The YC-14 featured an unusual technique in which the engines were mounted on the leading edge to blow across the wing's upper surface. With a 27,000-pound payload, the YC-14 could take off after a 1,000-foot run.

fly-off competition—the airplane you bought from the paper submissions was the airplane you got. This cumbersome procurement process, which caused development costs to balloon to as much as $3 billion, was used for the last time on what was to become the standard USAF air-superiority fighter, the F-15. Fortunately, the era of strict adherence to quantitative analysis had passed, and the Air Force was listening to protesting voices within its own ranks.

THE EAGLE

A new fighter had been needed since the mid-1960s. Despite the bad experience with the multirole TFX fighter that led to the F-111, the Air Force was considering the F-X, Fighter Experimental, a 60,000-pound multimission aircraft. A young, outspoken officer had appeared on the scene to argue vigorously for a new idea, one that would first alter, and then totally change, the Total Package Procurement concept.

Major John R. Boyd, an expert fighter pilot as well as the originator of many new air-to-air tactics, put forward his concept of a single-purpose air-superiority fighter that could out-turn and out-speed enemy fighters at all altitudes. His successful advocacy led to a redefinition of requirements, a sign of the remarkable change within the Air Force. After almost ten years of Department of Defense domination of procurement criteria, dissent from within the ranks was possible, and the service began to assert itself again.

The F-X had begun under TPP, but the changes advocated by Boyd shaped a year-long paper competition among three contractors, North

American Rockwell, Fairchild-Hiller, and McDonnell Douglas. The latter won with the design that became the F-15 Eagle, a new departure in fighter design that responded to all the lessons learned so painfully in Vietnam. Unlike its predecessor, the F-4, the Eagle's great maneuverability derives from its large wing area and high power-to-weight ratio. The pilot has superb, 360-degree visibility through a huge canopy covering the cockpit, which is sited well forward. A General Electric M-61A six-barrel Gatling gun provides firepower along with four Sparrow and four Sidewinder missiles.

The Eagle takes full advantage of the electronic revolution, being designed to work closely with AWACS (airborne warning and control system) aircraft, and incorporating the latest in pulse Doppler radar, inertial navigation, and a heads-up display (HUD) for instrumentation. And, again unlike the F-4, the F-15's engines do not produce long trails of exhaust smoke to give its position away.

The F-15 first flew on July 27, 1972, and became operational with the 58th Tactical Fighter Training Wing on November 14, 1974. It has since become the backbone of the USAF fighter force, as well as serving in the air forces of Israel, Saudi Arabia, and Japan.

THE F-16 FIGHTING FALCON

Even as the F-15 was in development, there were pressures for the development of an even smaller aircraft intended as a low-cost alternative to the $20 million

McDonnell Douglas followed the success of its F-4 Phantom with the F-15 Eagle, which incorporated all the lessons learned in more than a decade's operation of the Phantom. The F-15 was designed to counter the new generation of Soviet air-superiority aircraft. The aircraft was instantly popular with U.S. fighter pilots for its superb visibility, high maneuverability, and tremendous power-to-weight ratio.

Eagle. Boyd, now a colonel, joined forces with others in the Pentagon to form the "fighter mafia," a small, influential group dedicated to the concept of a lightweight fighter. Their efforts were first rebuffed as an intrusion on acquisition of the F-15, but the procurement pendulum had swung, returning to the "fly before buy" concept that had served so well for so many years, and the lightweight fighter they proposed was perfect for retesting the concept.

In the ensuing competition, the General Dynamics XF-16 won over the Northrop XF-17, but the latter was then developed in cooperation with McDonnell Douglas into a Navy lightweight fighter, the F/A 18 Hornet.

By this time, the XF-16 had overcome opposition within the Air Force staff (which preferred the procurement of additional F-15s), and was characterized by Chief of Staff General David C. Jones as a "swing-force" fighter, meaning that it would be able to perform air-to-ground missions as well as its originally intended air-to-air role.

The F-16 was selected as the standard fighter for Belgium, Denmark, Norway, and the Netherlands, becoming the largest international military co-construction program in history. Subsequently, it was adopted by Egypt, Israel, South Korea, Singapore, Thailand, Turkey, and Venezuela. It made its combat debut with Israel in the famous strike against the Osirak nuclear reactor near Baghdad, Iraq. The round-trip distance of 1,200 miles for that attack was accomplished without refueling. Later, it was used in combination with the F-15 with devastating effect in the invasion of Lebanon in June 1982. Eighty Syrian fighters and five helicopters were shot down without any Israeli losses, an incredible victory ratio, and a tribute to both the Eagle and the Falcon.

MODERNIZATION PROGRAMS

For the first sixty years of flight, new models of aircraft, both military and civil, were adopted for use in rapid succession. In the 1940s and 1950s, six new fighter systems were acquired in production quantities each decade. In the 1960s and 1970s, only two systems were procured each decade. Now, it looks as if only one new fighter, the Lockheed F-22, will be procured for the rest of the century. Larger aircraft have even greater longevity so that there are 707s and B-52s flying long decades after they left the production line.

The B-52 is probably the greatest example of extending the life of an aircraft design by updating its component systems. Over the years the bombing system has been replaced, the structure reinforced, new armament storage provided, and entire generations of electronic countermeasures introduced. More than forty years after its first flight, it still wins first place in some elements of the Air Force bombing competitions.

In the past, modifications were created when something broke on a weapons system, or some new requirement surfaced. Now, modifications are built into a system's master plan, and installed via a phased-improvement pro-

gram. One, called Pacer Classic, saved the forced replacement of the entire fleet of Northrop T-38r trainers by means of a special program that incorporated ten necessary modifications in a single package. In another example, the Boeing KC-135 tanker fleet will be able to operate well into the twenty-first century because of a $10 billion reengining program. The alternative was a $30 billion procurement of new tankers. In a similar way, when the airlift fleet was found to be deficient in capacity during the Vietnam War, the workhorse Lockheed C-141 was brought in to have a twenty-three-foot, four-inch-long section inserted in the fuselage, and modified with an in-flight refueling capability. The modification was equivalent to obtaining ninety more C-141s, at about one-tenth the cost of such a procurement.

Modernization is expensive. It currently costs about $3.6 billion a year, but it saves roughly three times that amount by expanding the capability of existing weapons systems, extending their service lives and avoiding new procurements.

The tails tell the tale. Each of these B-52Hs has a "stinger," a six-barrel 20mm cannon operated by a "tail gunner" whose seat is in the forward compartment with the rest of the crew. As the missions of the B-52 changed, the hallowed position of gunner was dropped from the crew, ending an era that had begun in World War I.

The boom operator's view of the beginning of an aerial refueling between a KC-135 and a B-52. Air refueling goes on every minute of the day, but it is never routine, for the danger of collision is always present.

DOING MORE WITH LESS—THE TOTAL FORCE CONCEPT

Even before the Vietnam War had ground to its painful end, then–Secretary of Defense Melvin Laird called for a total force concept, one that integrated the Air National Guard and the Reserves so tightly into the Air Force that they became equivalents of first-line regular units. It was not an entirely popular decision, and many people thought that it might be impossible to do. Over the years, the Air National Guard and the Reserves had frequently had to make do with obsolete equipment and lowered standards.

As has so often been the case with the Air Force, a leader emerged from the National Guard, one exactly right for the time, and perfectly suited for the task at hand: revising the Air National Guard from a politicized force that was often more a state flying club than a combat organization into an integral part of the USAF. His name was Winston P. Wilson, and he had more influence on the Guard component than any man in its long history.

The Air National Guard has its roots in the 1908 "Aeronautic Corps" of the New York National Guard. Over the course of eight decades it has survived budget cuts, wars, politics, and mobilizations, often because it was content to make do with obsolete aircraft and a paper mission.

During World War II, National Guard personnel were called into federal service. These Guardsman filled an important role, for although their experience might have been limited, it was far greater than that of the brand-new recruits pouring in. The Guard organizations served effectively as stiffeners to old units and as cadres to new ones. But the state governors were unwilling to give up the patronage implicit in an Air National Guard, and in 1946 the Army Air Forces had reluctantly agreed to form a dual-component Reserve system, to include both the Reserves and the state-controlled Air Guard units. The effect was to have many separate state air forces, all flying obsolete equipment, lacking a definite mission, and not prepared for immediate deployment into combat.

The Korean War revealed other deficiencies in the way the Air Force regarded the National Guard. Even though aviation elements of the Guard were mobilized and served as individual units, many of their key personnel were transferred to other Air Force assignments. The result was that the Guard units were called "Sunday soldiers" or "weekend warriors" and were looked down on by regular units.

In 1953 Brigadier General Winston P. "Wimpy" Wilson took over the direction of the Air Force Division, National Guard Bureau, leading it as Hap Arnold had led the USAAF, without regard for the niceties of administration but with a total focus on obtaining results. Over the next eighteen years—an unprecedented tenure for a military officer—Wilson put the Guard on a combat footing. An essential element of his leadership technique was paying attention to the details that mattered. Wilson changed the drill schedule from four

Wednesday nights a month to two Wednesday nights and one full weekend. The results were remarkable, and the system was widely adopted in all of the Reserve programs for U.S. armed forces.

It had been traditional for the Guard to be responsible for its own training, with predictable results. When called up, Guard units were often not able to meet the demands of active service, not because the personnel were not talented, but because they were not well trained. Wilson insisted that the Air Force provide the Guard with training as rigorous and as carefully evaluated as the training given its own units. The result was Guard units equal in every respect to regular Air Force units, and for the first time the Guard was included in national war plans.

From this initial benchmark, Wilson had a triumphant series of achievements capped by the assignment of first-line aircraft to the Guard. He saw to it that Air Guard units augmented active duty units in peacetime, so that there would be no lag time if the Guard was called up. When he retired as a major general in 1971, Wilson had changed a collection of rag-tag air forces into a fighting organization that constituted almost 20 percent of USAF strength, and which, as we will see, made invaluable contributions to the prosecution of the Persian Gulf War.

The history of the United States Air Force Reserve has been filled with as many ups and downs as that of the Air National Guard. Its origins go back to June 1916, when its primary role was to provide approximately 10,000 pilots who were graduated as RMAs, Reserve Military Aviators. After World War I, the drastic cuts in regular forces reduced the scope of the Reserves almost to the vanishing point. When World War II began there were about 3,200 reservists on active duty, including 1,500 pilots. The Reserve Officer Training Corps would have great impact on all the services; by June 1941 there were 58,000 Reserve officers in the Army, outnumbering regulars by four to one.

The drastic demobilization after World War II reduced the aviation Reserve units to little more than flying clubs, offering proficiency training in a handful of aircraft. It was not until 1948, at the direction of President Truman, that an Air Force Reserve program was established that trained reservists in tactical units designed for prompt mobilization. At the same time, the Air Force ROTC grew swiftly until by 1951 there were 145,000 cadets on campuses around the country.

Headquarters, USAF, regarded the Reserves primarily as a manpower pool, to be called upon in an emergency but not to be expected to go immediately into battle. When the Korean War broke out, 149,000 reservists were called to active duty, not without some bitter controversy. There were complaints that some Reserve units were poorly prepared, and that reservists had been called to go to Korea while many regulars remained on duty within the United States. A virtual mutiny occurred at Randolph Air Force Base, where

reservists protested having to fly war-weary B-29s in combat while regulars were assigned to more modern aircraft in the Strategic Air Command and stayed in the United States. Another source of friction was the fact that, like members of the Air Guard, reservists were assigned to any active duty organization that needed their talents, weakening the organic strength of the Air Force Reserve units.

Yet the invaluable service they rendered made a more extensive buildup of the Reserve force inevitable in the following years. In January 1955 a new program for fifty-one Air Force Reserve Force wings was established. The initial flying emphasis in the Reserve was on troop carrier and air-sea rescue squadrons, although for a time there were also bomber and fighter-bomber units. Later the Reserves would fulfill almost every Air Force role with distinction. Three Reserve rescue and recovery squadrons saved sixty-one lives following the eruption of Mt. St. Helens in 1980; later that year a Reserve Special Operation squadron, the 302d, rescued fifteen people trapped by fire on the balconies of the MGM Grand Hotel in Las Vegas. There were also numerous Reserve nonflying units, including medical and aerial port squadrons.

The Reserves were mobilized four times in the 1960s and again in 1970, but there began a natural drift toward the total force concept when Reserve units became associate units, maintaining and flying the aircraft assigned to regular Military Air Command airlift units. As with the Air National Guard,

the Reserves made their greatest contribution to the total force concept during operations Desert Shield and Desert Storm. Their ability hinged on the stringent training and education that has become characteristic of the Air Force.

The similarity between the MiG-29 and the McDonnell Douglas F-15 is striking. The MiG-29 has given flight demonstrations all over the world, and is available for sale to all comers.

THE TIDE BEGINS TO TURN

A resurgence in pride and capability came about in the USAF as the 1980s began. The sense of self-doubt over the Vietnam War faded away, at the same time that the civilian populace began to be more accepting. The decade after Vietnam had been one of introspection and reorganization as the force dropped in numbers from a peak of 904,759 in 1968 to 559,450 in 1979; the coil had been compressed to the maximum. The years that followed would see the Air Force rebound sharply in the biggest and most effective buildup of peacetime forces in history. It would also see the subtle but momentous transition from the concept of air power to that of space power.

Sam Lyons Jr.

CHAPTER EIGHT
Our Guns, Their Butter 1980—THE PRESENT

The decade of the 1980s opened with a totally new approach to air power as President Ronald Reagan and his Secretary of Defense, Caspar Weinberger, gained congressional assent to pour massive amounts of funds into the largest American rearmament program in peacetime history. This program had two goals, one overt and one covert. The first derived in part from our humiliation over the Iranian seizure of American hostages, which revealed how weakened our armed forces had become as a result of the unilateral disarmament policies of the Carter years. The weakness was exacerbated by abysmal intelligence work in the Middle East, a problem that would affect our dealings with Iraq and beyond. The Reagan administration was determined that the United States would in the future conduct its relations with other states from a position of strength. The second goal was subtly Machiavellian, for its aim was to bring the forty-year-long armament race to an end in the bankruptcy of the Soviet Union as it strained to match the United States buildup. Both goals were achieved; their full import is still to be determined.

In 1982, the task of leading the Air Force fell to the eminently qualified General Charles A. Gabriel. "Gabe" was almost certainly the most popular Chief of Staff in history, and the first since Tooey Spaatz to have a widely used, nonpejorative nickname. He was also one of the few to have flown combat missions in two wars—100 in Korea, where he shot down two MiG-15s, and another 152 in Vietnam. Gabriel and his successor, General Larry D. Welch, guided the complex melding of new aircraft, new spacecraft, higher levels of training, and the integration of the Reserve and Guard components into the total force concept. One of Gabriel's most daunting tasks was to remove the stake President Jimmy Carter had driven into the heart of the Rockwell International B-1B program.

THE B-1B LANCER

The B-52 had first flown in 1952, and over the years a number of follow-on aircraft had been proposed as replacements in its deep-penetration role. The

OPPOSITE:
One of the astonishing phenomena of the jet age is the thrust-to-weight ratios provided by the latest generation of enormously powerful engines. This Sam Lyons painting catches the Lead Solo pilot of the Thunderbirds in a vertical climb.

The Fairchild A-10, flying much higher than it usually does.

The visibility afforded the pilot of the McDonnell Douglas F-15 is unsurpassed.

OPPOSITE:

The F-15's power-to-weight ratio provides the means for vertical climbs like this.

The Rockwell International B-1B has, like the General Dynamics F-111, endured a controversial development program. Both aircraft had too much expected of them, and both have required time to mature. Faced with shortcomings in the electronic counter-measures equipment, B-1B crews have developed techniques to offset the deficiencies.

Lithe and swift in the air, the B-1B seems ponderous on the ground, with its gaping air intakes and complex landing gear.

B-52 had been supplemented for a time by the Convair B-58, a supersonic bomber of elegant line but crippling operating costs. The General Dynamics FB-111 had been foisted upon the Strategic Air Command as a partial way out of the general debacle resulting from McNamara's TFX brainstorm. The FB-111 ultimately proved extremely capable, serving for twenty-five years before being retired, a tribute to the airplane and the men who flew it—and the additional funds lavished on it. The 1960s also saw the long, expensive development of the XB-70, a high-altitude bomber whose mission was knocked out by the same kind of missiles that destroyed Gary Powers's U-2.

Hanging for years over the B-52 replacement drama was the specter of the B-1, the center of a controversial development struggle that made it a favorite whipping boy of the media. The inherent USAF love for the manned bomber had kept predecessors of the B-1 program going for a long time, despite the argument that the increased accuracy of the USAF intercontinental ballistic missiles made a follow-on to the B-52 unnecessary. The B-1 was given a new lease on life in the early 1960s, when the concept of the Strategic Triad gained favor as the most effective nuclear deterrent. The Triad comprised land-based ICBMs, missiles launched from submarines, and traditional bombers, still needed because they were the most flexible of the weapons and could be recalled in flight.

Design studies for a new low-level, high-speed bomber had begun in 1961; they continued for twenty years, under a variety of designations. A fitful start was made in 1974, with the first flight of the B-1. President Carter canceled production of the bomber in 1977, opting instead to convert the phantom bargaining chip of the cruise missile into a weapons system. In 1981, President Reagan reversed Carter's decision, authorizing the production of 100

Slipping into its element, the B-1B heads for the ground. Its ability to flash along the surface of the ground, masking its radar return by threading its way around mountains and through the valleys, makes it a stealth bomber in its own way.

B-1Bs as an interim bomber. Work on the cruise missile was accelerated, as was the development of the supersecret Stealth bomber, which would in time materialize as the Northrop B-2.

The highly modified B-1B was the first new bomber to join SAC in more than twenty years. With only 1 percent of a B-52's radar signature, the terrain-following B-1B made a very potent penetrator. Yet it was plagued by stories of its protracted development and by exaggerated reports of difficulties in testing, which the media seized upon to cast doubts on it. Every deficiency was magnified. Early fuel leaks are not uncommon in new aircraft—they occurred in the B-47 and the B-52, for example—but they were ballooned out of proportion for the B-1B. The fuel leaks were fixed but the stories were not. There were also initial difficulties with the terrain-following software, but these were corrected early on. The major deficiency, admitted to by SAC, is in the B-1Bs electronic countermeasures (ECM) suite, which has never performed as required. Despite this, the B-1B is known by the most knowledgeable people— its crews—to be the best operational bomber in the world today, one that justifies its long gestation period. Because of the level of technical sophistication and for security reasons, it is impossible to convey to the public just how the crews have taken up the slack for the bomber. Crew skills compensate for most of the deficiencies in the ECM. Crew members combine their intimate knowledge of the terrain and the disposition and techniques of enemy defenses to enhance the B-1B's capabilities. Skimming over the surface of the terrain in all weather conditions at near-supersonic speed, the B-1B crews know that they can penetrate enemy defenses almost with the ease of the Stealth bomber.

MISSILES AS THE PRELUDE TO SPACE

With the introduction of the intercontinental ballistic missile, the Air Force managed a cultural revolution within its ranks fully equivalent to the replacement of the horse by the tank in the land army. Although the ICBM did not replace the manned bomber, it did create a world of new requirements in research, recruitment, training, and career development. This subsequently proved to be an essential springboard to the Air Force's establishing a supremacy in space power that exceeded its own aspirations.

Curiously, while air power historically had its outspoken advocates in Billy Mitchell, Benny Foulois, and others, the reality of space power came almost silently upon the scene. A pertinent reason for this quiet approach was a series of international agreements outlawing weapons of mass destruction in space. Yet space is the ultimate high ground, essential for ballistic-missile warning (the current land-based warning system is openly regarded as inadequate by Air Force leaders) and for satellite operations. Control of space is necessary to protect U.S. and Allied space-based systems, and to negate, if necessary, any potential enemy's space systems.

The effort to achieve supremacy in space requires the same sort of internal Air Force adjustment as did the establishment of the missile fleet: persuading leaders to accept the new challenges, allocating an appropriate amount of the budget, and then fostering the inter- and intraservice cooperation to make it work. The rapid growth in capability and sophistication in the missile program provides an indication of how space power evolved.

THE ICBM ARSENAL

General Bernard Schriever guided the pell-mell race to create an initial ICBM capability, fielding the Atlas force in an amazingly short period of time. But this was only part of his achievement. As the Atlas was being modified for operational use, it was also adapted for use as a research vehicle and as a booster for Project Mercury test vehicles. Development was also proceeding on the Titan missile, which served as the missile heavyweight from 1963 through 1987, and was then designated as a primary boost vehicle for launching satellites.

The liquid-fueled Atlas and Titan missiles were interim systems designed to fill the gap until the deployment of the LGM-30 Minuteman, which began to enter SAC in 1962 and which reached a force level of 1,000 by 1967. As the Air Force had created almost instantaneously an Atlas missile force to deter the Soviet Union, it had simultaneously done the R&D and production to field a far safer, more efficient weapon, one that used underground launchers to protect against a preemptive attack, the Minuteman.

The silos for the three-stage, solid-propellant Minuteman were built in remote locations, and they offered instantaneous response to an enemy first strike. The Minuteman also offered new challenges to Air Force personnel in a

BOTTOM LEFT:
After almost three decades of service as a nuclear deterrent ICBM, the Titan missile has taken on a new life as a launch vehicle for satellites. This Titan IV launch is from Vandenberg Air Force Base, California.

BOTTOM RIGHT:
Although long retired, the Atlas missile provided the interim deterrent shield that allowed the development of the later Minuteman and Peacekeeper missiles.

variety of terms, ranging from technical expertise to the psychological ability to adapt to life in a silo. The demands placed upon families were equivalent to those on bomber crews in alert facilities. In usual Air Force style, the crews and their families adapted. In time many found the life attractive: the Minuteman bases were usually in areas where the cost of living was low and the hunting and fishing good. Minuteman crews took pride in their work, which they knew to be critically essential. Training and evaluation were continuous; practice alerts occurred with nerve-jarring frequency. In the twenty-four-hour watch there was inevitably slack time. Hundreds of officers and airmen used it to take correspondence courses to gain additional degrees. The Air Force provided other incentives in terms of competitions, recognition, and awards. Gradually, an esprit built up equal to that of the bomber crews.

The Minuteman fleet has been upgraded over the years so that there are now 450 Minuteman IIs and 550 Minuteman IIIs, the latter with three MIRVs (multiple independently targeted reentry vehicles). After a tremendous debate that raged for years, 50 of the Minuteman fleet have been replaced in their silos by the latest and most accurate ICBM, the LGM-118A Peacekeeper. Originally, there were to be 100 Peacekeepers, each with up to ten MIRVs. Funding problems and interminable arguments over deploying these in a mobile rail-garrison mode have limited the procurement to 50.

Limited development continues on a small ICBM (unofficially called Midgetman), but its ultimate fate depends upon the arms reduction talks that began between the United States and the USSR, and the program is now bogged down in the confusion attendant on the dissolution of the Soviet Union.

Supplementing the ground-based missile fleet is an array of airborne missiles, including the AGM-69 SRAM (short-range attack missile), the AGM-86B ALCM (air-launched cruise missile), and the new AGM-129 ACM (advanced cruise missile). Taken together, the ICBMs, air-launched cruise missiles, and traditional bombers constitute an internal Air Force triad for deterrence.

It was the expensive, time-consuming, and ultimately successful establishment of this triad that created the enormous infrastructure of physical and intellectual capabilities that brought about the Air Force domination of space. It is important to note that the Air Force has been deeply involved with space activities from the first. It might have had astronauts working in space long before the Space Shuttle if the Dyna-Soar project or the manned orbiting laboratory (MOL) had been approved. The Air Force has had an on-again, off-again relationship with the Space Shuttle, at times appearing to be against it, at other times being accused of taking it over. Yet with all this activity and development, an outspoken space advocate in the Billy Mitchell mold has never appeared on the scene, probably because the Air Force has become more sophisticated managerially and politically. To have trumpeted space power would have been foolhardy, running the risk of alienating the public and Congress. There were numerous potential sources of opposition—the other services, foreign countries, NASA, as well as the still powerful antimilitary movement. It was better to move quickly, but quietly.

The gradual acquisition of space dominance under the umbrella of the Air Force's own triad and the larger strategic triad enabled the United States to continue to deter aggression even when so totally preoccupied with a situation as grave as the Persian Gulf War.

AIR POWER IN THE GULF WAR

The bigger military budgets called for by the Reagan administration coincided with the advent of new equipment. F-15s and F-16s began to pour into Tactical Air Force units, the B-1B came on line with SAC, the Fairchild A-10

Even the Warthog can appear seductive in the right setting. These two A-10s are on the ramp, waiting for tomorrow's flights.

As with every design, the F-16 was soon tasked for multiple missions and began to be loaded down with new equipment and larger weights of ordnance. The design was modified to slightly lengthen the fuselage and enlarge the wing areas to accommodate the increased weight. The results were surprising—the already fantastic rate of roll was improved by as much as 80 percent. Foreign countries became interested in the aircraft, and after intense competition the F-16 was adopted by the Netherlands, Belgium, Norway, and Denmark. One important inducement in the selection was a coproduction program of unprecedented scale.

Aircraft designers try to make their aircraft as "clean" as possible by removing every element of drag they can only to see them loaded up with tons of ordnance. Here a heavily laden General Dynamics F-16 pulls away from a KC-135 tanker after refueling.

It is rare when events bear out an advocate's wildest predictions, but that was the case with AWACs in the Persian Gulf War. The Boeing E-3B Sentry was indispensable both in controlling UN coalition aircraft and in keeping track of any Iraqi aircraft that left the ground. The Sentry maintained a continuous radar picture of the battle zone from the Arabian to the Red Sea. The thirty-foot-diameter rotating radome has no adverse affect on flight characteristics. Naturally designated a High Asset Value target, the three Sentries on station were protected by F-15C Eagles.

entered service as a ground-attack aircraft, and airborne command and control was extensively developed at both strategic and tactical levels. The distinction blurs with the proliferation of types, which include the E-3B Sentry AWACS, EC-135 strategic airborne command and control, E-4B airborne command post, EC-130 airborne battlefield command and control, and E-8 J-STARS. All are capable of contributing to both strategic and tactical warfare.

When the Soviet Union began to show signs of dissolution, the military services had the foresight to plan war games envisioning a crisis in the Middle East. But a failure of intelligence gathering prevented them from anticipating Iraq's reckless adventure of August 2, 1990, when Saddam Hussein's forces swept into Kuwait, taking only hours to place the fourth-largest army in the world on the borders of Saudi Arabia. Had the Iraqi army rolled on, the ultimate victory in Desert Storm would have been delayed by months; fortunately, the show of strength by the United States and the political backing of the United Nations caused Saddam to hesitate. Despite what proved to be inadequate air- and sealift capacity, the United States was given time to build up forces by using the excellent Saudi Arabian port and base facilities.

On August 7, 1990, the first tangible sign of U.S. commitment

Sleek and black, the Lockheed TR-1A has a lethal appearance that belies its role as a reconnaissance aircraft.

Speed brake deployed, the F-15A comes in to land at a speed of about 120 knots (138 mph). Although slightly longer and with a four-foot greater span than its F-4 predecessor, the F-15 weighs less and has 20 percent more wing area. The F-15 was the only fighter in history to accumulate 5,000 flying hours before its first accident.

OPPOSITE TOP:

One lesson learned from the Vietnam War was that dogfighting was still an essential element of air superiority. The McDonnell Douglas F-15 was designed to be able to out-accelerate and out-turn any enemy fighter at all speeds and altitudes. A high thrust-to-weight ratio was critical, as was a ratio of low weight to wing area. The F-15 design was relatively simple—no swing wing, not even an extreme wing sweep, but plenty of area and superb visibility from the cockpit. Also important is the simplified structure of the F-15 compared to the F-41, which resulted in faster production and easier maintenance.

OPPOSITE BOTTOM:

A two-seat trainer version of the F-15 was produced first as the TF-15A, and then redesignated F-15B. A TF-15A flew nonstop from Loring Air Force Base, Maine, to Bentwaters, England, in 5.3 hours. It then flew 92 demonstration flights in forty-three days at the Farnborough Air Show, a remarkable demonstration of reliability for a new aircraft.

occurred when forty-eight F-15 Eagles from the 1st Tactical Fighter Wing made a dramatic nonstop flight from Langley AFB, Virginia, to Dhahran, Saudi Arabia. The F-15s, like most fighters, are uncomfortable to fly after two or three hours, so much so that the Japanese are installing in-flight massage units in their aircraft. The flight to the Persian Gulf took up to seventeen hours, with as many as nine in-flight refuelings en route. It was the most arduous and most effective "show the flag" effort in aviation history, deterring Hussein from plunging on into Saudi Arabia, as he easily could have done.

The F-15s were followed by a continuous buildup of forces. The drayhorse work was done by the Military Airlift Command, bringing in paratroopers, tanks, Patriot missile batteries, and all the incredible impedimenta needed for modern warfare. By the end of the campaign, almost 5 billion ton-miles of personnel and cargo had been flown, nearly ten times the amount carried in the Berlin Airlift.

The electronic surveillance of the battlefield was soon provided by Lockheed U-2Rs and TR-1As and Boeing E-3 AWACS aircraft. In a risky move, the two prototype Grumman/Boeing E-8A J-STARS aircraft were sent to the theater, six years ahead of their scheduled deployment date. The E-8As primarily maintain surveillance of the land battle, but supplement the AWACS in controlling the air battle. The J-STARS proved so efficient that the Iraqis were forced to stop moving their vehicles in convoys, and instead tried to spirit them along the desert floor in ones and twos. Demand for the J-STARS capability came from every side, as they proved to be the keystone of the execution of what would be a textbook air-land battle, including the dramatic role targeting of Scud missiles for F-15E "Strike Eagle" aircraft.

Over an excruciatingly long five and a half months, the United States exhausted every diplomatic effort to get Saddam Hussein to relinquish his hold on Kuwait territory. At the same time the United States was building up the most massive striking force since the Vietnam War. The Air Force reached its peak on the thirty-eighth day of the war, when it had 909 combat aircraft and 463 support aircraft in the battle.

During the long waiting period there occurred an incident that sent chills down the spines of professionals observing the war. The new U.S. Chief of Staff, General Michael Dugan, was summarily fired by Secretary of Defense Richard Cheney. Dugan was quoted on some remarks that did not coincide with the official White House position. Many made the immediate inference that his firing meant that this war was going to be run like the war in Vietnam, from the White House and the Department of Defense. If so, disaster loomed.

Fortunately, exactly the opposite was true; the most obvious mistakes of Vietnam were not going to be repeated. President George Bush and Secretary Cheney enunciated their policies, and then left General Colin Powell and the military commanders on the scene to carry them out. The rules of engagement made sense: every effort was to be made to avoid damage to civilian lives or property, but the war was to be fought as intensively as possible, with the idea of winning decisively in the shortest possible time. A coalition of forces was created and General H. Norman Schwarzkopf was designated Commander. He chose Lieutenant General (now General) Charles A. Horner as Commander, Central Air Forces, to coordinate all air operations of the coalition of the United Nations' forces. It was a brilliant decision, much harder politically than militarily, given the sensitivities not only of the coalition members but of the sister services, but it made all the difference. In Vietnam, confusion over target selection and attack routes ultimately resulted in the country being divided into "packages" that were assigned to the different services, a solution that was only partly satisfactory. Given the high level of participation by Allied forces in the Gulf War, particularly the outstanding British and French efforts, a single air commander was a necessity.

At 2:59 A.M., Baghdad time, on January 17, 1991, the situation seemed normal to the Iraqis. The standard patrols by AWACS and fighters were the only apparent activity. At 3:00 A.M., an air attack of unprecedented ferocity blasted Iraqi air defenses, communications, electrical power grids, and command bunkers. The Iraqi command and control and radar defense systems were blinded as Air Force MH-53E special operations helicopters, Army Apache helicopters, Navy Tomahawk missiles, and a combination of many kinds of radar-jamming aircraft swept over the border. Seven B-52G bombers on the longest bombing raid in history—a thirty-five-hour mission from Barksdale AFB, Louisiana—fired conventionally armed AGM-86C air-launched cruise missiles to strike critical communication and power facilities.

OPPOSITE TOP:
Early in its career, a specially prepared F-15 "Streak Eagle" set eight altitude and time-to-climb records, taking five previously held by the F-4, and three from the MiG-25. As one example, the F-15 climbed to 98,425 feet (30,000 meters) in 207.8 seconds, cutting 36 seconds off the MiG-25's best time.

OPPOSITE BOTTOM:
The wing of the F-15 is relatively simple, and does not have any leading-edge devices for lift augmentation. The aircraft's structure is designed for ease of both manufacturing and maintenance. Most of the electronics are in the forward fuselage section, while the fuel tanks, guns, and missile systems are in the middle section. The rear section houses the two Pratt & Whitney F100 PW-100 turbofan engines, which are readily accessible for maintenance.

*The streamlined contours of the Marines'
McDonnell Douglas AV-8B are totally
destroyed by its huge load of ordnance and
fuel tanks.*

*The McDonnell Douglas F-15 was flown
by both the U.S. and Saudi Arabian air
forces. Saudi Arabia fielded four F-15
squadrons, and took turns with USAF and
RAF flying four-hour combat air patrols. A
Saudi F-15 pilot shot down two Iraqi
Mirages, the only victories by other than
American pilots.*

One of the best-kept secrets in military history was the Lockheed F-117A Stealth fighter. Despite easily observed operations out of its Nevada base, the Tonopah Test Range, and despite three crashes, a veil was kept over the airplane for years. Its combat debut in Operation Just Cause in Panama was not entirely auspicious, but its unparalleled work in the Persian Gulf War made it immortal as a warplane.

Its shape not too different from that of the classic paper glider, a Lockheed F-117A turns toward California. The unconventional profile of the Stealth fighter led to early speculation that it was unstable and difficult to fly. The comments from the pilots who flew it in combat totally refuted this.

More than eighty B-52 were used in the Persian Gulf War, operating from several different airfields; only one was lost, not due to enemy action. The BUFFs carried a load of fifty-one 750-pound M-117 bombs to hammer the Republican Guard. Never considered a beautiful aircraft, the B-52's lines have been altered over the years with turrets and fairings for new equipment. Yet its repeated successes have lent it an air of nobility.

The B-52's wings droop on the ground, and on the takeoff roll, they fly before the rest of the aircraft. The black smoke from the eight engines is characteristic of the old warrior. In the Persian Gulf War, B-52s proved to have a devastating effect on the morale of Saddam Hussein's Republican Guard. The BUFFs flew sorties from far-flung bases—Barksdale Air Force Base, Louisianna; Wurtsmith Air Force Base, Michigan; Diego Garcia in the Indian Ocean; and others.

The Sikorsky MH-60 helicopter shown here symbolizes the whole range of helicopter activities of the Gulf War. The MH-60 was used for both taking in and bringing out Special Operations teams on covert activities, and for making rescues behind enemy lines. The MH-53 sister ships, equipped with Pave Low systems, were assigned in pairs to accompany four Army AH-64 attack helicopters on their mission to destroy two air defense sites more than twelve miles inside the Iraqi border. The MH-53s used global positioning navigation equipment to get the Army helicopters on target.

Simultaneously, Lockheed F-117A Stealth fighters began their deadly attack, opening a path for the other bombers. These 117s, only 2.5 percent of the force, took out 30 percent of the toughest targets, hitting thirty-seven the first night. There is no indication that they were ever tracked by Iraqi radar. The arduous F-117A missions were always flown at night, averaging five and a half hours, with more than thirty minutes exposure to continuous antiaircraft fire. Despite the danger of enemy fire and the incredible swiftness of the attacks, the bombing accuracy averaged an amazing 85 percent, and the loss rate was zero. The F-117A proved invulnerable.

The public, almost as stunned as the Iraqis by the continuous television presentation of flawlessly executed attacks, responded with Super Bowl enthusiasm as a wave of patriotism washed over the country. But to the troops it was no Super Bowl; it was a deadly business, with hazards attendant on everything from high-gross-weight takeoffs to blacked-out, radio-silent, night in-flight refuelings. In the inferno of antiaircraft fire over Baghdad, each arcing trace was potentially a "Golden BB" for crewmen, the shot with their names on it. Although the Iraqis had lost their capability for accurate fire control, they laid down barrages of SAMs and antiaircraft fire that filled the skies and made random death a real probability.

Curiously, the first air-to-air victory of the war went to an unarmed

ABOVE:
A cockpit shot of then Lieutenant General Charles A. Horner, the man who commanded air operations in Operation Desert Storm. General Horner now heads the USAF Space Command.

LEFT:
Stealth qualities derive from both active and passive elements. The active elements are familiar electronic countermeasures that date back to World War II. The more interesting passive elements of the F-117A include the angular shapes that comprise its external form, the radar-absorbing material from which it is built, and the measures taken to reduce infrared and acoustic signatures. The multifaceted, angled shapes shown here deflect incoming radar signals, so that they are not reflected back to the tracking radar set. The F-117A has six different kinds of radar-absorbing material sprayed on or used in sheeets applied in different thicknesses on various parts of the aircraft.

OPPOSITE:

Operation Desert Storm gave a new lease on life to another old soldier that had been slated for retirement. The F-4 Phantom, operating as a reconnaissance aircraft and as a Wild Weasel, proved itself once again. Wild Weasel F-4Gs used the HARM (High-speed Antiradiation Missile) against Iraqi radar systems. The oldest reconnaissance plane to see service was the venerable RF-4C from the Alabama Air National Guard. RF-4Cs are now on average over twenty-five years old—a long time to be pounding in at supersonic speeds.

After the official first flight on February 2, 1974, the Air Force announced plans for acquiring at least 650 F-16s. The single-engine Fighting Falcon employed the same F100 power plant as the F-15, submerged in unique blended wing and fuselage design. The F-16's wing avoided the weight and cost of a variable sweep mechanism, using instead automatically variable camber, with the leading and trailing edges moving to adapt to a specific flight condition.

Without doubt the most sophisticated and effective electronic warfare aircraft in the world is the General Dynamics/Grumman EF-111A Raven. In fulfilling the SEAD (Suppression of Enemy Air Defenses) mission, the Ravens blacked out the enemy's radar and electronics with their powerful ECM equipment. This EF-111 is from the 390th Electronic Countermeasures Squadron from Mountain Home Air Force Base, Idaho. Of the ten EF-111As participating, only one was lost.

USAF EF-111A Raven radar-jamming plane. An Iraqi Mirage fired a missile at it; the Raven turned and dived to evade the missile, pulling out a few hundred feet above the ground. The Mirage, in hot pursuit, failed to pull out and crashed into the ground behind the Raven.

Blinded by the radar jammers, shot down when encountered, the crushed and bewildered Iraqi Air Force was defeated. In its first day, the USAF had launched more sorties than the Iraqi Air Force had flown in eight years of war against Iran. The Iraqis were unable to cope with the onslaught and, with a

Missiles have shown the same surprising longevity as airframes. The first contract for the AIM-9 Sidewinder was awarded in 1951, and it went into operational service in 1956. Widely copied around the world, the Sidewinder, much improved, is still in production. Here a Phantom fires the AIM-7 Sparrow, which also entered service in 1956. It has since been continuously improved, being transformed over time into totally new versions like the Shrike anti-radar missile.

few exceptions, declined combat. They sat on the ground until their shelters proved vulnerable, and then elected to fly to safety in the bosom of their recent enemy, Iran.

The story of the Gulf air war has been told often. It is sufficient to call attention to some factors that are sometimes overlooked. If it had ever been in doubt, the concept of the total force, the aggregate employment of regular, reservist, and Air National Guard assets, had been demonstrated convincingly. By February 1, 1991, 17,500 reservists were on active duty for the Gulf War, flying and maintaining first-line combat-ready equipment like A-10s, C-5s, C-130s, C-141s, F-16s, and KC-135s. One in four reservists was a woman, reflecting contemporary social conditions, and posing a genuine problem in Middle Eastern culture. The reserves plunged into combat with the A-10s, attacking every sort of ground target, including Scud missiles. Reserve units flew more than 5,200 combat sorties without any losses.

Similarly, the Air Guard's motto, "Always Ready, Always There," was fully proved in the Gulf War by the 12,500 men and women who responded to the call of duty, 5,000 of whom went to the Gulf. The very first American air-craft to land in Saudi Arabia after the Kuwait invasion was a Mississippi Air National Guard C-141. When the air war started, Guard F-16s flew 3,550 missions and dropped 3,500 tons of ordnance. The reconnaissance RF-4s flew 360 combat missions, while KC-135 tankers off-loaded 200 million pounds of fuel in 14,000 hookups with aircraft of all the coalition. It was an impressive showing by true citizen-soldiers.

A less personal factor that loomed large in the conflict was the affirma-

Among the many additional tasks the veteran Lockheed C-130 has assumed is that of tanker. Here a KC-130 executes a maneuver that would have been considered impossible thirty years ago, the aerial refueling of a helicopter, in this case a Sikorsky Jolly Green Giant.

The ability to carry huge ordnance loads was built into the A-10's specifications. The Warthog can carry an amazing variety of weaponry, and always has its 30mm cannon to fall back upon.

BOTTOM LEFT:
The shark-tooth insignia was first seen in World War I; it was made internationally famous by the American Volunteer Group, the Flying Tigers, in World War II, and appeared again in Vietnam and in the Persian Gulf War on this Fairchild A-10.

BOTTOM RIGHT:
One of the most critical factors in the victory in the Persian Gulf was the success of the Boeing AWACS, which guided the vast formations of coalition aircraft all during their battles.

The General Dynamics F-16 Fighting Falcon was begun as a low-cost, light-weight fighter that would supplement the heavier, more expensive F-15. The Soviet Union was continuing its practice of producing a wide variety of types in large numbers, and some analysts felt that they might prevail through sheer weight of numbers over American aircraft of superior quality. The F-16 quickly developed into an all-weather air-superiority aircraft with the capability for precision ground attack. Intended originally as an experiment, the F-16 has grown into the largest fighter production run in the Western world.

The Air Force flight demonstration team, the Thunderbirds, were equipped with F-16s that proved perfect for the air-show circuit. Their extreme agility enabled the Thunderbirds to perform their entire repertoire of maneuvers within the airfield perimeter, and the shape lent itself perfectly to the Thunderbird paint scheme.

tion that *complex* was no longer synonymous with *unreliable*. To the contrary, the newest and most sophisticated systems—the F-117A, the EF-111A, the F-15E, the J-STARS—proved to be far more reliable than anyone could have predicted, being maintained at an average 90 percent in-commission rate versus a standard peacetime expectancy of 60 to 70 percent. Another factor was the imaginative use of new equipment and new tactics. The F-15, originally designed as a day-superiority fighter, excelled at night attacks that the pilots termed "tank plinking."

Older weapon systems fared well too. The Boeing KC-135 tankers, with an average age of more than thirty years, refueled aircraft constantly, as did the more modern McDonnell Douglas KC-10s. The General Dynamics F-111, the subject of bad press for many years, covered itself with glory, dropping 7.3 million pounds of precision-guided ammunition in forty-two days, and taking out 245 hardened aircraft shelters, hundreds of bunkers and bridges, and as many as 1,500 tanks and personnel carriers. One of the most unusual F-111 "victories" occurred when two GBU-15 TV-guided 2,000-pound bombs were steered into an oil-pumping manifold to cap a sabotaged Kuwaiti well that was spilling oil into the sea, a case of bombs preventing an ecological disaster. Other older aircraft also got a new lease on life. The McDonnell Douglas F-4G, working as a Wild Weasel in a hunter-killer team with General Dynamics F-16s, devastated enemy SAM sites, using cluster-

The McDonnell Douglas F-15E Strike Eagle is the most versatile strike aircraft in the world, combining all of the basic F-15 attributes as an air superiority fighter with a tremendous weapons load for ground attack. In the Persian Gulf War it had three principal tasks: attacking the Republican Guard's tanks and artillery, hunting for Scud launchers, and carrying out deep-ranging strategic missions into Iraq. Laser targeting pods for the "smart bombs" were scarce—initially only five were available for the forty-eight F-15Es assigned to the theater. F-15E pilots found that cluster bombs were the best weapon against the Scuds.

The Northrop B-2 takes a different approach to stealth than the Lockheed F-117A or YF-22. The flying wing B-2 has more subtly rounded curves, and in its construction makes greater use of radar-absorbing materials.

bomb units, conventional bombs, and Maverick and HARM missiles. The venerable B-52Gs once again proved their worth as flying artillery, able to place tremendous amounts of bombs on troop concentrations, especially Saddam's crack troops, the Republican Guard. Each B-52 carried fifty-one M-117 750-pound bombs; a cell of three aircraft could churn a strip of sand one mile wide and one and a half miles long, killing the troops in its path and demoralizing those nearby. And perhaps most heart-warming of all, the ugly, often derided Fairchild A-10 "Warthog" used missiles and guns not only to suppress enemy armor, killing twenty-three tanks in one day, but in air-to-air combat. Captain Bob Swain, a reservist pilot of the 706th Tactical Fighter Squadron, shot down an Iraqi helicopter to score the first-ever A-10 air-to-air kill.

There were two key factors in the successes achieved with both new and old aircraft. The first was the arduous, realistic training that had gone on for so many years. The service members had spent their nights and weekends away from their families, in long deployments, practice exercises, and endless hard work. The second and more important factor was the quality of the personnel flying and supporting the aircraft. For an extended period of six months, located in a foreign environment with extraordinary climatic and cultural differences, the men and women of the Air Force maintained a level of esprit and morale that made the crucial difference. Aircraft and equipment were simply *not allowed* to go down for maintenance; no matter how many hours or how much ingenuity it took, the weapons were ready for launch on schedule. Back in the United States, electronic repairs would be made by pulling out and replacing an entire system unit, even if only one component on one circuit board was the cause of the problem, the "black-box out/black-box in" method. But supplies were short in the Gulf, and replacement black boxes were not always available. The mechanics would then pull the malfunctioning unit, take it apart, and replace the malfunctioning circuit boards in time for takeoff.

The Air Force and all the services employed the usual means to sustain morale—as many creature comforts as possible, frequent telephone contacts with families at home, and the assurance of service support in case of difficulty. But the prime factor in morale was much more fundamental. The men and women believed they were fighting for a just cause, and they knew they were being allowed to fight to win. Much more had been learned from Vietnam than anyone realized. Saddam Hussein had counted on the American public to manifest a Vietnam War mentality and demand the recall of its troops. That did not happen.

In the process of victory, a new condition emerged, one that was recognized at the time only by a very few persons at the top of the command structure, but which has since become more obvious. It is that air power has been raised to another level, that of space power.

AIR POWER BECOMES SPACE POWER

Space is the natural extension of the USAF's operating medium. The Air Force operates over 90 percent of all military space systems and supplies almost 50 percent of the U.S. total space budget, including NASA's share. And although there are no weapons in space, the use of space is now integral in every form of combat, from precision bombing to Special Operations Forces operating in radio silence behind enemy lines.

Air Force Space Command (AFSPACECOM), with headquarters at Peterson Air Force Base, Colorado, is tasked to use space as a force multiplier for weapon systems and for gathering global information. A remote-sensing satellite was used to give U.S. commanders an overall view of the situation.

The Navstar Global Position System (GPS) satellites were used to position air crews for parachute drops and to locate pickup zones for special

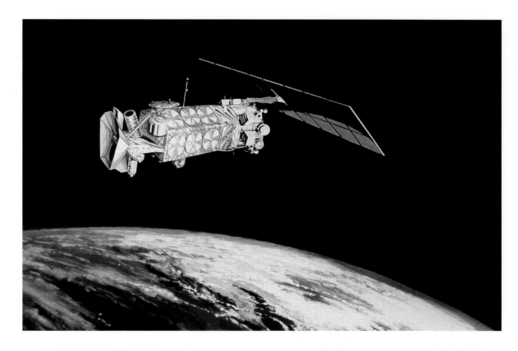

In combat, weather information is almost as critical as instant communication; the Defense Meteorological Satellite Program provides it in detail.

The advent of space power brings about a new image, one that some find less romantic than the airplanes of the past. Yet the ability to communicate instantly around the globe is crucial to decision making, and ultimately to making war. This is a Navstar Global Position System satellite that permits uncanny navigation accuracy.

operations forces in both Operation Just Cause, the invasion of Panama, and in the Persian Gulf War. Individual soldiers carried GPS terminals in their backpacks. Standard navigation and weather satellites were used to brief the aircraft crews of all services with the optimum flight paths. Communications satellites made everything work—everyone from the soldier at the point of combat to the aircraft waiting to deploy was in touch.

The GPS satellites are the best example of the precise control that space-based equipment can provide. Twenty-one satellites are planned in a system that will have continuous coverage over the entire earth. When the system is fully operational any user will be able to plot his or her position anywhere in the world to within a thirty-foot radius.

DESERT STORM

Space power came of age with Desert Storm, when space systems became an integral part of an enormous battle and proved crucial to its outcome. Its net effect was to make the operational combat commands importunate customers for space services in the future.

As the buildup in the Gulf proceeded, a critical shortfall in available communication channels soon occurred. There were simply too many people with too many radios to handle with existing equipment. The shortage was relieved by the adroit exercise of space power. To offset the shortage in communication channels, AFSPACECOM personnel at Falcon AFB, Colorado, sent the signals to turn on the rocket motor of a reserve Defense Satellite Communication System II satellite that was in stationary orbit over the Pacific. The huge satellite was shuttled westward to a point over the Indian Ocean, the first ever repositioning of a satellite to support combat operations. The new satellite capability instantly provided an abundance of communication channels, so that satellites had become the primary means for *intra*theater as well as intertheater communications.

The Navstar Global Position System provided the means by which allied land, sea, and air forces could navigate to a point, and then fire with unprecedented accuracy. In preceding wars, it had been impossible to know with precision not just where the enemy was but even where your own forces were. In the Persian Gulf War the Special Operations Forces, roving with Lawrence-of-Arabia dash behind enemy lines, depended on GPS in all their aircraft and helicopters. Air Force F-16s, operating in the ground-attack role, used GPS to arrive at the Initial Point on their bombing runs, then switched to another electronic marvel, the LANTIRN (Low-Altitude Navigation and Targeting Infrared for Night) system to complete their runs. GPS was used by other services as well, the Navy using it in particular for the standoff land-attack missile (SLAM), the Army for guiding everything from tanks to meal trucks.

The one deficiency of the space power revolution in the Gulf was an insufficiency of receivers. The systems were so new that it hadn't been possible to produce enough to satisfy every requirement, and some individual soldiers went to private companies for them. There were, however, enough to position the Air Force for its triumphant victory in the Gulf.

THE ECSTASY AND THE AGONY—TRANSITION INTO THE FUTURE

The triumph in the Persian Gulf briefly brought unalloyed ecstasy to the men and women of the Armed Forces, just as it did to civilians at home. They had fought a good war and won with minimum losses. The expensive equipment that had been so controversial over the years proved itself. In the process of countering Iraq's invasion of Kuwait, the United States had established itself unmistakably as the world's sole superpower.

The timing was remarkable. A marvelous mixture of important events were jumbled together in the last decade of the twentieth century, impossible to separate and difficult to determine as to cause and effect. The Berlin Wall fell to the Joshua's horn of freedom, and Communism dissolved like a sugar cube in hot tea. In the process, leaders were deposed, tyrants executed, wars begun and ended. Woven into all of this Cold War tapestry was the Air Force's absolute assertion first of air and now of space supremacy.

Forging the sword of the armed forces to fight the Cold War had starved essential social programs; with the Cold War over, the sword could be beaten into a plowshare for social justice. Even as the Gulf War was being fought, plans were being made to reduce all of the armed services by 25 percent or more in size. Even as the Air Force was conducting strikes against Baghdad, studies were underway to change its mission to fit within new funding guidelines.

The planning dictated that the great organizations that won the victories, laden with tradition and battle honors, would be deactivated and relegated to history. They included the Strategic Air Command, the Tactical Air Command, and the Military Airlift Command.

For many people, the most incredible change was the dissolution of the Strategic Air Command, perhaps the single greatest reason for success in the Cold War. Three generations of Americans had grown up in the security of Curtis LeMay's creation. Without ever dropping a nuclear weapon in anger, SAC accomplished its mission. It had withstood the turbulence of the times for forty-six years, changing its role to become a dropper of iron bombs when necessary, but never losing sight of its goal of nuclear deterrence.

Almost as startling was the deactivation of the Tactical Air Command, tested and proven in Vietnam, and brought to the height of its powers in the Gulf War. In the same way, the Military Airlift Command, whose distinguished lineage extended from flying the Hump to the Berlin Blockade to performing relief work in Russia, was no more.

Because satellites are unmanned, their lift-offs do not convey the drama to the layman that a Space Shuttle launch does. Yet to the scientists and technicians involved in the satellite programs, each launch is vital. Here the workhorse Delta II rocket lifts off from Cape Canaveral.

Part of the reason for deactivation of these fine old commands was the blurring in distinction of tactical and strategic operations in the Gulf War. Nominally tactical fighters like the F-15E had been assigned strategic targets, while the B-52 strategic bomber had been employed on tactical bombing missions. There were many other examples, such as the use of ground-attack A-10s, usually frontline aircraft, far in the enemy rear to strike Scud missile carriers.

SAC, TAC, and MAC were replaced by two new commands, reduced in size and streamlined in structure, and combining elements of the old organizations. The first of these is the Air Combat Command (ACC), which combines former SAC and TAC elements for integrated combat operations. Its focus is to be on deterrence and limited wars; its mission is to project U.S. power around the world. The second new organization is the Air Mobility Command (AMC), which will combine the airlift elements of MAC with about half of SAC's former tanker force, forming a team with global reach.

Many other changes have occurred, including the merger of the Air Force Systems Command and the Air Force Logistics Command into the Air Force Material Command (AFMC). This was the least painful of the reorganizations, for both of the former commands had common roots in even older units at Wright-Patterson Air Force Base.

On the briefing charts, the dissolutions and recombinations could be presented painlessly, with new symbols easing out the old. It was far different for the personnel involved, for implicit in the changes was a reduction in force. Immediately before the Persian Gulf War, the Department of Defense had placed a "stop loss" order into effect, preventing troops from retiring or separating. Immediately after the war, it began working on the reduction of a million military and civilian employees from all the armed forces. The Air Force must reduce from its 1987 strength of 607,000 to 430,000 by 1997, a 29 percent reduction. As the cutback began, men and women who had joined with plans for full careers in the service were suddenly forced out, even though many of them had been decorated for their actions during the Gulf War.

The irony of making drastic changes in the size and shape of a military force that has just scored the most decisive victory in its history is not lost on the man behind the changes, Chief of Staff General Merrill A. McPeak. Having listened to all the arguments about not fixing something that isn't broken, the general insisted that with the inevitable reductions in the budget, changes had to be made, and made quickly.

The budget reductions will have other effects. Within a few years the Air Force will have 40 percent fewer bombers, 50 percent fewer ICBMS, and 30 percent fewer fighters. Instead of maintaining a defensive force in Europe, the United States will now maintain a "presence," a force sufficient to gain time until reinforcements can come from the United States. The old wing structure, which had perhaps sixty aircraft of a single type of bomber or fighter, has been modified with a view to assisting this new strategy. Now new units especially intended to intervene in brushfire wars are being established. They will combine fighters, tankers, reconnaissance and AWACS planes, and B-52s. The maintenance and logistic problems are expected to be resolved with advanced managerial methods, placing heavy reliance on computer programs for tracking spare-part inventories and forecasting maintenance needs. As the Air Force consolidates and decentralizes, cutting staff and merging commands, it is also trying to manage an abrupt decline in procurement. The problem is far more serious than a potential deficiency in numbers; the very existence of a defense industry itself is in question.

Current United States strategy, as explained by the Joint Chiefs of Staff, is dependent upon ample warning time of a new threat, in order to be able to "reconstitute" our industrial base and our armed forces. In essence, the definition of warning time has been drastically changed. It used to refer to the thirty minutes that SAC would have to get bombers into the air upon notification of an impending ICBM attack. Now warning time for "reconstitution" is four years—the amount of time necessary to gear up industry and to mobilize forces that have been disestablished.

Four years might not be enough. Some industries—those supplying electro-optical gear, computer chips, and other high-tech materials—might not exist anymore. The United States already has a critical reliance upon foreign suppliers, principally Japan, our ally today but perhaps a bitter trade enemy ten years from now. Japanese writers have already asserted that Japan can control the world's superpowers through its production of critical components. The F-16 fighter and the M-1 Abrams tank both depend upon computer chips from foreign sources, and these are just two examples.

The entire situation is distressingly reminiscent of England's after World War I, when the infamous "Ten-Year Rule" was placed in effect. Proposed originally but later opposed by Winston Churchill, the Ten-Year

*Takeoff from Palmdale, Callifornia: the
B-2 lifts off the ground before a distant
admiring gallery. Heat radiating from the
B-2's engines is carefully masked in flight.*

*The B-2 proved to be stable, just as comput-
er simulations had predicted it would be. The
stability is also ensured by computers that
artificially augment its stability with hundreds of control inputs per minute, none of
which are perceptible to the pilot. As a result,
refueling operations like this were much easier
than anticipated.*

OPPOSITE:

*While the concept of swept-forward wings is
not new, having been tested in Germany in
1944 with the Junkers Ju 287 bomber, the
ability to use the concept effectively depended
upon the development of new materials,
structural techniques, airfoils, and fly-by-
wire flight-control systems. The Grumman
X-29 is a test vehicle designed to investigate
the use of advanced composite materials,
variable-camber wings, relaxed static stability, a close-coupled canard surface, and a
forward swept wing with a supercritical
airfoil. The design is inherently unstable,
and can be piloted only through the medium of computers that continuously provide the control inputs necessary to
offset the instability.*

At one time there were perhaps half a dozen "X"-planes flying during the same period of time in the United States—the X-1A, X-1E, X-2, X-3, X-4, and X-5 were all roughly contemporary. One of the few "X"-planes now flying is the Grumman X-29, of which two examples have been built. Results of the X-29's highly successful flight testing are being provided to the U.S. aerospace industry.

Not yet a "fly-by-wire" aircraft, the F-15 uses a hydraulic flight-control system with two different linkages, one electric and one manual, which provide redundance as insurance against battle damage. For all its complex systems, the F-15 is surprisingly easy to fly; pilots go solo in the single-place version after only two flights in the two-seat F-15B. Here artist Mike Machat captures an F-15 from the 5th Fighter Interceptor Squadron about to pounce on two Russian Bear reconnaissance planes.

Rule assumed for budgetary purposes each year that there would be no war in the next ten years, so military spending could be cut to the bone. The result was a defense force so weak that Great Britain had to acquiesce to a series of humiliating diplomatic defeats leading to the Munich agreement, and culminating ultimately in World War II.

The Cold War is over; the hazards to world peace are not. If the Air Force and the other military services are cut to the levels currently forecast, the United States will be at risk in the twenty-first century.

WHAT DOES THE FUTURE HOLD?

Besides risk, the future holds promise. The heart of the technological revolution, the computer, will continue to beat faster in future years, evolving at a rate greater than the average person's comprehension. As a rough analogy, the com-

Self-portrait of the photographer at work, a Chris Zeibold photograph of Chris Zeibold in an F/A-18.

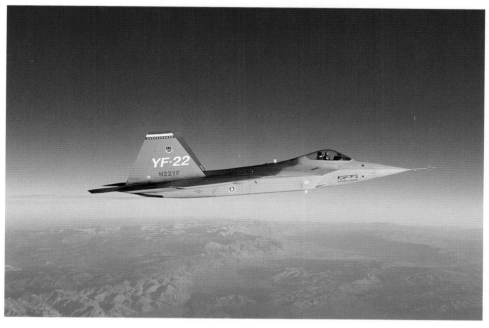

The Lockheed YF-22 incorporates elements of stealth in its design, yet its greatest innovation is its capability for sustained supersonic cruise speeds without the use of an afterburner.

puter today is roughly as advanced over its rude beginnings as World War I fighter planes were over the Wright Flyer. The improvement has been significant, but we are still at the first rung on the ladder of change. The advances in computers will fuel advances everywhere, in aerodynamics, electronics, and communications. Our current radars and electro-optical sensors will seem primitive within ten years or less. Further along, the computer will be the key to exploiting the energy of antimatter, perhaps as a propulsion system for space travel.

In the near term the Air Force will bring the Northrop B-2 Stealth bomber, the Lockheed YF-22, and the McDonnell Douglas C-17 into its inventory, each in limited numbers because of their cost. A little further along, we will see the National Aerospace Plane (NASP). It is currently under development as the X-30. Unlike today's Space Shuttle, which must be launched

The Air Force has left the vertical takeoff fighter to the Marines for development; the McDonnell Douglas AV-8B Harriers did well in the Persian Gulf War.

Design competitions sometimes lead to unforseen results. The competition for the Air Force F-16 led indirectly to the McDonnell Douglas F/A-18, shown here in Marine service.

The two Lockheed YF-22 prototypes are ready for dawn test flights at Palmdale, California.

Contrary to expectations, the Northrop B-2 Stealth bomber proved to be very easy to fly, and refueling tests with the McDonnell Douglas KC-10 Extender proceeded smoothly. The manufacturing techniques developed for production of the B-2 were as sophisticated as the aerodynamics of the aircraft itself. No matter what happens to the B-2 program itself, the new methods and materials developed for its production will fundamentally affect the design and manufacture of future civil and military aircraft.

The successor to the F-15 and F-16 is the Lockheed F-22, an aircraft of unprecedented capability. The F-22 will form the backbone of the country's defense for the next thirty years.

with a huge, expensive, and dangerous rocket system, the NASP will be able to take off conventionally from a runway, climb into space orbit, and return.

In the longer term, just as aircraft once faced a sound barrier, so do new technological developments face a cost barrier. It may be that systems revealed as attainable in research and development programs may be beyond the capabilities of one country, or even a coalition of countries, to sustain. A major effort is being made to contain new system costs within realizable boundaries, but the twin circumstances of a decline in threat and an almost geometric rise in cost may drive the Air Force away from its quest for equipment with continually improved performance. It may instead turn toward a maintenance mode, in which existing systems are improved incrementally over long periods of time. Given that the product of a still-primitive jet-engine technology, the B-52, will almost certainly have a fifty-year service life, it is not inconceivable that the weapons systems introduced during the next twenty years might endure for a century, given good maintenance and continuous improvement.

There is a vast public sentiment, both scientific and romantic, for a return to manned space exploration, including establishing bases on the moon as a prerequisite for the exploration of Mars. The Air Force has already joined in the research necessary for stunning new technical achievements. If the economy permits, it could well carry off a mission to Mars before 2020. But in the face of pressing social problems, the budget may dictate against such a project. If so, the Air Force can put Mars on hold and concentrate on a less glamorous but more necessary role as national defender, using proven weapons.

It is comforting to realize that no matter what the coming challenges are, no matter how low the budget levels sink, the success of the Air Force depends on attracting the same sort of leaders and members as those who have served it so well in the past. In all its stormy existence, as a fledgling Air Service in World War I, as a gigantic force in World War II, as the winner of the Cold War, the Air Force has always managed to get the right people in the right jobs at the right time. It will continue to do so in the future.

Acknowledgments

Words cannot express how very grateful I am to the many people who helped me create this book. Without them it would have been impossible; with them it was a pleasure. I deeply regret that I was not able to reproduce in full so many of the marvelous accounts they provided me about individuals, units, and battles. Just reading them was a tremendous education, and although the full accounts may not be evident, I have synthesized much of what was given me, and translated it into the text and captions. It would be wonderful to relate something also of the individuals who provided it, for many of them have fascinating stories to tell. Instead, I am forced by their sheer numbers to acknowledge them in a very abbreviated fashion.

Let me thank first of all the wonderful people who provided the photographs for the book. I raided Jay Miller's collection; in his usual openhanded style he let me cart off boxloads of material. John T. Correll, editor in chief of the Air Force Association's *Air Force* magazine, was similarly gracious, and it was a privilege to work with the AFA librarian, Pearlie Draughn, who is both extremely knowledgeable and very helpful. The pictures taken by professional photographers speak for their talent and skill, from veterans like Fred Bamberger, Warren Bodie, Bob Esposito, and Howard Levy, to the new guard like Bob DeGroat, Robert F. Dorr, Charles Filippini, George Hall, Philip Handleman, Randy Jolly, Russell Munson, Larry Sanders, Eric Schulzinger, and Erik Simonsen. And I want to give a special salute to the many service and corporate photographers who took pictures and were not given credit at the time.

There were many historians and other individuals who helped me find photographs and background material. I am grateful to Col. Fredric C. Lynch, who marshaled historians in the Fifteenth Air Force for me; Col. Wayne Pittman, USAF (Ret.); George Cully, Aero Historian Association; Diana G. Cornelisse, Headquarters, ASD; prolific author and expert Jeff Ethell; Hugh Burns and Jeff Rhodes, Lockheed; C. John Amrhein, Northrop; Lon Nordeen, McDonnell Douglas; Harry Gann, McDonnell Douglas and American Aviation Historical Society; M. Sgt. Daryl E. Green, Grissom AFB; T. Sgt. Lionel L. Harvey, March AFB; Capt. Robin Grantham, Fairchild AFB; Frederick Johnsen, McChord AFB; Eric Falk, General Electric; M. Sgt. Ernest F. Morgan; Andrew Biscoe; Christina Blazina; Terry Monrad, Martin Marietta; Donald Hanson, McDonnell Douglas; Carl L. Harris, Bell Helicopeter; Gary DuPriest, Brooks AFB; Col. Philip W. Corbett, Scott AFB; Wally Meeks; Lucien Mather; Dennis Parks, Experimental Aircraft Association Aviation Foundation library; John Burton, EAA, veteran author and airman; C. V. Glines, Eric Hehs, and Bill Williams, of *Code One*, General Dynamics; Dr. Michael Fopp, Director, RAF Museum; Regina G. Burns, Archivist, U.S. Army Aviation Museum, Fort Rucker; R. T. Smith, who provided an uninterrupted supply of documentary and photographic material; James Wallace, Smithsonian Institution; Larry Wilson, National Air and Space Museum; Dana Judge, Grumman Aircraft; Ellen Kaplan, Richard D. Whitmyre, and J. G. O'Connor, United Technologies; Ray Wagner and Ron Bulinski, San Diego Aerospace Museum; Linda Winkler, Defense Finance and Accounting Service; Col. Glenn L. Nordin, USAF (Ret.), editor of *Daedalus Flyer*; Gerald F. Vessely; Joe Mizrahi, Sentry Books; David L. Moffat; Col. Frederick W. Morgan, Peterson AFB; Capt. Mark Brown; Milt Furness, Dr. Paul Spitzer and Marilyn Phipps, the Boeing Company; Gerard Pahl, Kalamazoo Aviation History Museum; Herbert Foster; Margie Rawlins; Col. George S. Howard, USAF (Ret.); Richard Riding, editor of *Aeroplane Monthly*; Brother James, Holy Cross Abbey; W. L. Oversend; Esther Oyster, Historian, 319th Bomb Squadron; O. H. McKagen; Lt. Col. Fred Zimmerman, USAF (Ret.); Carlton and Betty McConnell; and many others who called or wrote, and whose names I will find again as soon as this has gone to print. To all I have inadvertently omitted, forgive me.

Alice Price of the Air Force Art Collection responded with her usual efficiency and dispatch, as did Mike Machat, who was instrumental in providing slides of the paintings that are included. Mike was able to give me examples of the work of Jerry Crandall, James Dietz, Jack Fellows, Keith Ferris, Nixon Galloway, Roy Grinnell, Craig Kodera, Sam Lyons, William Phillips, and his own fine work. Keith Ferris, the dean of American aviation art, not only made some of his work available but provided insight from his memories of the early days of his family life in the Air Corps. Dr. Luther Gore was also helpful with aviation art, as were Bern Kovit and Philip Handleman.

I could not have been more fortunate in my support from the publishing side, at Simon & Schuster, where it was a pleasure to work with Robert Bender and Patricia Leasure, just as it was with Marsha Melnick, Susan E. Meyer, William Broecker, and Ross Horowitz of Roundtable Press. It is a privilege and a joy to be associated with the book's designer, Nai Chang, and I'm proud to have worked with him. Leo Opdycke and Henry Snelling provided wonderful editorial advice, and as always, I relied on the sound counsel of my agent, Jacques de Spoelberch.

Like everyone who has ever known or read of him, I have tremendous respect and admiration for Gen. James H. Doolittle, who provided the foreword as graciously as he has provided seven decades of inspiration to aviation. And I wish to thank Lee Ewing, who generously and ably wrote the introductory note. To all—and especially to anyone whose name I have forgotten—thank you from the bottom of my heart.

WALTER J. BOYNE
Ashburn, Virginia

Credits

Abbreviations: T—top; M—middle; B—bottom; L—left; R—right.

Courtesy Air Force Association, 17M, 30B, 75T,B, 127L,M,R,

Author's collection, 39, 45, 47, 56T,M, 64, 72M,B, 91T,B, 99T,B, 100T,B, 102, 103T,M,B, 107, 108L, 109B, 112, 114B. 117B, 120L, 133B, 135, 141T, 152T, 162, 163T, 165, 167T, 168T,B, 180T, 181L,R, 183B, 190B, 191, 192B, 194, 195T, 197RT, 200B, 203T,M,B, 204T,M,B, 205T, 206T,M, 209, 212B, 214M, 215T, 217L,R, 219, 220, 258, 283, 284-85, 295, 322T,B

Author's photo, 248, 233T, 234, 236, 248T, 252, 294B

Fred Bamberger photo, 113, 115B, 118T,M,B, 119T,B, 145

Warren Bodie Collection, 32B, 128, 150, 192T, 215M, 278

Boeing Aerospace and Electronics, courtesy Milt Furness, 261, 264

The Boeing Company, courtesy Paul Spitzer/Marilyn Phipps, 205B, 224R, 225L,R, 262, 279

Merv Corning painting, courtesy Alice Price of the Air Force Art Collection, 36

Bob de Groat photo, 157T

Jim Dietz painting, 12

Experimental Aircraft Association, courtesy Dennis Parks, 122M, 132

Charles Filippini photo, 2, 267

William A. Ford photo, courtesy *Air Force* magazine, 313BR

Courtesy Francis Thompson Films, 19

Nixon Galloway painting, 126, 218

General Dynamics, Code One, courtesy Bill Williams/Eric Hehs, 138, 149B, 172B, 179

General Electric, courtesy R. Eric Falk, 94T,B

Roy Grinnell painting, 62, 63

Grumman Aircraft Corporation, 26-27, 30T; courtesy Dana Judge, 323, 324T

Fred Johnsen photo, 74

Randy Jolly photo, 79, 229, 308T,B, 310B, 313BL, 315T

Courtesy Terry Gwynn Jones, 34, 95T

Kalamazoo Aviation History Museum, courtesy Gerard Pahl, 153

Pete Knox photo, 156, 158, 159T, 174B

Howard Levy photo, 6, 58, 59TL, 65T, 65B, 66T, 66B, 67, 68T,M,B, 69T,M, 73M,B, 77T, 124-25, 158, 159T, 174B, 182M, 207R

Lockheed Corporation, 328B; courtesy Jeff Rhodes, 133T, 149T; courtesy Eric Schulzinger, 182T, 210, 214T, 307T,B, 325B, 326-27B

T. Sgt. Jose Lopez photo, courtesy Air Force Association, 300T, 304T,B

Sam Lyons painting, 176, 290

Mike Machat painting, 177, 324B

Courtesy Martin-Marietta, 235L

McDonnell Douglas, courtesy Harry Gann, 114T, 121, 122B, 139, 141B, 195B, 196, 207L, 211, 215B; photo by Chris Zeibold, courtesy Lon Nordeen, 293, 306T, 326T, 327T

Kirk McManus collection, via Jay Miller, 33

Courtesy Messerschmitt-Bölkow-Blohm, 163B

Jay Miller Collection, 28, 29T,B, 37, 38, 49, 51T, 52, 55, 56B, 57, 59TR, 59B, 61T, 69B, 72T, 81, 84, 90L,R, 92, 101, 108R, 109T, 115T,M, 116T,B, 117T, 129, 130, 131, 141M, 144, 155, 167B, 171, 180B, 182B, 183T, 190T, 193, 200T, 202, 208TL,TR,B, 212T,M, 214B, 216T,M, 232T,B, 233B, 235R, 237T,B, 239, 240, 241, 242, 245, 247T,B, 248M,B, 265T, 268, 269, 271, 273T,B, 274, 276T,B, 277, 280, 288, 289, 302, 303T,B, 313T, 314T,B, 320

Jay Miller photo, 136, 216B, 231, 244, 265B

Sgt. David S. Nolan photo, U.S. Air Force, 310T

North American Aircraft photo, courtesy Air Force Association, 166

William S. Phillips painting, 198, courtesy Alice Price of the Air Force Art Collection, 260

Albert Piccirillo photo, courtesy the Norm Taylor Collection, 223T

Ryan Aeronautical Collection, courtesy William Wagner, 120R, 227

Courtesy Karl Schneide, 73T

Eric Schulzinger photo, 123

Carl Schuppel photo for the Experimental Aircraft Association, 122T

Erik Simonsen photo, 77B, 78, 254-55, 256-57, 263, 272, 299, 309B, 315B

Douglas Smith painting, 80

U.S. Air Force, 197RB, 213, 281, 292T,B, 297R, 300M,B, 306B, 308M, 309T, 311, 312, 313M, 328T; courtesy Air Force Association, 8, 17T,B, 20, 21, 22T,B, 31T,B, 32T, 51B, 83L,R, 86, 95B, 97, 106T,B, 111, 142, 148, 152B, 157B, 159B, 160, 170, 172T, 173T,B, 174T, 186L,R, 187L,R, 197L, 199, 223B, 224L, 253, 294T, 301; courtesy Capt. Mark Brown, Peterson AFB Public Relations, 297L, 317T,B, 319; courtesy Diana G. Cornelisse, HQS, ASD, 23, 89, 104; photo by A1C Marty Edelstein, courtesy Air Force Association, 259; photo by Larry Groom, courtesy Air Force Association, 222; courtesy Col. Fred Lynch, 206B

U.S. Army Aviation Center, Fort Rucker, Alabama, courtesy Regina Burns, 61B

Courtesy Warner Bros., 151

Chris Zeibold photo, 325T

Suggested Reading

Anderton, David A. *History of the U.S. Air Force*. New York: Military Press, 1989.

Arnold, Henry H. *Global Mission*. New York: Harper & Bros., 1949.

Ballard, Jack S. *Development and Employment of Fixed Wing Gunships, 1962–1972*. Washington, D.C.: Office of Air Force History, 1982.

Baumbach, Werner. *The Life and Death of the Luftwaffe* (reprinted as *Broken Swastika*). New York: Ballantine, 1967.

Berger, Carl, ed. *The United States Air Force in Southeast Asia, 1961–1973: An Illustrated Account*. Washington, D.C.: Office of Air Force History, 1984.

Boyle, Andrew. *Trenchard: Man of Vision*. New York: W. W. Norton, 1962.

Boyne, Walter J. *Boeing B-52: A Documentary History*. London: Jane Publishing Co., 1981.

———. *The Leading Edge*. New York: Stewart, Tabori & Chang, 1986.

———. *The Smithsonian Book of Flight*. Washington, D.C.: Smithsonian Institution Press, 1987.

Christienne, Charles, and Pierre Lissarrague. *A History of French Military Aviation*. Washington, D.C.: Smithsonian Institution Press, 1986.

Coffey, Thomas M. *Hap*. New York: Viking Press, 1982.

———. *Iron Eagle: The Turbulent Life of General Curtis Le May*. New York: Crown Publishers, 1986.

Copp, Dewitt S. *Forged in Fire*. Garden City, N.Y.: Doubleday & Co., 1982.

———. *A Few Great Captains*. New York: Doubleday & Co., 1980.

Craven, Wesley Frank, and James L. Cate, eds. *The Army Air Forces in World War II*, vols. I–VII. Reprint, Washington, D.C.: Office of Air Force History, 1983.

Futrell, Frank. *The United States Air Force in Korea, 1950–1953*. Washington, D.C.: Office of Air Force History, 1983.

Galland, Adolf. *The First and the Last*. New York: Henry Holt, 1954.

Glines, C. V. *From the Wright Brothers to the Astronauts: The Memoirs of Major General Benjamin D. Foulois*. New York: McGraw-Hill, 1968.

Goldberg, Alfred, ed. *A History of the United States Air Force, 1907–1957*. Princeton, N.J.: Van Nostrand, 1957.

Gross, Charles Joseph. *Prelude to the Total Force: The Air National Guard, 1943–1969*. Washington, D.C.: Office of Air Force History, 1985.

Hansell, Haywood S. *The Air Plan That Defeated Hitler*. Atlanta: Hansell, 1972.

Littauer, Raphael, and Norman Uphoff, eds. *The Air War in Indochina*. Boston: Beacon Press, 1972.

Maurer, Maurer, ed. *The U.S. Air Service in World War I*, vols. I–IV. Washington, D.C.: Office of Air Force History, 1979.

———. *Aviation in the U.S. Army, 1919–1939*. Washington, D.C.: Office of Air Force History, 1987.

Mitchell, William. *Memoirs of World War I: From Start to Finish of Our Greatest War*. New York: Random House, 1960.

Momyer, William W. *Air Power in Three Wars (WW II, Korea, Vietnam)*. Washington, D.C.: Office of Air Force History, 1985.

Murray, Williamson. *Luftwaffe*. Baltimore: Nautical & Aviation Publishing Co., 1985.

Prange, Gordon W. *At Dawn We Slept: The Untold Story of Pearl Harbor*. New York: McGraw-Hill, 1981.

Shiner, John F. *Foulois and the U.S. Army Air Corps, 1931–1935*. Washington, D.C.: Office of Air Force History, 1983.

Walker, Lois E., and Shelby E. Wickam. *From Huffman Prairie to the Moon: The History of Wright-Patterson Air Force Base*. Dayton: Office of History, Wright-Patterson Air Force Base.

Index